DICTIONARY OF MUSIC

DICTIONARY OF MUSIC

NIRMALA DEVI

ANMOL PUBLICATIONS PVT. LTD.
NEW DELHI - 110 002 (INDIA)

ANMOL PUBLICATIONS PVT. LTD.
4374/4B, Ansari Road, Daryaganj
New Delhi - 110 002
Ph.: 23261597, 23278000
Visit us at: www.anmolpublications.com

Dictionary of Music

First Published, 2004

ISBN 81-261-1842-3

PRINTED IN INDIA

Published by J.L. Kumar for Anmol Publications Pvt. Ltd., New Delhi - 110 002 and Printed at Mehra Offset Press, Delhi.

Preface

This dictionary compiles very succinct and judiciously selected terms covering the entire field of music such as instruments, compositions, technical terms, musical forms, periods, styles, movements, musicology and musicologists, etc. The Indian Music is given an elaborate treatment. It also includes the life sketches of famous Indian musicians of yore days..

The growing interest in medieval and Renaissance music is reflected in the coverage of this dictionary.

Meticulous efforts are made to write the entries in a clear and lucid style to provide both straightforward definitions and invaluable background information.

The presentation throughout has been aimed at sustaining the interest of readers while enriching their vocabulary in music.

The kind help and cooperation extended by Mr. J.L. Kumar Managing Director, Anmol Publications Pvt. Ltd., New Delhi is gratefully acknowledged.

—Editor

A

A (Eng.; Ger.; It., Fr., la).

(1) Sixth note (or submediant) of scale of C major. Practice of using letters A to G for successive octaves dates.

(2) As abbrev. A. = alto, associate.

(3) Indication of a Transposing Instrument, on which the note written C sounds as A (and correspondingly with other notes): e.g. clarinet in A, or, colloquially, A clarinet.

A. Term used analysis to symbolize the first section of a piece. So e.g. ABA represents a piece having one section followed by a different section followed by a repeat of the first.

A, a(It., Fr.) To, at, with, etc. So a 2, a 3, etc., indication either that a piece has been written in so many parts, or that a single line of music is to be played by so many instruments in unison; so also a Cappela, a Piacere, a Tempo, etc. (in all such see under next world).

Abendmusiken (Ger.). Evening musical performances.

Abgesang (Ger.), **'Attersong'**. Concluding portion of stanza of Minnesinger or Meistersinger song.

Absolute Music. Music without direct reference to anything outside itself, i.e. not having words and not being illustrative Music depicting story, scene, etc. Most music is in this category. Also called abstract music. Opposite is programme music.

Absolute Pitch or **Perfect Pitch.** The term used for the gift of re-cognizing pitch of any note heard, or of singing note at any pitch without help from instrument.

Abstract Music. Same as Absolute Music.

Academy. A teaching institution of Music.

A Cappella (It.), 'in the church style'. Term applied to choral music without accompaniment.

Accelerando (It.), 'quickening (the time)'. Abbrev. Is accel.

Accent:

(1) The rhythm of music is made clear by accent. On the whole, accent recurs at regular intervals, e.g. in 4/4 time on 1st beat of bar, and with less force on 3rd; in 3/4 on 1st beat of bar. However, it has been by no means universal; there has been no reason why accent should coincide with 'strong' beats. Accent signs:

>	Normally indicates strong accent
— —	Stress or pressure
∧ ∨	heavy pressure.

Other abbreviations indicating strong emphasis; sf, sfz (sforzando, 'forcing'), sfp or fp (sforzando piano or forte piano, an accent followed immediately by piano), rf or rfz(rinforzando, 'reinforcing');

(2) French term for Nachschlag.

Acciaccatura (It., a crushing):

(1) An 'extra note which is struck just before (or simultaneously with) the main note, but immediately released.

(2) Name is now applied to short Appoggiatura, an ornamantal note of minimum duration, sounded immediately before, or simultaneously with, main note. Notated by auxiliary note in smaller type with stroke through stem.

Accidental. A sharp, flat, double- sharp, double-flat, or natural sign which is occurring temporarily in the course of a piece, and not forming part of the key-signature. It conventionally refers only to the bar in which it occurs not to any succeeding bars, unless repeated there.

Accompaniment. Subordinate part(s), usually instrumental added to principal part(s). May be mere duplication. Where a piece has been scored for equal partners, e.g. sonata for violin and piano, piano part should not be regarded an accompaniment.

Accompany. To perform with another performer, but in a subordinate capacity. When the performers are thought of as equal partners, e.g. in a violin and piano sonata, then accompany and its deriv- atives are to be avoided.

Accordion, Piano-accordion. Refers to the portable reed organ, which was invented by Friedrich Buschmann of Berlin,1822. Sounds get produced by metal reeds freely vibrating within frames, air being supplied by bellows operated by player pushing and pulling instrument – hence nickname, 'squeeze-box'.In accordion, both hands press studs, producing single notes or chords; in piano-accordion, right hand plays on keyboard. It is much used in informal music making, very rarely elsewhere.

Achtel (Ger., eighth part). Eighth-note, quaver.

Acoustic. This term is sometimes used to distinguish a 'normal' (non-electric) instrument from its electric counterpart – e.g. acoustic guitar.

Acoustic Bass. The term used for the organ stop in which pipes of sixteen-foot pedal stop sound with rank a fifth above, producing Resultant tone on octave below sixteen-foot pipes.

Acoustics. Refers to the science of sound. Sound involves impact on ear of air vibrations set in motion by:

(1) Vibration of elastic material,

(2) Vibration of air column in pipe, or

(3) Vibrations electrically produced or transmitted. Elastic material may be (a) gut string or wire (string instruments, keyboard instruments except organ family), (b) reed(s) (oboe clarinet), (c) membrane (vocal chords in voice, lips in brass instruments, skin of drum) (d) solid body (bells, triangle, xylophone etc).

Intensity of note may be determined by amplitude of vibration; greater amplitude gives louder sound.

Pitch of note may be determined by frequency of vibration low frequency gives low note etc. On the whole short strings or pipes produce higher frequency.

Resonance of note depends on presence of auxiliary material (e.g. belly of violin) or air column (e.g. in woodwind instruments) that vibrates in sympathy or by direct contact with original vibrations e.g. of string or reed).

Quality of note depends on complex character vibrations. Most instruments, when single note is played, in fact produce very faint 'overtones' of the Harmonic Series; richness of quality depends on number and selection of these overtones.

Actions:

(1) The operation of mechanical or other devices used in construction of musical instruments – e.g. tracker action.

(2) Mechanism of keyboard instrument, esp. pressure required to sound note.

(3) Distance between strings and fingerboard in stringed instrument, dictated by height of bridge.

Act Tune. 17th, 18th centuary term which is used for instrumental music played between acts of play.

Acute. Refers to the ornament in 17th centuary English music.

Acute Mixture. The organ stop, which is giving overtones, tuned slightly sharp.

Adagietto (It., a little adagio). Not quite so slow as Adagio.

Added Sixth. The term used for the addition of a sixth to major or minor triad, e.g. in C major, A is added above triad of C-E-G.

A deux Cordes (Fr.; It., a due cordes). On two strings.

Adlib. (Lat., ad libitum). At discretion, to be performed as the performer wishes-especially meaning that strict time need not be observed, or that the inclusion of a particular voice or instrument in the ensemble is optional.

A Due (It.), 'in two parts.' Generally written a2:

(1) In wind parts reveals that single melodic line is to be played by two instruments in unison;

(2) In string parts reveals that passage in two parts is to be played divisi (term normally used now). So also a 3, a 4.

Aeolian Harp. It is zither- like instrument having strings of different thickness all tuned to same note. Not played, but placed outside to catch wind; wind makes strings vibrate with various harmonies depending on speed, producing series of chords. Known in ancient times; name derives from Aeolus, god of winds.

Aeolian Mode. The mode, which may be represented by the white keys of the piano from A to A.

Aeolina, Aeoline. The soft organ stop, resembling sound of Aeolian harp.

Aerophone. The term used scientifically to classify an instrument in which a vibrating column of air produces the musical sound – including pipe-organ, accordion, etc., as well as conventional mouth-blown wood-wind and brass instruments.

Affektenlehre (Ger.). Refers to the system of musical aesthetics formulated in Germany in 18th centuary, and widely accepted. Maintained compositions should be judged by extent to which they portrayed and aroused certain emotions.

Affetto (It.). Affection.

Affettuoso (It.) 'affectionate', i.e. with tender emotion.

Affrettando (It). Becoming faster or more agitated.

Agitato (It). 'Agitated', i.e. restless and wild.

Agous Dei (Lat.), 'Lamb of God'. Concluding portion of musical setting of Roman Mass. In Requiem Mass, is followed by Lux Aterna.

Agogic. Term, which is describing deviations from strict tempo and rhythm necessary for subtle performance of musical phrase.

Agrement (Fr.) = Ornament

Ai (It). At the, to the (pl.).

Air. A Simple tune for voice or instrument.

Ais and **Aisis** (Ger.). A sharp and A douple sharp respectively.

Ai (It.) To the.

Alala (Sp.). Type of Galician folk melody, which is sung in free rhythm and often ornamented with grace notes. It appears to have melodic affinities with plainsong.

Alberti Bass. The spreading-out of a left-hand keyboard chord in a rhythmical pattern.

Alborada (Sp.; Fr. Aubade). The 'morning song'. Form of music for bagpipes and side-drum popular in Galicia.

Aleatory. This term is confined to compositions in which random chance genuinely plays a part in performance (cage), not to those in which a decision of the performer replaces a decision of the composer.

Alla Breve (It.). Term which means that Breve is to be taken as standard of mensuration instead of Semibreve, i.e. that music is to be performed twice as fast as notation would suggest.

Allargando (It.). Broadening, becoming slower.

Alla Tedesca (It.). Short for alla danza tedesca, i.e. in style of German dance or Allemande or either type.

Alla Turca (It.). 'In the Turkish style'.

Alla Zingarese (It.). In style of gypsy music (from zingaro, a gypsy).

Alla Zoppa (It.). 'In a limping manner', i.e. syncopated Applied especially to rhythm known as Scotch Snap.

Alankaras. Alankara is a "Varna" and expands and adds to the beauty. Alankaras are meant for the practice of the pupil. It develops the most intricate and difficult movements. The mixture of the notes going upwards and downwards and the passages while developing the art of music are the special features of an Alankara. There are many kinds of Alankaras in various combinations. These alankaras give very good training to the beginner.

Alap. This is just the analysis of a rag or melody. Elaboration in different varieties which are strictly within the boundary and the limits of law, provided for this systematic development of the notes form the main feature.

Allegretto (It., a little allegro). Plot quite so lively as Allegro.

Allegro (It.). The lively, i.e. rather fast (but not as fast as Presto).

Allemande. The term used for the dance-movement often opening the baroque suite, in moderate 4 – 4 times; it was divided into two sections, and usually began with a short note just before the bar- line. The term is French for 'German' but this has been not the same as a German dance.

Allentando (It). 'Slowing down '.

Allmahlich (Ger.). Gradual, gradually.

Allongarese (Fr). In style of Hungarian (gypsy music).

All' Ottava (It). At the octave (below or above).

All' Unisono (It). 'In unison', i.e. 2 or more instruments are to play the same notes.

Alphorn. The wind instrument having a straight wooden tube sometimes as much as 12 ft. long. It sounds one Harmonic Series only (like a bugle) with very powerful tone, and is used in Switzerland for attracting cattle (and tourists). The German name is Alphenhorn.

Alt

(1) In phrase in alt (from Lat., alto, in the height), applied to notes from G above treble stave to F above that; notes in octave above are said to be in altissimo;

(2) (Ger.), Alto.

Alteration

(1) The term used for the conventional augmentation of value of breve, semibreve or minim in mensural notation before 1600. Rhythemic Modes, Mensural Notation.

(2) The chromatic alteration is raising or lowering of note of scale by means of Accidental.

Althorn (Ger.). Brass instrument of Saxhorn family.

Altissimo (It., very high), preceding entry.

Alto (It., high).

(1) An unusually high type of adult male voice, employing falsetto.

(2) The lower type of female voice – so designated in choirs, elsewhere usually contralto; also, sometimes, the corresponding child's voice;

(3) In a 'family' of instruments, is having ranged approximately that of an alto voice.

American Organ. Type of Reed, orange in which air is sucked in through bellows. (U.S. term: cabinet-organ).

Differs from harmonium in that in latter air is forced through reeds, whereas in former it is drawn through by suction. American organ is nearer in tone quality to organ, but is less expressive than harmonium.

Amore, d'; Amour, d' (It., Fr.). Term applied to some old instruments indicating and ingratiating tone (literally, 'of love').

Amoroso (It). Lovingly, tenderly.

Anacreon, opera-ballet by Cherubini, libretto by R. Mendouze. First perf. Paris, 1803. Now known mainly for overture.

Anche (Fr.). The reed, reed instrument, reed pipe (in organ).

Ancient Cymbals or Antique Cymbals. Small cymbals, usually found in pairs, producing definite notes. Much used by dancing girls in Ancient World. Produce soft, delicate sounds.

Ancora (It., cp. Fr. Encore). Still, yet: ancora pitu presto, still more quickly.

Andante (It.), 'going moving'. Now generally used of a moderate tempo, inclining to slowness ('at a walking pace') rather than actually slow. Hence used as title of piece or movt. In this tempo. Piu andante means 'moving more', i.e. slightly faster.

Andhra Desa. It is also famous for Dappu Vadyams. This is a sort of drum played in folk festivals generally by the Dhobi class. Playing on this instrument creates excitement. The crowds who are assembled to watch, also dance to the rhythm, in the way of offering homage to the village deity.

Andantino (It, a little Andante). The term apparently indicating either a little slower than andante, or (now more usually) not quite so slow as andante.

Anglaise (Fr.). Short for dance anglaise English dance, dance in quick duple time, one of dances of foreign origin (cf. Polonaise) introduced in 17th cent, and so incorporated in suite as one of Galanterien or optional dances added to normal allemande, courante, sarabande, gigue. Term was also applied to other dances of English origin.

Algoza. This is an instrument peculiar to the Punjab. It has a pair of Bansuris having one mouth to blow and is played simultaneously by one man with four fingers using both hands.

Anglican Chant. The type of the harmonized melody used for psalm- singing in the Church of England. The melody is four-square in itself, but made metrically irregular by having to accommodate a varying number of syllables.

Animato (It). 'Animated' lively.

Anschlag (Ger.)

(1) Lit. 'touch', i.e. either way in which player depresses keys of keyboard instrument or way in which they respond;

(2) An ornament, sometimes known as double Appoggiatura, consisting of 2 successive grace notes, one lower than principal note, the other a second above it. Notated by 2 small notes, first played on beat. First note is normally either repetition of preceding note or second below principal note.

Answer. A musical phrase appearing to respond to another – particularly in a Fugue, where the first entry of the main theme is called the subject and the second (at the interval of a fifth upwards from the subject) is called the answer, and so alternately. If the answer exactly reproduces the subject (apart from the displacement of a fifth) it is called a real answer and the fugue a real fugue; if the internal intervals of the subject are (as usually) slightly modified in the answer, so as to keep the music within the key, then the answer is a tonal answer and the fugue a tonal fugue.

Anthem. Short solemn vocal composition (hence national anthem, authorized for expression of patriotic sentiment).

Anticipation. The term used for the sounding of a note before the chord of which it forms part, so that at first it is heard as a discord with the preceding chord.

Antiphon. The part of Roman Catholic and Greek Orthodox church services sung as responses between single and many voices or between two groups of singers; hence antiphonal, descriptive term for musical effects drawn from the use of groups of performers stationed apart. Term Antiphonal derives from practice of alternating performance between 2 sets of singers.

Antiphonal

(1) Book containing music sung by choir in Office of Roman Church i.e. in all services other than Mass (music for Mass is contained in Gradual).

(2) Now word is applied to musical effects brought about by groups of performers being positioned in different places in auditorium or on platform – one group 'responding' to other group(s).

Anvil (Fr, enclume: Ger.,Amboss; It., ancudine). The instrument which is composed of steel bars strunk with hard wooden of metal beater. Intended to sound like blacksmith's anvil.

A Piacere (It.). 'At pleasure', same as Ad Libitum.

Appollonicon. Refers to elaborate type of Barrel, Organ, with keyboards for 6 performers and stops imitating orchestral instruments.

Appoggiatura (It., a leaning)

(1) The musical ornament (chiefly 18th century, now obsolete) consisting of unharmonized auxiliary note falling (or, less frequently rising) to an adjacent note, which is harmonized or implied to be so.

(2) The term used in modern harmonic analysis for accenting non- harmonized, note like the D in the first example (whether or not notated in the above obsolete way) adjacent to following harmonized note less accented than itself.

A Punta D'arco (It.). With the point of bow.

Arabesque (Fr., Eng.; also Arabeske; Ger.). The title borrowed from visual art and sometimes given to short piece with decorative qualities.

Archet (Fr.), Bow.

Archi (It.), lit, 'bows'. Refers to any group of stringed instruments played with bows.

Archlute. The generic name for a long-necked Lute with extra bass strings.

Arch Viol. The 17th-centuary, keyboard instrument designed to resemble several viols played with one bow; not successful.

Arco (It.). Bow (of a stringed instrument); (instruction to) play with the bow (cancelling the instruction Pizzicato).

Aria (It.). Air song, especially one or some complexity in opera or oratorio; 'da capo' aria, one in which the first section is finally repeated after a contrasting section.

Arie (Ger.). Air, Aria.

Arietta (It.). The diminutive of Aria. Short song (or instrumental piece), simpler in character and structure than aria.

Ariette (Fr.). A term indicating an operatic song of considerable dimensions and great vocal display.

Arioso (It.), aria-like, i.e. 'normally' sung (as distinct from Recitative) though not necessarily constructed according to the formal balance normally accorded to an Aria. The term is occasionally used as a title.

Arpa (It.), a Harp.

Arpeggio (It, from preceding). The chord (on piano, etc.), which is performed 'spread out' – i.e. the notes sounded not simultaneously but in succession (nearly always starting at the bottom) as normally on the harp.

Arpicordo (It.), Early name for Harpsichord.

Arpo (It.), harp.

Arrange. To set out for one performing medium a composition written for another. (Normally this indicates stricter fidelity to the composer's notes, and less artistic licence, than does Transcribe).

Arrangement.

(1) Adaptation of a piece of music to make it suitable for perf. by forces other than those of which it was originally composed.

(2) Harmonized setting for voices or instruments, of existing melody. Folk song provides obvious material for such treatment.

Ars Antiqua (Lat, old art). The term for the style of Western European medieval music (based on Plainsong and organum) practised e.g. by Perotin and preceding the Ars Nova.

Art of Fugu, The (Ger., Die Kunst der Fuge). Work by Bach, a series of fugues and canons all on the same theme –

showing prodigious resource in contrapuntal technique. No instrument is indicated, but the work was demonstrably intended for keyboards (harpsichord or organ) – though versions with other instrumentation have been made by several 20th-century musicians.

As (Ger.). Aplat.

Asavari. This melody asavari, according to some scholars is connected with snakes and snake-charmers, they say, in olden days. The snake-charmers used to play on their mouth instrument called Been, this melody, to overpower the snakes and catch them.

It is a melancholy tone of unhappy love. Her beloved has not come back to her. So, she calls the snakes with her charm to come and console her.

The literal meanings of this raga Asavari they say, is 'Asi' a snake,'Ari' is an enemy.

This is a morning raga.

Assai (It.). Very; allegro assai, very quick.

A Tempo, 'In Time'. Used to restore normal tempo of piece after rallentando, allargando, a piacere etc., or after section marked at faster or slower speed than that indicated at beginning of piece.

Atonal. Not in any key; hence atonality, atonalism. As a systematization of atonal music there developed twelve–note music.

Atonality. The term, which is often, used loosely of music, whose harmony appears unfamiliar, but properly applied to music, which rejects traditional tonality, i.e. which abandons use of tonic or key- centre to which all notes and chords of piece are related.

Attacca (It.) attack (verb), *i.e.* go on to the next section without a break; so also attacca subito (immediatly).

Attacco (It.). Short figure used as subject for imitation in figure or other polyphonic composition.

Aubade (Fr.) Morning song (cp. Serenade). Often used as title of short instrumental pieces.

Aug. Abbreviation for augmented as applied to intervals.

Augment

(1) To supplement the numbers of a performing group; so 'augmented choir', etc.

(2) To 'increase' certain intervals.

(3) To subject a melody to augmentation.

Augmentation. The treatment of a melody in such a way as to lengthen (usually doubling) the time-values of its notes. The device is used, e.g., in some fugues.

Augmented. The term applied to a type of interval regarded as an 'increased' version of a certain other interval.

Augmented Interval. The following intervals can be augmented by sharpening upper, or flattening lower, note: major second, major third, fourth, fifth, major sixth, major seventh, octave. Augmented fourth, takes place between 4th and 7th notes of every major scale; other augmented intervals necessitate notes foreign to key.

Augmented Sixth. See Augmented interval. So-called chord of augmented sixth has 3 forms hallowed by tradition, known respectively (for no good reason) as Italian, French, German: A flat, C, F sharp; A flat, C, D, F sharp; A flat, C, E flat, F sharp. Since on keyboard, it is impossible to distinguish between F sharp and G flat, last of 3 may also be treated as Dominant seventh chord (in this case in key of D flat): A flat, C, E flat, G flat.

Augmented Triad. The chord composed, in simplest form, of 2 major thirds, e.g. C, E, G sharp. Notes of chord can also be arranged as follows: E, G sharp, C; or, G sharp, C, E.

Aulos, generic term used by ancient Greeks for any wind instrument (Lat., tibia). Term used more particularly for double reed instrument, most important wind instrument of ancient Greeks. Played in pairs, with reeds held inside mouth.

Aural Training. Purpose of aural training is to teach pupils to recognize sounds and rhythms they hear to write them down on paper. Ability to do this is indispensable for study of harmony and counterpoint, and essential for any musician.

Autoharp. Refers to the kind of zither in which chords are obtained by pressing keys that stop or damp strings.

Ave Maria (Lat), 'Hail Mary', prayer to Virgin used in RC Church, often set to music, e.g. by Liszt. Schubert. Gounod.

Auxiliary Note. In harmony, a note which forms a discord with the chord with which it is heard, but is 'justified' because it lies adjacent (higher or lower) to a note of the chord which is heard immediately before and after.

Ave Maria (Lat., Hail, Mary). Roman Catholic prayer of partly biblical source. It has been variously set to music.

Ayre. The old spelling of air, retained in modern English for a type of English song practised (e.g. by J. Dowland) about 1600—having its main melodic interest in the top vocal line, with accompaniment for lute (or other voices), usually strophic.

B

B (Eng.; Fr., It., Si; Ger., H):

(1) Refers to the seventh (or leading) note of scale of C major. In German nomenclature, B is B flat and H is B natural;

(2) As abbrev., B = Bass, Batchelor (B. Mus. B. or Mus. B = Bachelor of Music).

B. Mus. The abbr. of Bachelor of Music.

Baal Shem. Refers to the suit for violin and piano by Bloch, subtitled 'Three Pictures of Chassidic Life': named after Baal Shem Tov (Master of the Good Name), 17th-century founder of the Jewish pietist sect of Chassidism.

Baba Haridas. Haridas Baba's name will be familiar to all those who have studied the life of Tansen of Hindustani music fame.

Haridas Swami lived in Brindavan, teaching the worship of the Lord through musical knowledge to all those who went to him, most magnanimously. He also taught this noble art to Miyan Tansen.

After Tansen had attained fame, once the Emperor Akbar asked him who his teacher was, meaning thereby, "if the disciple himself was so great the guru should be really still greater", and desired to see him.

Now, Baba Haridas would not like to exhibit this skill mastery before any man, however great he might be. He would only sing to God.

So Tansen quietly took the emperor to Brindavan and left him in a hiding place and went alone to pay his humble respects to his esteemed guru, and started singing before him deliberately and cleverly, making some mistakes purposely so as to make his guru sing. The guru at once burst out began to sing in order to correct his pupil, who was committing such blunders, to his great surprise and disappointment.

Emperor Akbar, who was concealing himself nearby, could hear the Swamiji's exquisite music and was very much impressed. In fact the music was so enchanting that he had to ask Tansen, "why he had not learnt exactly like his guru". To this Tansen's witty answer was, "My guru sings only to the God, whereas, I have to sing to human beings at their command".

Such were the heights of the musical talents of Haridas Baba, and Tansen had mastered his art under the able guidance of a noble teacher of calibre.

There are no records available to know how long Haridas lived. But it is believed, he left his mortal coil at Brindavan during the lifetime of his great disciple Tansen.

Baborak. Bohemain national dance that is consisting of alternating sections of 3/4 and 2/4 times.

Baby Grand. The smallest size of grand piano.

Bacchetta (It., pl-ette, stick). Refers to the drumstick.

Bach. German family of musicians. Bach without prefaced name or initials indicates Johann Sebastian Bach and contemporaries.

Bach Trumpet. The modern instrument which is designed to make practicable the playing of high, florid trumpet parts in works of Bach and contemporaries.

Bachianas Brasilerras. The term used for name of series of works by Villa-Lobos combining Bachian procedures with elements of Brazilian traditional music.

Backfall. The term current in 17th-centuary. England for short Appoggiatura, where ornamental note has been one degree of scale above principal note. Double back fall was equivalent to slide taken from above, i.e. with

2 ornamental notes above principal note.

Bandinage or Badinerie (Fr.). The 'frolic', term which is used in 18th centuary for quick, frivolous move in duple time, e.g. in Bach's suite in B minor for flute and strings. It is one of optional dances or Galanterien in suite.

Badinerie (Fr., a teasing). The term used for the title of certain quick 2/4 movements in the 18th century, e.g. in Bach's Suite in B minor for flute and strings.

Bagatelle (Fr.), 'trifle'. Short piece, which is usually (but not necessarily) written for piano, and usually of light, humorous or whimsical character. Bethoven composed 3 sets of Bagatellen for piano (op 33, op 119, op 126 – 26, pieces in all).

Bagpipe (s). The term used for the reed-pipe instrument for which wind is stored in a bag, either mouth-filled, or filled by bellows under player's arm; the former type is the louder. Similar types are found in other countries; most are having one or more drone pipes (giving unaltered bass-notes) as well as a pipe for the melody (chanter).

Bagpipe

Baguette (Fr.). The drumstick.

Balalaika. A type of Russian plucked instrument, which is usually with three strings and triangular body; made in various sizes and used singly and in bands for folk music, etc. Cp. Domra.

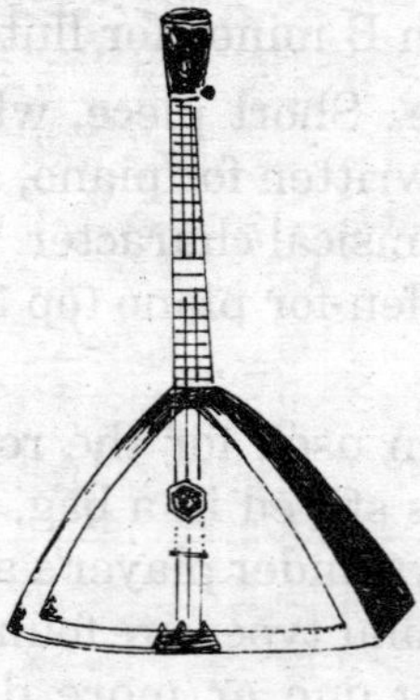

Balalaika

Ballabile (It.). To be danced; in a dancing manner.

Ballad:

(1) Narrative song, which is either traditional or (as in the 19th centuary.) written in imitation of traditional forms. From 16th to 19th centuary, words of ballads, frequently dealing with contemporary events, were printed on sheets and sold at fairs etc.

(2) Sentimental drawing-room song of late 19th, early 20th centuary.

(3) Instrumental piece = Ballade (2).

Ballade (Fr.) :

(1) Refers to the type of medieval French verse with refrain at end of stanza, frequently set to music by

trouveres, or, with more complexity, by polyphonic composers;

(2) In 19th, 20th cent., instrumental piece, sometimes of considerable length, of lyrical, romantic character. Chopin pioneered this type of ballade.

Ballad Opera. Type of opera, in which dialogue gots interspersed with songs set to popular tunes (often actually taken from words of well-known composers).

Ballata (It.). A form of 14th-century Italian poetry and music.

Ballet:

(1) The form of dancing of Italian origin, becoming established at French court in the 16th century, and evolving into a recognized art-form with its own traditional technique and conventions; it normally uses orchestral music (specially composed or otherwise) and appropriately full resources of stage decoration. The term is now used in Britain for almost any piece of stage dancing having an artistic purpose and substantial length; but in the U.S.A. It is commonly with held from works not based on the 'classical' technique of dancing e.g. the so-called 'modern dance'.

(2) An alternative spelling of Ballett, and so pronounced.

Ballet (It, balletto). Refers to the composition for several voices, mainly homophonic in character, generally with refrain to words fa la.

Balletto (It.).

(1) See ballet.

(2) The dance movt. In suite.

(3) Ballet.

Ballo (It). A dance; Overtura di Ballo, idiosyncratic title of a concert-overture by Sullivan, 1870, using dance rhythms.

Bamboo Pine. Refers to the simple wind-instrument of recorder type, which is used mainly educationally, players after making their own instruments; sometimes just called pipe.

Band. Refers to a numerous body of players, especially of wind or percussion instruments – Brass, Military, Dance, Percussion bands, etc. The use of the term for a full or string orchestra has been obsolete or colloquial.

Banjo. Refers to the fretted instrument of five or more strings, plucked with fingers or plectrum.

Bar.

(1) A metrical division of music which is marked on paper as the distance between two vertical lines; so 'two beats in the bar', etc.

(2) Such a vertical line itself. But two vertical lines close together, indicating the end of a piece or section, are called even in English double bar, not (double bar line.).

(3) A medieval German unit of song-construction, two similar sections being followed by one in contrast.

Bar. Abbreviation or Baritone (voice).

Barber-shop Singing. The term used for the singing of home-made arrangements of sentimental songs by amateur male quartets.

Barcarolle (Fr., from It.). Refers to a boating-song, especially of the kind associated with Venetian gondoliers; song or instrumental piece suggestive of this, in swaying 6/8 time.

Bard. Celtic minstrel, whose duties incl. Composition of extempore songs in honour of patron.

Baritone

(1) The man's voice of a range intermediate between tenor and bass.

(2) Of 'families' of instruments indication of a range below the 'tenor' type, e.g. baritone saxhorn, baritone saxophone.

(3) Name used in braas bands as abbreviation for baritone saxhorn.

Barkarole (Ger). Barcarolle.

Barocco, Barock (It. Ger.). Baroque.

Baroque. This term used to describe characteristics of musical style roughly corresponding to this, c. 1600-1750. The term baroque organ is applied to the type of this period, more brilliant in tone and less heavy than 19th century type, with lighter wind-pressure and greater reliance on mutation stops.

Barrage (Fr.). The use of chords played Barre on the guitar.

Barre (Fr.). (Chord on guitar, etc.) Played with one finger laid like a rigid bar across all strings, raising the pitch of all these equally.

Barrel-organ. Refers to automatic organ in which projections on a hand-rotated barrel bring into action the notes required – i.e. a genuine pipe-organ though limited to a number of pre-set tunes like a musical box.

Baryton. An obsolete stringed instrument, which is resembling bass viol but having sympathetic strings like the viola d'amore.

Basant (Rag.). It is a lively raga connected to spring season., It is a dancing melody. It is visualized as Radha the female figure carrying a spray of yellow colour in a tray made of flower and a garland to offer to her lover at the time of mirth and gay merriment. Raga Basant portrays also as a beautiful youth bedecked with flowers.

This raga suggests the joyful emotions of human beings at the advent of spring. It is one of earliest seasonal melodies.

Basic Set. Term used in twelve-note technique for the note-row or series (comprising all twelve notes within the octave) in its original chosen order—i.e. not in an order arrived at by using the row backwards, or upside-down, or both.

Bass

(1) The lowest male voice.

(2) The lowest note or part in a chord, a composition, etc.

(3) The lower regions of musical pitch generally-especially in antithesis to treble.

(4) Of a 'family' of instruments. Having low range, e.g. bass clarinet. Bass saxophone; bass flute, usually a misnomer for alto flute.

(5) Colloquial abbreviation for double-bass, or (military and brass bands) for the tuba (either size and indicating F below middle C as top line but one of the staff (and so sometimes also called F clef.)

Bass drum (or Long Drum). The large shallow drum of low but indefinite pitch; used in symphony orchestras, military bands (where it may be carried), dance-band (the drum-stick usually worked by pedal), etc.

Bass Fiddle. The colloquial term for double-bass.

Bass (Fr.). Bass; base chantante = Basso cantante.

Bassef Horn. Instrument of same type as clarinet but lower in pitch down to the F at the bottom of the bass staff. It is a transposing instrument. The origin of its name is said to be from a South German term for 'small bass', the basset-hounp being so named after its voice.

Basso (It.) Bass. So basso cantante ('singing'), a bass voice suitable for lyrical rather than dramatic parts in opera; basso profondo (not profundo), a bass voice of unusually low range.

Bassoon. The bass woodwind instrument found in the orchestra and military band, occasionally also as soloist and in chamber music; having a double reed, thus related to the oboe.

Baton (Fr. Baton). The stick used by conductor to indicate time and expression.

Batterie (Fr.). Battery also percussion section of orchestra.

Battery. The collective term for percussion instruments.

Battuta (It.)

(1) 'Beat'. A battuta, in strict time. Senza battuta, without any regular beat, i.e. in free time (e.g. in recitative).

(2) Particularly 1st beat in bar, hence 'bar'. Ritmo di tre battute, 3-bar rhythm, i.e. with main accent falling at beginning of every 3 bars.

Be (Ger.). The flat.

Bearbeitung (Ger.). The arrangement.

Beat

(1) Refers to the unit of measurement in music, indicated in choral and orchestral works by motion of conductor's stick. Number of beats in bar depends on time-signature and on speed of movt Movt, in 4/4 time may have 8 beats if very slow, 4 if speed is moderate, 2 if very fast. In exceptional cases may only be 1 beat in bar; this occurs most frequently in very quick movts, in 3/4 or 3/8 time.

(2) Early English name for various ornaments.

Beatrice Et Benedict. The opera by Berlioz, libretto by composer based on Shakespeare's Much Ado About Nothing. First perf. Baden-Baden, 1862.

Be-bop. Type of jazz (of agitated character) cultivated in 1940s, mainly by small groups.

Bebung (Ger.). The vibrato used on clavichord. Finger repeatedly presses key without releasing it, varying tension of string, so producing minute variations of pitch.

Becarre (Fr.). Natural.

Becken (Ger.). Cymbals.

Bee's Wedding. The see songs without words.

Begleitung (Ger.). The accompaniment.

Bel Canto (It., beautiful singing). Term used—often vaguely—by teachers, 'authorities' on singing, etc, with reference to the finely cultivated voice, especially implying suitability to the agile yet smooth voice-production demanded in the operas of Bellini, Donizetti, etc.

Bell:

(1) Heavy reasoning vessel in hollow cup-shape found in churches, etc., and rung either directly by hand-ropes or by Carillon;

(2) An orchestral instrument usually in the form of a free-hanging tube ('tubular bell') struck by hand with small hammer—a set of such bells sometimes spanning as much as an octave (see also Glockenspiel);

(3) The open end of a wind instrument, at the opposite extremity to the mouthpiece.

Bell Anthem. The name given to 'Rejoice in the Lord always', anthem for voices and strings by Purcell; beginning suggests tolling of bells.

Bell Lyra or **Bell Lyre.** Refers to portable glockenspiel played in military bands. It is having metal bars attached to lyre-shaped frame with handle. Player holds handle in one hand, mallet in other.

Bell Tree. Refers to a set of small bells, which are mounted vertically on long rod. Usually played by running stick along set, producing arpeggio.

Belly. (Fr., table). Refers to the upper part of sound box of string instrument. It is often known as 'table'.

Bemol (Fr.) = Flat.

Ben Bene (It.). Well, very.

Benedictus (Lat) :

(1) Refers to the second part of Sanctus of Roman Mass;

(2) Refers to the canticle Benedictus Dominus Israel ('Blessed be the Lord God of Israel').

Berceuse (Fr.). The Cradle–song; instrumental piece suggestive of this.

Bergamasca (It., also in other languages as bergmasque, bergmask, etc.):

(1) Tune and chord-sequence, e.g. as ground bass;

(2) The folkdance from Bergamo;

(3) Now a term used by composers with only the vaguest picturesque significance.

Bergertte (Fr.). Light-French song cultivating an idealized pastoral style (like Dresden-China shepherdesses). From Fr. Berger, shepherd.

Bes (Ger.). B double flat.

Bestimmt (Ger.). Decisively.

Bewegt (Ger.). 'moved', i.e. with animation (It., mosso). Bewegter, faster (It., piu mosso). Massig bewegt, at moderate speed.

Bezifferter Bass (Ger.). A figured bass.

Bhajan. Bhajan is a devotional type of song. It is very old-fashioned type of music sung in praise of any deity or the Lord. Saints like Tulsidas, Surdas and Meerabai composed and sang such devotional songs. These are still sung all over and are most popular.

Bhangra. It is folk tune of the Punjab. Women folk sing this and the men dance. Emphasis is given more on the rhythm than melody. The little melody needed for it is sometimes provided by a bowed instrument called

Chikara. Dholak songs geets are very common in Punjab. Tappas which are usually sung by a group of people are observed during merry-making festivities.

Holi songs are also sung like in other regions in their own peculiar style. Their Kawwalis and Heers are typical Punjabi specialities and are liked by people of all other regions too.

Bhirav (Rag). Rag Bhirav expresses a feeling of peace and harmony and is supposed to drive away fear.

The visual picture that is given, shows Lord Siva sitting in a meditative mood, with his companion Parwati who is seen applying sandal paste on his body. This raga is sung in the early hours of the morning. It gives peace of mind.

Bicinium (Lat.; bis, twice, and canere to sing). The term used in 16th, 17th centuary for composition for 2 voices or (later) 2 instruments.

Bilawal. The character of this melody is a lady putting on her jewels, getting ready, to meet her lover. Her maid attendant assists her, holding a tray of toilet requisites. The lady prays to the God of Love, while still dressing, that she should look the best among the ladies to win the love of her mate.

This is sung in the morning time.

Binary. In two sections; binary form, classification used of a simple movement which is in two sections, the first modulating to another key and the second returning to the original key. (Cp. Ternary).

Bird Organ. Miniature foreinner of barrel organ originally made to teach songbirds to sing tunes. Later versions imitated bird song and were built into cages of mechanical birds.

Bis (Fr.), 'twice' (Lat., bis). Indicates that passage-over which word is written, is to be played twice.

Bisbigliando (It., whispering). This term means repeating the notes softly and quickly, as a special effect in playing the harp.

Biscroma (It.). Thirty-second-note, demisemiquaver.

Bitonality. The use of 2 keys simultaneously, whether indicated by different key signatures or not. However, clear distinction is between 2 keys, ear instinctively seizes on any points they may have in common.

Biwa. A Japanese form of lute, normally with 4 silk strings.

Black Pudding. Another name for serpent.

Bladder And String. Folk instrument which is consisting of inflated bladder attached to pole. Taut string is fastened to each of end of pole, passing over bladder, and is bowed to give sound.

Blanche (Fr.). The minim.

Blaser, Blasinstrumente (Ger.). The wind instruments. Blasmusik, music for wind.

Blech (Ger.). Brass (section of an orchestra); Blechmusik, brass band, music for brass.

Blechinstrumente (Ger.). Brass instruments.

Block (percussion instrument). See Temple Block, wood block.

Block Chords. Refer to harmonic procedure whereby notes chords move simultaneously in 'blocks', instead of different contrapuntal directions. Debussy used device in Plano pieces; subsequently adopted by many modern jazz pianists, inch. Dave Brubeck, George Shearing.

Blockflote (Ger.; Fr., flute-a-bec). A recorder or breaked flute.

Blue Note. A note of the scale (especially the third and seventh) characteristically flattened in jazz and in light and serious music indebted to jazz idiom.

Bocca Chiusa (It.; Fr., bouche fermee). This term means singing with closed lips.

Boehm. See also bohm (alternative spelling).

Bochm System. Woodwind key-mechanism.

Bogen. The 'bow – in string parts used, like arco, to contradict preceding pizzicato.

Bolero. Spanish dance, usually with a triplet on the second half of the first beat of bar; accompaniment includes dancers' voices and castanets.

Bolshol Theatre. Moscow's principal opera and ballet theatre; the present building opened in 1856. (Bolshoi means large, great).

Bombard. The double-reed instrument, now obsolete: bass of shawm family.

Bomhard (E). The name given to the larger instruments of the obsolete shawm family. (Pommer is an alternative form).

Bombarde. The organ reed stop of great power made at 8ft, 16ft and 32ft pitches.

Bombarda (It.). Euphonium.

Bombarde. A sixteen-foot reed stop on the organ.

Bombardon

(1) The name formerly given in brass and military bands to the two types of bass tuba used in those bands.

(2) The organ stop similar to bombarde.

Bones. The percussion instrument which is used in black-faced minstrel shows, etc; a pair of small bones held between the fingers and clicked together rhythmically, like castanets. Orig. made of ox rib; known since medieval times.

Bongo (pl bongos). The small Cuban usually played in pairs with fingers.

Bongo. The single-headed small drum (both tunable and non-tunable varieties exist) struck with the finger; familiar in Latin-American dance bands and occasionally used elsewhere. Usually in sets of 2 or 3 (plural pongos).

Boogie-woogie (sometimes just 'boogie'). Jazz style, special type of piano blues. Became popular in late 1930's, early 1940's. Characterized by continuous sharply rhythmic ostinato bass played by left hand, while right hand provides melody, adhering to 12-bar period, though with great rhythmic variety and improvisation within that framework.

Bore. The diameter of tube of wind instrument.

Borre, Borree, Borry. The old English spellings of bourree.

Bouche Fermee (Fr.). With the mouth closed, i.e. (as instruction to singers) humming.

Bourdon (Fr.), lit. 'burden':

(1) Drone bass e.g. that produced on lowest strings of hurdy-gurdy.

(2) Soft organ stop, using stopped pipes generally of 16 ft tone.

Bourree (Fr.). The dance-movement (found e.g. in the baroque suite) in quick double time beginning with an up-beat.

Bouzouki. The fretted string instrument of Greece. Played by plucking strings with much use of tremolo to prolong notes.

Bow (Fr., archet; Ger., Bogen; It., arco). The instruments of viol and violin families are played with bow, consisting of horse-hair strung on wooden stick. Name derives from fact that orig. shape of stick was convex. Tension of hair can be varied by adjustable nut at one end of stick. Shape of bow has varied: modern bow came in at end of 18th centuart. Longer than earlier bows; stick tapers towards point (i.e. end furthest from hand, as opposed to heel) and is slightly curved towards hair. Bows used for viola, cello and double-bass are similar to violin bow, but progressively heavier; cello and double- bass bows are progressively shorter.

Bowed Harp. The primitive violin, first depicted in 12th-century. Norwegian carving. Held vertically on knee; its 2 to 4 strings were played simultaneously to give drone beneath melody. Very similar to crwth.

Bowing. In general, technique of playing string instrument string instrument with bow. In particular, method of playing notes or passages, indicated by conventional sings: ▯ indicates down-bow, i.e. arm moves from left to right, and V indicates up-bow, i.e. arm moves right to left. Strong down-bow ensures good attack. Increased pressure possible with up-bow, after bow has already touched string, helps produce steady crescendo.

Br., abbr. Or Ger., **Bratsche** (N), i.e. viola(s).

Brace. The vertical line, generally accompanied by bracket, used to join 2 or more staves together.

Branle, **Branle**. French dance-movement in 2/2 time, something like the gavott; it is called brawl in Shakespeare.

Brass. The collective term for musical instruments made of brass or other metals and blown directly through a cup-shaped or funnel- shaped mouthpiece. (This excludes saxophone, because the air is actuated through a reed and not directly; it excludes flute, even if made of metal, because it has no such mouthpiece. Woodwind. Basic brass requirements of the symphony orchestra have been 4 horns, 2 or 3 trump sets, 2 tenor and 1 bass trombone and 1 tuba; heavy brass, inexact and unhelpful term for trombones and tuba.

Brass Instruments (modern) (1) double B flat tuba (2) B flat euphonium (3) sousaphone (4) trombone (5) bugle (6) cornet (7) trumpet (8) French horn (9) Wagner tuba.

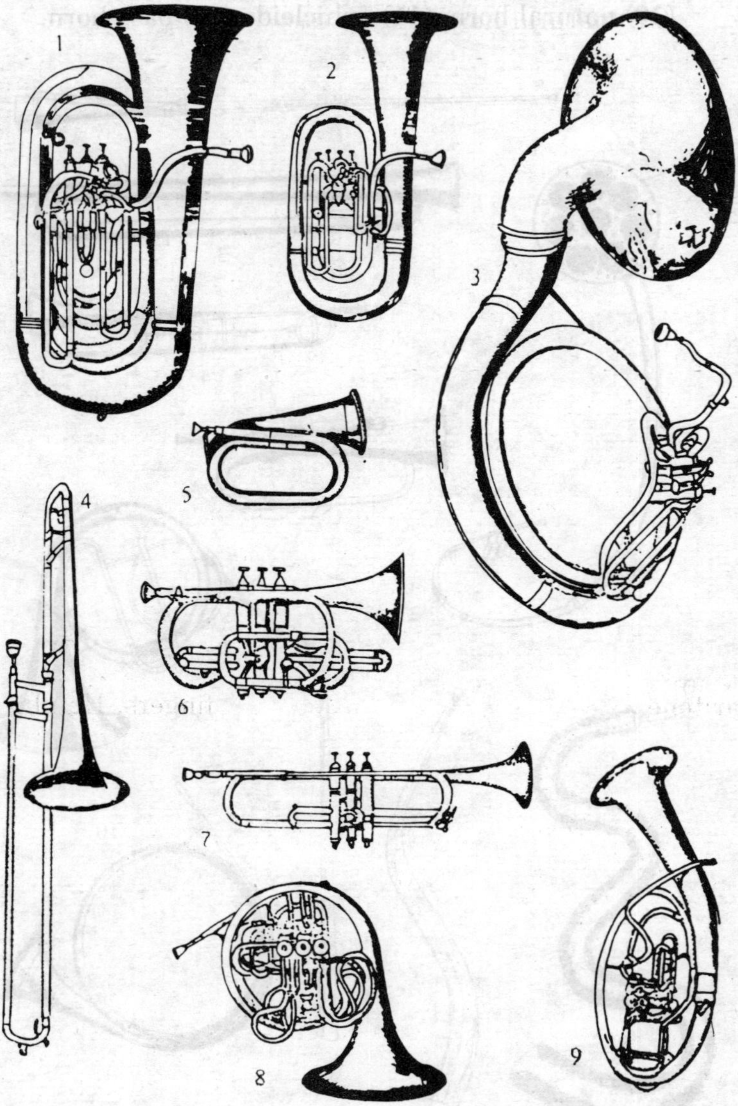
1
2
3
4
5
6
7
8
9

Brass Instruments (old) (1) 1 or (2) buisine (3) Alphorn (4) Slide trumpet (5) Key bugle (6) hand horn (7) Serpent (8) tenor cornett (9) Straight cornett (10) natural horn. (11) ophicleide (12) bass horn.

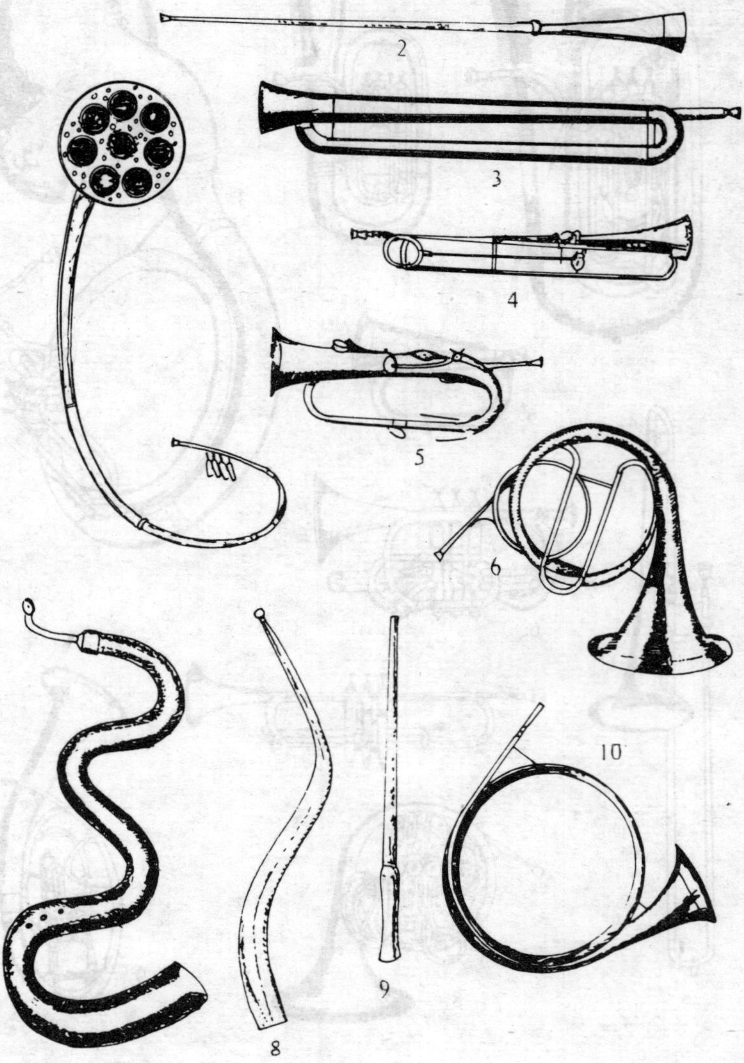

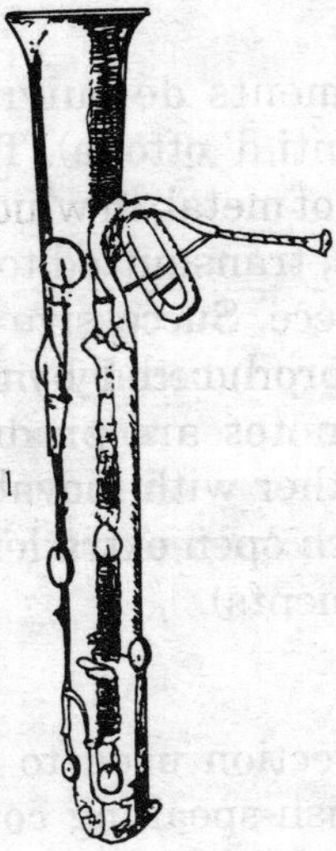

11

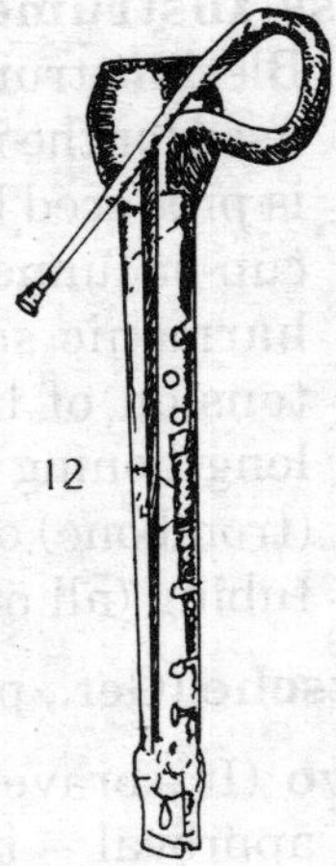

12

Note: nos (7) (8) and (9) are not, strictly speaking brass instruments but are related, being blown through cup – shaped mouth pieces.

Brass Band. The combinations of brass instruments only (Military Band) has woodwind too with or without percussion; in many countries made up of a fairly rigid combination of cornets, flugelhorn, tenor and baritone saxhorns, euphoniums, trombones, and tubas.

Standard organization is: 1 E flat cornet, 8 B flat cornets flat flugelhorn (tereble saxhorn), 3 E flat saxhorns, 2 B flat baritones, 2 euphoniums, 2 tenor trombones, 1 bass trombone, 2 E flat bombardons (bass tubas), 2 B flat bombardons. With exception of bass trombone, all instruments are treated as transposing instruments, parts being written in treble clef.

Standards of performance of brass bands are extremely high, and are maintained by competition festivals dating from early 19th centuary. More recently, distinguished composers have written tes pieces for these. There being little music of quality written for brass bands, normal repertory largely depends on arrangement.

Brass Instruments (Fr., instruments de cuivre; Ger., Blechinstrumente; It., strumenti d' ottone). The term used for the instruments made of metal, in which sound is produced by vibration of lips, transmitted to tube by cup-or funnel-shaped mouthpiece. Successive notes of harmonic series have been produced by increased tension of lips. Intervening notes are produced by lengthening sounding tube; either with movable slide (trombone) or with valves which open extra lengths of tubing (all other brass instruments).

Bratsche (Ger., pl. en). Viola.

Bravo (It., brave, fine). The interjection used to express approval – invariable in English-speaking countries, but brava, bravi, brave in Indian for a female performer, male performers, female performers, respectively.

Bravura (It.), lit. 'bravery', 'swagger'. In music, term implies display; bravura passage requires some feat of virtuosity by performer.

Break

(1) A change in tone-quality encountered in some voices and wind- instruments in passing between different registers.

(2) A short solo passage, usually improvised, in a concerted jazz piece – i.e. a cadenza.

(3) (Verb) of the voice, to undergo that change in quality and compass which comes to a young male's voice in puberty (better spoken of as to change, as break suggests that something has been destroyed and lost).

Breit (Ger.). Grandly broadly—used to describe manner, not tempo, of performance.

Breit (Ger.). Broadly, grandly—an indication of manner of performance, not (except) incidentally of speed.

Breve (Lat., brevis, 'short'), orig. Introduced in early 13th centuary; as notes of still shorter value were introduced it became longer. Now longest note, still occasionally used: equal to 8 minims.

Brevis (Lat.). The short: missa brevis.

Bridge

(1) On a violin, viol, guitar, etc, the supporting piece of wood which holds the strings up from the belly of the instrument, and transmits their vibrations to the body of the instrument.

(2) In a composition, a section (usually bridge passage) the main function of which has been to link together (sometimes partly by a change of key) two passages more important than itself.

Brilliant (Fr.) Brillant (It.). Brilliant (direction for performance).

Brindisi (It.). The drinking-song, toast.

Brillant, **Brillante** (Fr, It.). Brilliant (as a direction for performance, particularly in solo music).

Brindisi (It.). Coast, drinking-song (e.g. in Verdi, s 'La traviata').

Brio (It.). Vigour; con brio, Vigorously.

Brise (Fr.). The 'broken'—used of arpeggio in keyboard and harp music, and detache bowing in string music.

Broken Chord. A chord of which the notes are not all played simultaneously, but one after the other (or a few followed by another few. Similarly broken octaves, a passage of alternate notes an octave apart—especially in piano-writing.

Broken Consort. An old English term for an ensemble of instruments of more than one family.

Broken Octaves. Refer to passage of octaves performed not simultaneously but alternating between 2 registers—much used in piano music.

Browning. A type of English variation form current about 1600 based on a tune 'The leaves be green, the nuts be brown'.

Brunette (Fr.). The amorous pastoral song; current in late 17th, 18th centuary.

Brustwerk (Ger.). Refers to one of manuals in old German organs, with stops of quieter tone than those on Great organ (Hauptwerk). Also known as Brustpositiv. No exact English equivalent.

Buda-budakku. In Andhra Desa Buda-Budakku a small drum-like instrument is also seen. It is held in one hand and with particular movements it makes peculiar rhythmic sounds. Usually the village street beggar who goes about from street to street uses this to invoke the presiding deity to shower blessings upon his patrols.

There is also a snake-charmer's wind-pipe, made of pumpkin shell (hollow) tagged to a pair of bamboo reeds with holes. The snake charmer blows the instrument with his mouth and plays on the reeds with fingers. He plays on this when he wants to make the snake dance with its hood raised.

Buffo (It.; tem; buffa), comic; opera buffa, comic opera. A noun, means comic actor or singer.

Bugle. A brass instrument with conical tube and cup–shaped mouth –piece, used for giving military signals.

Bugle A Clefs (Fr.). Key bugle.

Buhne (Ger.). The stage or theatre.

Bund (Ger.). The term applied to clavichord in which each note has separate string.

Burla, Burlesca (It.; Fr.; burlesque; Ger., Burleske), lit. 'Jest'. Short piece of lively and frolicsome character. Also applied to extended composition in playful style.

Byzantine Music. The music of Christian church in Eastern Roman Empire. Music of Byzantine liturgy survives in notation of ancient origin. Correspondences between Byzantine and Gregorian music show early influence of Eastern Church on Western; further contribution to West was organ, though used in Byzantium only for secular purposes.

C

C (Eng., Ger.; Fr., ut, do; It., do).

(1) The key-note or tonic of scale of C major;

(2) As abbrev = cantus (It., canto), contralto, con (with), col or colla (with the); C. B. = col Basso, indicating cellos are to play with double-basses; C.B. = contrabasso (double-bass); C.F. = Cantus Firmus.

(3) C clef, ornamental form of letter C, indicates middle C.

C.A. The abbrev for coll' acro (with the bow).

Cabaletta (It.), (1 e.g. as in Rossini). The short operatic song in simple style; (2, e.g. as in Verdi) the final, quicker section of an aria or duet made up of several (usually 2) sections.

Cabinet Organ (US). The American organ.

Caccia (It.). Hunt; for above da caccia: for corno da caccia.

Cachucha. Spanish solo dance in 3/4 time, with rhythm somewhat like bolero.

Cacophony. The sounds of the utmost dissonance, usually used in derogatory sense.

Cadence. A progression of chords (usually 2) giving an effect of closing a 'sentence' in music. Thus perfect cadence, progression of dominant chord to tonic chord; plagal cadence, subdominant to tonic; imperfect cadence, tonic (or other chord) to dominant; interrupted cadence, dominant to submediant (or to some other chord suggesting a substitution for the expected tonic chord); Phrygian cadence, progression (deriving from the Phrygian mode) which, in the key of C major, leads to the chord of E major (and correspondingly with other keys).

Caenza (It. Candence but pronounced as English and used in different sense), solo vocal or instrumental passage, either of an improvised nature or in some other way suggesting an interpolation in the flow of the music – particularly, today, in concertos for solo instrument and orchestra.

Caisse (Fr.). The drum; grosse caisse, bass drum; caisse clair, side drum; caisse roulante or caisse sourde, tenor drum.

Cakewalk. US dance originating in Negro slave plantations, with musical elements foreshadowing ragtime; became generally known from late 19th century.

Calando (It.). Refers to giving way, both in volume and speed; i.e. combination of diminuendo and ritardando.

Calinda, La. Orchestral piece by Delius (excerpt from his Negro opera 'Koanga'); a dance taking its name from an actual Negro dance imported by African slaves to the American continent.

Calliope. The organ powered by steam instead of air. Can be played manually or operated mechanically. Its very loud sound makes it suitable for use in fairgrounds.

Cambiata (It.). Short for nota cambiata, changed note. Used mainly of 16th-centuary counterpoint, term implies use of dissonant note where one would expect consonant note. Currently used in 2 senses:

(1) Of an accented passing dissonance. Palestrina's music occurs on even beats of bar in descending passage; other composers show greater freedom in its use;

(2) Of a sequence of notes, also known as 'changing note group'.

Camera, Da (It.), for the room–either (1) as distinct from da chiesa, for the church, or (2) as implying music for a small gathering, exactly as 'chamber music' does.

Campana, Campane (It.). Bell, bells.

Campanology. The study of bells or art of bell ringing.

Canarie, Canaries, Canary. The term used for an old dance in triple time (a type of jig), having a prominent dotted rhythm.

Can-Can. The Parisian dance, sometimes supposedly salacious, in quick 2/4 times.

Cancrizans (made-up Lat.), crab-wise. The term is used (apparently through defective observation of crabs, which move sideways) to indicate a back-to-front order of notes (i.e. retrograde motion); canon canrizans, a canon in which the imitating voice gives out the theme not as the first voice gave it but with the notes in reverse order.

Canon. The contrapuntal composition, or section of a composition in which a melody given by one voice (or instrument) is repeated by one or more other voices (or instruments) each has entering before the previous voice finished, so that overlapping results.

Cantabile (It.). Refers to 'singable'. Applied to instrumental piece, which indicates that player should make music sing.

Cantando (It.). Refers to 'singing'. Same as cantabile.

Cantata (It., a sung piece). An extended choral work with or without solo voices, and usually with orchestral accompaniment.

Cantatrice (It.). The woman singer.

Canticle

(1) A hymn with bibilical words, other than from the Psalms, used in Christian liturgy (distinct from anthem, not on a liturgically obligatory text); so, analogously.

(2) A concert work with a religious or quasi-religious text– term used.

Cantiga. Spanish or Portuguese folk song. Over 400 Cantigas de Santa Maria (hymns of the virgin) were collected by Alfonso the Wise (1221-84), King of Castile and Leon (1252-84).

Cantilena (It.). A smooth song-like melodic line.

Cantillation. Unaccompanied chanting in free rhythm– term used particularly of Jewish liturgical chanting.

Canto (It.). Song, melody; col canta indicates that accompanist takes tempo from singer.

Cantor (Lat), 'singer'. Chief singer in choir; or director of music in cathedrals, and similar establishments (Eng. 'chanter' or 'precentor').

Cantoris (Lat., of the singer, i.e. of the precentor). Refers to that section of the choir in a cathedral, etc., which is stationed on the north (i.e. precentor's) side of the chancel; opposite of decani.

Cantus (Lat.). Song melody; cantus firmus (pl. cantus firmi), fixed song, i.e. the 'given' melody borrowed from religious or secular sources.

Cantus Firmus (Lat.; It., canto fermo), 'fixed song'; pre-existing melody used, often in long notes, as foundation of polyphonic composition.

Cantus Planus (Lat.). Plainsong.

Canzona, Canzone (It.)

(1) Any song;

(2) Specifically, a type of medieval Italian poem, and hence a musical setting of this;

(3) Type of short instrumental piece, especially of the 16th to early 18th centuries.

Canzonet. The term used c. 1600 for a light song for one or more voices, and later, for an English solo song not from an opera.

Canzonetta (It.). Refers to little song, light song.

Capella. The incorrect spelling for Capella.

Capo (It., head). A device used on the finger-board on a suitar to shorten the strings equally in order to facilitate playing in various keys – i.e. a form of movable nut.

Capotasto (It.). The 'head (capo) of finger-board (tasto)' of string instrument. Also, mechanical device which has been consisting of cross bar of wood, metal or ivory (Fr., barre), for shortening all strings simultaneously and hence raising pitch; simplifies performance of pieces in extreme keys, but only particle on instruments with frets.

Capriccio, Caprice (It., Fr.). The term applied – caprice being also used as English – to various types of lively light piece, and specially to a 17th-century keyboard work in lively fugal style.

Carmen (Lat.). The song; the plural is carmina.

Carillon

(1) The set of bells hung in bell tower, struck by hammers connected to keyboard and pedal board, or to automatic mechanism powered by clockwork or electricity, so producing tune;

(2) The organ stop with bell-like sound.

Carnival of the Animals (Fr., Le Carnival des animaux). The satirical suite by Saint-Saens for 2 pianos, string quintet, flute, clarinet and xylophone (though often played by full orchestra), described as fantaisie zoologique.

Carol. An English traditional song or joyful character (apparently in its medieval origins a danced song). The Christmas carol is only one type.

Cassa (It.). The drum; gran cassa, bass drum; cassa rullante, tenor drum.

Cassation (It., cassazione). The term used in 18th centuary. For instrumental suite which is suitable for open-air performance, thus similar to serenade or divertimento.

Castanets. Refers to the percussion instruments of 2 hollowed-out wooden surfaces rhythmically clicked together by the fingers of Spanish dancers; in the orchestra the clicking pieces of wood are often mounted for convenience at the end of a small stick, which is shaken.

Castrato (It., castrated). The term used for male singer who has sexual organs modified to allow development of a powerful voice in soprano or contralto range.

Catalogue D'oiseaux (Fr., Bird catalogue). The set of 13 piano pieces by Messiaen, each portraying a French bird.

Cavatina (It.)

(1) Operatic song in slow tempo, either complete in itself or followed by faster, more resolute section.

(2) A rather slow, song-like instrumental movement – title.

CB. Abbrev. of contrabassi (double basses).

Cebell. The gavotte-like dance, found in England in 17th-century.

Cedez (Fr.). The term means 'give way', i.e. go a little slower.

Celere (It.). The term means quick. Celerita, speed; celeramente, quickly.

Celesta. An instrument looking like small upright piano but having hammers striking metal bars giving bell-like sound.

Cello. Bowed four-stringed instrument, one of the family (of which the principal member is the violin) which superseded the viols in the 17th and 18th centuries; has compass from C two octaves below middle C, upwards for more than 3 octaves.

Cembalo (It.)

(1) Dulcimer.

(2) Abbrev. Of clavicembalo.

Cents. The units by which musical intervals are measured. Cent is 100th of semitone in well-tempered scale; octave contains 1200 cents.

Ceol Beag (Gaelic, 'little music'). The class of music for Scottish bagpipes, consisting of marches, strathspeys and reels. Ceol meadhonach ('middle music'), consists of folk songs, lullabies, laments, slow marches etc. Ceol mor ('big music'), consists of salutes, gatherings, laments and commemorative tunes: also known as pibroch.

Ces (Ger.). C flat.

Ceses (Ger.). C double flat.

Ch. The abbr., for choir (as a manual on the organ); chm., abbr., for choir-master.

Chaconne. The piece (originally for dancing) in slow 3-beat time, in which composers often chose to repeat a given theme over and over again in the bass (i.e. a ground bass). In such works, the theme is harmonically implied even at those points when it is not actually present. The term is applied by modern historians also to vocal numbers having a similar pattern of repetition.

Chacony. 17th-centuary. English version of Chaconne.

Chair Organ. The term used in 17th, 18th centuries, for small organ (Fr., positif) used in conjunction with larger instrument, 'great organ'. Two orig. separate, but became incorporated, being played on different manuals.

Chaitanya. With the coming of Chaitanya Maha Prabhu, Bengal saw the revival of Bhakti Movement towards 1485 A.D. to 1533 A.D.

Chaitanya was born at a place called Navadweepa about hundred miles from the city of Calcutta.

He was a very active Kirtan singer, who popularized the Nama Kirtan, with the help of accompaniments like the Ektaras (a single-stringed instrument) a Khole, (a type of drum) and Kartal i.e. cymbals, made of metal, to give rhythm.

His devotional songs had a special significance and appeal, as they were drenched in super-devotion combined with lively music of celestial nature.

The whole preaching consisted of intense musical activity with songs set in simple ragas and Tals, sung by a group of people in its correct spirit, which was its peculiarity.

Chaitanya Maha Prabhu used to lead a party of followers, throughout the streets singing in choruses and playing in ecstasy creating an atmosphere of sanctity and sacredness all over, with holy vibrations.

Chalumeau (Fr.). The generic term for rustic reed-pipe.

Chalumeau (Fr.) :

(1) An obsolete instrument, forerunner of the clarinet;

(2) The lowest register of the clarinet, with a distinctively 'dark' tone-colour.

Chamber Music. The music intended for a room (in fact, called by Grainger 'room music', very sensibly), as distinct from a large hall, theatre, church, bandstand, ballroom, etc; hence, particularly, music calling for 'intimate' presentation, having only a few performers, and treating all these as soloists on equal terms.

Chamber Opera. The opera written for reduced forces, suitable for performance in more intimate theatre than grand opera house.

Chamber Orchestra. The small orchestra (not necessarily consisting only of strings), performing Chamber Music.

Chamber Opera. The term sometimes used for an opera with few singers and a small orchestra.

Champetre (Fr.). The rural, rustic.

Change ringing. The British practice of ringing church bells by teams, of which each member pulls the rope controlling one bell; thus with 3 bells the number of available changes (i.e. variations of the order of pulling) is 6 (= 3×2×1), with 4 bells it is 24 (= 4×3×2×1), etc.

Chanson (Fr.). The song, for either single voice or vocal ensemble. Also applied, like Air, instrumental piece of vocal character.

Chant. In general, music, which is sung in accordance with, prescribed ritual or tradition.

Chanter or Chaunter. Refers to part of Bagpipe: pipe with finger holes on which melody is played, as opposed to 'drone' pipes, which merely sustain single notes.

Chanterelle (Fr.). Highest (E) string of violin, or highest string of similar instruments.

Character Piece (Ger., Charakterstuck). Instrumental piece, esp. for piano, portraying specific mood, attitude, place, literary conception etc.

Charleston. The king of fox-trot, orig. Dance of SUS Negroes. Characteristic rhythm divides 4/4 bars into dotted crotchet followed by quaver tied to minim.

Chef D'attaque (Fr.). The leader of orchestra.

Chef D'orchestre (Fr.). The conductor.

Chekker (Old Fr., eschaquier). The keyboard instrument with strings, used in 14th-15th centuaries.

Chest (of viols). A set of various sizes—usually 6 instruments in all.

Chest Voice. Refers to that 'register' of the voice which gives the feeling to the singer of coming from the chest—i.e. the lower register, contrasted with Head Voice.

Chevalet (Fr.; Ger., Steg; It., ponticello). Bridge of string instrument.

Chiaro, Chira (It.). Clear. Chiaramente, clearly, distinctly, chiarezza, clarity, distinctness.

Chiesa (It.). 'church. Used in 17th, early 18th centuaries to distinguish music suitable for performance in church from that suited to secular surroundings.

Chimes. The small set of bells. Stone chimes known since ancient times; orchestral equivalent is tubular bells. Wind chimes or Aeolian bells are hung in open air to strike against each other and sound as wind blows.

Chimta. This has iron flat plates each about three feet long, joined and tied together on one side, is generally played on happy occasions. Traditional to the players of Punjab folk music.

Chinese Block. Hollowed block of wood struck with druw-stick to give hard resonant tap. Also known as wood block, clog box, tap box.

Chitarra (It.). The guitar.

Chitarrone. Large Lute.

Chiusa (It.), closed; (of horn notes). 'Stopped' by the placing of the hand in the bell.

Choir:

(1) A body of singers, especially in a place of worship;

(2) Part of a church where singers are seated;

(3) Usual abbreviation for Choir-organ.

Choirbook. Refers to the large medieval manuscript volume, which has been designed so that separate parts of choral composition could be read by number of singers standing in front of lectern. Music not written in score: parts written separately on 2 facing pages (thus saving space). Use inevitably declined in favour of more practical system of separate Part-Books.

Choir-organ (or simply choir). The division of an organ (a manual and the equipment controlled by it) having predominantly soft stops. (Originally, chair-organ, the pipes being placed behind the organist's chair or stool.)

Chopsticks. Anonymous short quick-waltz tune for piano, playable with two outstretched forefingers, or with the little fingers if the hand is held vertically like a chopper.

Chor (Ger.), Choir, Chorus.

Choral:

(1) Adj. Used in music involving chorus, e.g. choral symphony;

(2) (Ger.), Plainsong (Gergorian chant);

Chorale. Ger. Choral, i.e. type of traditional German metrical hymn- tune for congregational use.

Chorale Cantata. Type of church cantata, which makes use of text and melody, of Lutheran hyman or chorale.

Chorale Fantasia. The organ piece in which chorale melody is freely treated.

Chorale Prelude. The generic term for piece of organ music based on hymn, tune.

Choral Fantasia. Work by Beethoven for piano solo, chorus and orchestra consisting of theme and variations, with improvisatory introduction for piano.

Choral Symphony. Either:

(1) A symphony in the normal sense but using a chorus as well, or

(2) A work of symphonic dimensions but written for voices alone.

Chord. Any simultaneous combination of not hotes – but sometimes defined as any simultaneous combination of not less than 3 notes. (Whether the notes form a Concord or discord is irrelevant: the term chord is not related to these.).

Chording:

(1) (satisfactory or unsatisfactory) Intonation of a chord by several performers, e.g. a choir;

(2) In composition, the spacing of the intervals in a chord;

(3) (U.S.) The provision of chords, e.g. on a guitar, to accompany a melody.

Chordophone. The term scientifically used to classify an instrument in which a vibrating string produces the musical sound; e.g. harp, violin, piano.

Chord-symbol. Type of simple harmonic notation used e.g., by guitarist in playing pope music: e.g. C7 means a chord of the minor 7th on C (i.e., C – E – G – B_6), but no stipulation is made as to which note should form the basis.

Choreographic Poem. The symphonic poem intended as score of ballet.

Chorton (Ger.), 'choir pitch', i.e., pitch to which organs in Germany were formerly tuned. Pitch was neither constant nor universal.

Chorus

(1) A substantial body of singers not all singing separate parts;

(2) Colloquial term for the Refrain of a song, in which chorus (in the first sense) often joins;

(3) Term figuratively used for a group of instruments, or organ stops, used in the manner of a chorus.

Chromatic. Refers to pertaining to intervals outside the diatonic (major or minor) scale; chromatic scale, ascending or descending by semitones.

Church Cantata. The cantata written for actual performance during church service, though not forming part of the liturgy – e.g., those by Bach.

Ciaccona (It.). Chaconne.

Cialamello (It.). Shawm.

Cibell or Cebell. The dance form in gavotte rhythm, current in England in late 17th, early 18th centuries.

Cigany. (Hungarian) 'Gypsy'.

Cimbalom. The form of Dulcimer used in Hungary. It is consisting of series of metal strings strung on pegs fixed on to wooden box. Strings are struck with sticks held in player's hands.

Cimbalom (Hung). Large concert Duleimer (having horizontal strings struck with hammers, and damping mechanism) used in Hungarian popular music and in certain works indebted to this.

Cinelli (It.). The cymbals. More usual term is piatti.

Ciphering. The continuous sounding, through a mechanical mishap, of a note on the organ.

Circle of Fifths (Ger., Quintenzirkel). The term used for clockwise arrangement of the 12 keys in order of ascending fifths. Thus, beginning with C, order of major keys would be C, G, D, A, E, B, (or C flat), F sharp (or G flat), C sharp (or D flat). A flat, E flat, B flat, and F. After 12 such steps, orig. key is reached again. Composers have sometimes used circle of fifths as source of inspiration.

Circular Breathing. The technique of sustaining note on wind instrument by breathing in while playing note.

Cis (Ger.). **C** sharp. **Cis cis, C** double sharp.

Cistre (Fr.). Cittern.

Cittern (also cither, cithern). The plucked, wire strung instrument (used for popular music c, 1550-1700) with strings set in pairs tuned to the same note (like lute) but built with flat back (like guitar). An earlier name is citole.

Clair de Lune (Fr., Moonlight). The piano piece by Debussy (later subjected to multifarious arrangements).

Clarion (Fr.). Bugle. Also 4 ft trumpet stop on organ.

Clarionet. The obsolete spelling of Clarinet.

Clairsearch. Irish Harp. Portable gut-strung type was developed in Ireland in 19th centuary; has finger levers instead of pedals.

Claribel, Claribel Flute (or clarabella). An organ stop of flute-like tone.

Clarinet. The woodwind instrument with single reed and normally a wooden (exceptionally a metal) body, in use since mid-18th century; constituent of symphony orchestra, military band, dance band etc.

Clarino (It.). The name used for high, florid 17-18th-century trumpet and horn parts.

Clarinet. (1) pibgorn (2) clarinette d'amour (3) chalumeu (4) clarinet (5) tarogato (6) modern basset horn (7) bass clarinet (8) Heckelclarina (9) old basset horn (10) saxophone.

Clarion. 4 ft trumpet stop on organ.

Clarone (It.). Bass clarinet.

Clarsach (Gael.). Ancient small Celtic harp, revived in the 20th century for folksong accompaniment.

Classical Music. The term 'classical' is used by historians to distinguish music which accepts certain basic conventions of form and structure, and uses them as natural framework for expression of ideas, from music which is more concerned with expression of individual emotions than with achievement of formal unity, i.e. Romantic Music. In practice, term is generally restricted to 18th, early 19th-century music. As works of masters of this period are constantly performed and have stood test of time, they are also 'classical' in sense in which one speaks of 'classics' of literature. This meaning of term is applied to any well-established work.

Claves (Sp.). A pair of wooden sticks beaten together to mark the rhythm in Latin-America dance music, etc.

Clavicembalo (It.). Harpsichord. (The term literally means 'keyed dulcimer' and is normally abbreviated to cembalo.).

Clavichord. The soft-toned keyboard instrument having strings hit by metal 'tangents'.

Clavicytherium. The rare obsolete instrument of harpsichord type with strings perpendicular, as in the upright piano.

Clavier. Keyboard, or manual (of an organ).

Clef. The sign which fixes the location of a particular note on the staff – and hence the location of all other notes; placed normally at the beginning of each line of music and at any point where a new clef cancels the old. The Treble clef fixes the note G above middle C; the Alto and Tenor fix middle C; the Bass fixes the F below middle C. Other clefs are obsolete, but the Soprano lingered well into the 19th century.

Cloches (Fr.). Bells.

'Clock' Symphony. The nickname of Haydn's Symphony no 101 in D major. In slow movt., accompanying instruments suggest ticking of clock.

Clos. The medieval term used in dance music, and similarly structured vocal pieces, to indicate final cadence at end of repeated section, in contrast to intermediate cadence used when section is performed first time.

Close. A cadence; full close, perfect cadence; half-close, imperfect cadence.

Close Harmony. Harmony in which the notes of a chord lie near together – this sometimes implying, e.g., in popular close-harmony trios, etc., that the supporting harmonizing notes keep as near to the melody as possible without any particular logic of harmonic progression.

Cluster. A group of adjacent notes on the piano keyboard played together, e.g., with the forearm flat.

Coach Horn. The straight horn, 3 to 4 ft-long, comprising conical wide-bore tube of copper and funnel-shaped bell. Played with cup mouthpiece.

Coda (It, tail). In musical analysis, a section of a movement considered to be added at the end as a rounding-off rather than as a structural necessity.

Codetta (It, little tail). In musical analysis, a rounding-off passage which does for a section of a movement what a Coda does for a movement.

Colla Parte (It.). 'With the part', i.e., accompaniment is to follow any modifications of tempo made by soloist.

Colla Punta dell' Arco (It.). With the point of the bow.

Coll Arco (It.). 'With the bow'; abbrev arco. Used in string music to contradict previous pizzicato (plucked with finger).

Colla Voce (It.). 'With the voice'. Same as colla parte, but applied only to accompaniment of vocal solo.

Coll'Ottava (It.). Double at the octave (above and below).

Colophony. Same as Rosin.

Coloratura (It.). Term applied to an agile, florid style of vocal music or to its performance; coloratura soprano, soprano with voice suited to this.

Colour. The word used, by analogy with painting, to describe individual tone-quality of instruments and voices, or their association together, e.g., orchestral colour.

Colour Symphony. A symphony by Bliss, 1922—its 4 movements being interpretations of Purple, Red, Blue, and Green, in the light of heraldic associations.

Colour-organ. Term used in English for the light-projecting instrument.

Colpo (It.). Stroke; colpod'arco, stroke of the bow.

Combination Pedals

(1) A device for bringing into action several rows of organ pipes by admitting air to soundboard on which they are placed;

(2) Also used in same sense as Composition Pedals.

Combination Tone or Resultant Tone. The faint note resulting from sounding two notes simultaneously. Two different kinds:

(1) Difference tones, resulting from difference between frequencies of notes sounded.

(2) Summation tones (fainter then difference tones), resulting from sum of their frequencies.

Comes (It.). 'Companion'. Name given by older theorists to second part to enter Canon or Fugue; first part known as dux (leader).

Common Chord. Major or minor Chord in root position.

Common Metre (in hymns). The metre of a four-line stanza having 8, 6, 8, and 6 syllables per line.

Common Time. Refers to 4 Quarter-Notes (crotchets) to the bar, written 4/4 or c.

Communion. Refers to antiphon sung after communion at Mass.

Comodo (It.). 'Convenient', i.e. at convenient speed, neither too fast nor too slow. Often combined with allegro.

Community-singing. Singing by the public at a meeting, a sporting event, etc. So community songs, those suitable for such occasions.

Comodo (It., easy). Easily flowing, leisurely.

Compass. The range of a voice or instrument from the highest to the lowest note obtainable; chromatic compass, the range in which a complete Chromatic scale is playable.

Competition Festivals. Refers to the meetings for competitive performance (with or without prizes) of choral music, songs, chamber music and also instrumental music.

Composition,

(1) Individually created music piece, thus not applied to folk songs or arrangements;

(2) Act of writing music.

Composition Pedals. Set of metal pedals, or buttons operated by feet, used in organ to bring stops into action without having to draw them by hand. Each pedal also puts out of action any other stops that happen to be drawn.

Composition Pedal. Refers to foot-operated or hand-operated lever on the organ bringing into action a pre-selected group of stops simultaneously.

Composition Pistons. Similar in action to compositions pedals, but are placed below manuals and controlled by fingers or thumbs.

Compound Time. Time in which each beat in bar is divisible into 3, e.g. in 6/8, 9/8 and 12/8 there are respectively 2, 3 and 4 dotted crotchet beats, each divisible into 3 quavers. Opposite has been simple time, e.g. 2/4, 3/4, 4/4, where each beat is crotchet, divisible into 2 quavers.

Comprimario. A (male) singer of supporting roles in Italian opera. The feminine form, comprimaria, is less often encountered.

Con (It.). 'With'; con affetto, with tender emotion; con amore, lovingly; con anima, with spirit; con brio, vigorously; con fuoco, with fire.

Concert. A substantial performance of music before an audience (other than in conjunction with a stage performance, or as part of a religious service or similar ceremony, etc.); a performance by 1 or 2, however, is called not concert but Recital, and the latter term is sometimes extended a little.

Concertant (Fr.), **Concertante** (It.):

(1) As adj., used to describe work, either for orchestra or for 2 or more instrument, in which one or more solo parts are prominent;

(2) It word concertante, as noun,—sinfonia concertante.

Concertante, (1 Fr.). See preceding entry; (2, It.). In a concerted form; sinfonia concertante, term used for a work for solo instrument(s) and orchestra with the implication that the form followed is nearer that of the symphony than of the concerto.

Concertate, Concertata (It.). Concerted (masc., fem. Forms). The term 'concertato style' is used by some historians for the new style of ensemble writing (vocal or instrumental) or the early 17th century founded on the practice of Continuo.

Concerted. Refers to a performance by several people on more or less equal terms so a concerted number (more usually called 'ensemble') in an opera.

Concertato (It.). Concertante. Coro concertato, group of solo singers forming contrast to full choir.

Concert Band. American type of band of woodwind, brass, and percussion instruments for which works have been expressly written by Hindemith, Schoenberg, and various American composers.

Concerted. Applied to piece in which parts all have more or less equal importance.

Concert Halls. The word concert means the performance of vocal or instrumental music. Any public performance of music has come to be known as a concert.

It is a foreign word borrowed by us like so many other things. The earliest concerts had been those of cultural learned programmes with audiences to watch.

In India, these are known as Sangeeta Sabhas, Ganeka Talsas, or Sangeeta Sammelans.

These concerts were originally meant to create interest in the general public and to make them music-minded while entertaining them.

But now such performances are largely attended by a vast number of music-lovers especially in the South. But still in the North, classical music has not attained that same popularity.

Nowadays, of course, large cities are very enthusiastically arranging concerts and it has become a fashion too.

Ever since the inception of the All India Radio stations in our country, music has attained a degree of excellence and greater popularity over the public. All India Radio is catering all kinds of programmes to suit the needs and tastes of the folk in general.

There are twenty-eight A.I.R. stations in all, spread all over the country, catering all kinds of music and trying to bring both the systems together. Through the radio, large numbers among the common people also have begun to appreciate classical and light classical music. In this way, it is doing a great service to the country and the nation. The map showing the places where radio stations are existing now is given at the end of this book.

The Saturday night concerts of National programmes are really a boon to music-lovers. It is such a pleasure even to go and listen to the music from the studios direct, watching the performer, because of its beautifully designed, specially constructed halls with acoustics and sound-proof studios.

It is the grandeur of the halls with such advantages, which add to the charm of the singer and attract large crowds.

Even these studios in our All India Radio stations are not sufficiently big to accommodate larger number of people for concerts. After all, how much can the All India Radio alone do?

As in Europe and other places, we in India also (in big cities) must build good, beautifully designed, luxurious concert halls with extensive platform, large enough to hold and orchestra groups of players, with sound- proof walls and roofs, with proper acoustics, and special loudspeakers, microphones, etc. on the European model. The engineers should show all their genius and skill by building concert halls on the lines of opera-houses in Europe.

The hall must hold at least a thousand or more people at a time. It is a pity that even a city like Delhi has not got one hall of this nature. The hall must be well furnished with artistic comfortable seats and magnificent structure, which can inspire the performer and create aesthetic sense and pleasure to hear more, and more in the listeners.

Japan and other Eastern countries, which have followed the lines of European music, have reached the forefront in its musical and other activities. Beautiful theatres, cultural halls, etc. are built with revolving stages and acoustics in a magnificent manner. We can learn so much from them.

Concertinto (It.).

(1) A group of soloists in concerto grosso (17th, 18th centuries);

(2) The work of one or more solo instruments with orchestra less formal in structure, than ordinary concerto.

Concert Instruments. Instruments (incl., all string and keyboard instruments) whose notation is at same pitch as music sounds (also called instruments in C). Other are termed as Transposing Instruments.

Concert-master. First violin (Eng., leader) of orchestra.

Concertize. To give concerts.

Concertmaster. The first violinist of an orchestra (following German term Konzertmeister).

Concerto (It.; Fr., concert; Ger., Konzeer),

(1) Orig. (late 16th to early18th centuries.), work for one or more voices with instrumental accompaniment, either for figured bass or with addition of other instruments.

(2) Work for several instruments, supported by figured bass and offering opportunities for contrast (17th, early 18th centuries), esp.;

(3) Concerto grosso, orchestral work in several

movements., with passages for group of solo instruments (concertino) as contrast tottutti for main body. Favourite solo group consisted of 2 violins and cello (accompanied, like tutti, by figured bass), but many other combinations are found;

(4) Solo concerto (i.e. for one instrument with orchestra) dates from early 18th centuary, when violin was most favoured solo instrument.

Concerto Grosso (It., great concerto). Type of orchestral work prevalent in 17th and 18th centuries usually (but not always) having an interplay between the large body of instruments ('concerto' or 'ripieno') and a smaller group ('concerto') each with its own continuo – as distinct from the modern concerto, in which only one soloist (rarely more, and anyway not a group) provides the contrast with the orchestra.

Concert Overture. Refers to form originating in 19th centuries. Consisting of orchestral piece similar to overture to opera or play but intended purely for concert room. Often have title and programme.

Concert Pitch. The conventional term for standard international pitch, according to which A in middle of treble clef is fixed at 440 cycles per second. Brass bands use higher pitch.

Conch Shanku. It is generally used in the temples and other worship places. The temple ritualistic music with its continuous flow of offerings made to God is nicely depicted from this. A constant stream of wind is supplied by the performers.

Concitato (It.). Agitated.

Concord. Refers to combination of sounds agreeable to ear-opposite of Discord. However, as interpretations of what has been agreeable have varied widely, any precise definition or list of concords is arbitrary and has no absolute validy.

Concrete Music (Fr., Musique concrete). Type of quasi-musical organization of real, 'concrete' sounds (from nature or man-made environment) recorded and arranged on tape.

Conduct. To direct a performance with the motions of a baton or the hands.

Conducting. The direction of performance given by group of singers or players or both. Involves not only precise indications of speed, dynamics and phrasing, but also careful preparation to ensure balance is correct and that intentions of composer are adequately represented.

Conducts. In medieval music, a type of secular vocal composition having one 'given' part (Cantus Firmus) to which other parts were set in close harmony—the 'given' part being either specially composed or taken from some other secular work, not from plainsong.

Conga.

(1) Tall narrow drum, usually single handed and played with fingers, often in pairs.

(2) Dance in which people form long winding line.

Conjunct. Opposite of disjunct. Both terms refer to succession of notes of different pitch. Melody is said to move by conjunct motion if notes proceed to adjacent degrees of scale (e.g. opening of 'Three Blind Mice'), and by disjunct motion if notes form intervals larger than a second.

Consecutive. Term applied to harmonic intervals of like kind succeeding one another e.g. C struck with the E above, and than F struck with the A above would give consecutive thirds.

Consecutive Intervals. If any interval between 2 parts is followed immediately by same interval between same 2 parts, 2 intervals are described as 'consecutive' or 'parallel', e.g. C played with E above followed by G played with B above are consecutive thirds; C played with F above followed by E played with A above are consecutive fourths, and so on.

Conservatoire, -torium, -tory. The school of musical training— originally in Italian, conservatorio,meaning an orphanage where children were 'conserved' and given musical and other training.

Conservatory. The school specializing in musical training.

Console. The part of organ from which player controls instrument, i.e. keyboards, pedals, stops, music desk, etc.

Consonance. The consonance and dissonance provide valuable contrast in music, one suggesting repose, the other stress. However, interpretations have always varied as to which intervals or chords are consonant and which dissonant. Traditionally major and minor thirds, perfect fourth, perfect fifth, major and minor sixths and octave are classed as consonant, and all other intervals (e.g. second, diminished fifth) as dissonant.

Con Sordino. (It). 'with mute' (abbrev. consord). Countermanded by senza sordino (abbrev. senza sord).

Consort. The old English word for a group of instruments; whole consort, all of one family; broken consort, of mixed families.

Continuo (It., abbr. of basso continuo). A type of accompaniment played from a bass-line, most commonly on a key board instrument. From the bass-notes, the player worked out the correct harmonies, sometimes aided by numerical shorthand indications provided by the composer.

Contra-, Contre-, Kontra-. Italian, French, and German prefixes signifying (of an instrument) 'lower in pitch' usually about an octave lower.

Contrabass.

(1) As prefix, indicates instrument built octave lower than normal bass of family, e.g. contrabass trombone ;

(2) As noun—Double bass.

Contrabasso. (It.). The double bass.

Contradanza. (It.). Contredanse.

Contrabactum. In medieval music, vocal composition in which orignal words are replaced by others of different character (e.g. sacred by secular and vice versa).

Contrafagotto. (It.). The double Bassoon.

Contralto. Lower type of female voice.

Contrapunctus (Lat.):

(1) Counterpoint;

(2) Piece of Contrapuntal style.

Contrapuntal. Pertaining of Counterpoint.

Contrasts. The violinist using 2 instruments, one of normal tuning (G, D, A, E) and the other tuned G, D, A, E, b.

Contrebasse (Fr.). Double bass.

Contrebasson (Fr.). Double bass.

Controfagatto (It.). The double-Bassoon.

Coperto (It.). Covered, e.g. of drums muffled with a cloth to give a muted effect.

Cor (Fr.). French horn, generally known simply as Horn.

Corda (It.; pl. corde). A string. So, in piano-playing, una corda (1 string)—instruction to play With soft pedal, this pedal achieving its effect (on grand pianos) by causing the Hammers to hit only 1 instead of 3 strings to each note.

Corda Vuota (It.). Open string.

Corde (Fr). String. Instruments a cordes (or cordes alone), string instruments. Quatuor a Cordes, string quartet. Corde a jour, corde a vide, open string. A la corde, play with bow kept on string, so playing legato.

Cor De Basset (Fr.). Basset Horn.

Cori Spezzati (It.), 'divided choirs'. Term used of antiphonal choruses which are characteristic feature of Venetian church music.

Cornamuse (It.). Bagpipe.

Cornemusa (Fr.). Bagpipe.

Cornemuse (Fr.). Bagpipe.

Cornamuto Torto (It.). Krummhorn.

Cornet

(1) Brass wind instrument with 3 valves, resembling trumpet but squatter in Appearance, of wider bore, and easier to play compass from E below middle C Upwards for about 2½ octaves—can be switched to become an instrument in A, half a tone lower.

Cornett. The old wooden or ivory wind instrument having a cup-shaped mouthpiece (like modern brass) but finger-holes (like modern wood-wind).

Cornet a Bouquin (Fr.). Obsolete cornett.

Cornet a Pistons (Fr.). Modern cornet.

Cornett (Fr., cornet a bouquin; Ger., Zink; It., cornetto). Wind instrument, entirely different from modern cornet. Normal type was slightly curved and made of wood or ivory, with holes stopped by fingers, and cup-shaped mouthpiece. Made in several sizes, commonest having compass of 2 octaves from A below middle C, with possible extension upwards.

Cornett-ton (Ger). The pitch used by German Stadtpfeifer.

Corno (It.). Horn.

Corno Di Bassetto (It.). Basset horn. Pseudonym under which Bernard Shaw wrote music criticism in The Star and elsewhere.

Coro (It.). Choir, chorus; also used of body of instrumental players.

Corona (It., Lat., crown). Pause sign placed above note, so called because it resembles crown.

Cortamente. 'Shortly'.

Counterpoint. Refers to the simultaneous combination of 2 or more melodies to make musical sense, one melody then being spoken of as the counterpoint of or in counterpoint to another.

Countersubject. The melody which is designed as counterpoint to subject (principal theme) of Fugue. First appears as continuation (in same part) of first statement of subject, thus normally occurring in association with answer (second statement of subject, in different part); thus it is both continuation of subject and contrast to it. Association continues regularly until Exposition is complete.

Counter-tenor. Highest male voice (also known as alto), produced by using head register.

Couning Dance. The name given to a traditional English dance of popular origin.

Coup D'archet (Fr.). The stroke of the bow, the attack with the bow.

Coup De Glotte (Fr.). The stroke of the glottis, a method of vocal 'attack' counselled by some teachers of singing.

Coup De Langue (Fr.). Tounging.

Couple (verb). On the organ, to contrive that the stops normally controlled by one Manual have been available also on another manual (or on pedals); that the striking of one note should also cause the sounding of the same note an octave Higher or lower.

Coupler. A device which is used to augment resources of organ. Couplers, which are less controlled by stops or tabs, have been of 3 kinds:

(1) octave and sub-octave couplers, which automatically double in octave above or below any note played;

(2) manual couplers, which enable player to combine resources of 2 manuals.These couplers also exist as octave and sub-octave couplers;

(3) pedal couplers (Fr., tirasses), which operate in similar way to manual couplers.

Couplet. Refers to stanza of a poem, the music being repeated for each successive stanza—so on operatic song may take the form of couplets.

Courante. Short for danse courante, running dance. Lively dance in triple time.

Cow' Bell. As used in orchestra, square bell struck with stick to emphasize beat.

Cow-horn. Refers to a brass instrument (roughly of Horn type, but valveless) Made to imitate the sound of a rustic horn and used in Britten's Spring Symphony.

Crash Cymbal. The suspended cymbal struck with stick to produce brilliant crash.

Crescendo (It., growing). Increasing in loudness.

Crescendo Pedal. The pedal on organ which when applied adds successively more and more stops.

Criticism, Musical. The reasoned discussion, in a periodical or book, of public performances or compositions, new or old.

Croche (Fr.). The Eighth-Note, quaver.

Croche, Monsieur. The imaginary person invented by Debussy as mouthpiece for His own critical opinions.

Croma (It.). The quaver. Hence adj. cromatico not only means chromatic', but in 16th centuary was applied to composition making liberal use of black notes.

Crook. Refers to the piece of tubing inserted into brass instrument between mouth-piece and body of instrument. Pitch of instrument varies according to size of crook. Thus horn with A crook will sound major third higher than with F crook.

Croon. To sing softly and sentimentally into a microphone, as in dance bands.

Crooning. The soft, sentimental style of singing through microphone, supported by dance band.

Cross-fingering. Refers to fingering the ascending or descending scale (on woodwind instruments) in a way that goes against the normal order of lifting up and putting down successive fingers.

Cross Relation. The US equivalent of False Relation.

Cross Rhythms. The conflicting rhythmic patterns performed simultaneously.

Crotales.

(1) Set of small bells to chromatic scale and played with sticks;

(2) Cymbals antiques;

Crotchet. Time-value, fourth part of semibreve and twice value of quaver.

Crumhorn. (Ger., krumm, crooked). Type of curved, cylindrically- bored, double-reed wind instrument current; made in at least 6 sizes of different pitch (a fourpart consort was standard).

Crwth (Welsh). The equivalent to obsolete English word crowd as musical instrument, Medieval and later British stringed instrument shaped like a lyre but played with a bow, surviving longest in Wales; an ancestor of the violin family.(Sometimes Misleadingly called 'bowed harp'.)

Csardas. Hungarian dance, consisting of slow, melancholy section (lassu) followed by fast, vivacious section (friss).

Cuckoo. The short pipe with single finger-hole, giving 2 notes a major third apart in imitation of cruckoo's call.

Cuivre. 'Brassy'. Indication to brass players to play with harsh, blaring tone.

Curtal. The name given in 16th, 17th centuries to small bassoon. Larger form, roughly Corresponding to modern bassoon, was called double curtal.

Curtal. (I). The old English name for obsolete family of wind instruments, the bass member surviving longest.

Cycle. The name given to set of works especially songs, intended to be performed as a group and often linked musically or by other means.

Cyclic Form.

(1) Refers to form of a work in which a theme does duty (often in new guise) in more than one moment—e.g. Franck, Symphony; Elgar, Symphony no.1; form of any work with more than one movement.

Cymbal. The percussion instrument consisting of a plate of metal which is usually either struck with drumstick (single stroke or roll) or clashed against another Cymbal.

Czardas. Incorrect spelling of Csardas.

D

D. The symbol in Tonic Sol-Fa notation for the first degree (tonic) of the scale, pronounced doh.

D. The second note (or supertonic) of scale of D major (Eng., Ger.; Fr., re; It., re).

Dal Segno. (It.). 'From the sign', i.e. go back to point in music.

Damper. The piece of felt, glued to strip of wood, which covers piano string and prevents it from vibrating.

Damping Pedal. The soft pedal (of piano).

Dance Band. The band that plays for strict tempo dancing. Usually consists of brass section of trumpets and trombones, reed section of saxophones doubling clarinets, and rhythm section of piano, bass and drums.

Dance of the Hours. Ballet music from Act 3 of Ponchielli's opera "La gioconda".

Dance-poem. The description sometimes given by composers to a substantial orchestral work intended for ballet and having narrative interest.

Danse. (Fr.). The term means dance.

Dantal. This instrument of Uttar Pradesh consists of one long steel rod shaped like the horse-shoe, two parts when struck on the rod, produce musical sounds and also rhythm.'Khaharwa' tune is played more popularly on this.

Danza Tedesca (It). 'German dance'.

Danza (It., Sp.). The dance.

Darbari Kanada. This is a majestic heroic raga symbolizing fighting in the battle, depicting a victorious, courageous, and bold figure holding a sword in one hand and pulling the reins of his horse by the other. This is a powerful and melodious raga with a forceful personality. This must be sung about the first part of the night.

Daruvus. These are mostly connected to dance dramas or operas, narrating some episode or a story, full of words. These have become out of fashion and are not so much in use. Merattur Venkata Rama Sastri has composed a number of daruvus in the Telugu language.

There are Tamil daruvus too. The main character is all centred in the sahitya. These also have the divisions of pallavi, anupallavi and charana like other songs.

These are all the different forms of music of the Karnataka system—which are the most stimulating and interesting works of our great composers.

Dauer (Ger.). Duration. Dauernd, 'enduring, i.e. lasting, continuing.

Dead March. Any funeral march.

Debile, Debole (It.), **Debile** (Fr.). Weak.

Decani (Lat., of the dean). Refers to that section of the choir in a cathedral, etc., which is stationed on the south (i.e. dean's) side of the chancel; opposite of Cantoris.

Decimctt. The piece for 10 instruments or voices.

Decrescendo (It.). The 'decreasing', i.e. getting softer, opposite of crescendo.

Degree. The position of note in given scale (major or minor) is classified by its degree, e.g. in scale of C major, C is 1st degree, D 2nd degree, E 3rd degree (etc.) of scale, until 1st degree (C above) is reached. Alternative terms for 1st to 7th degrees are Tonic, Supertonic, Mediant, Subdominant, Dominant, Submediant, Leading-Note.

Dehors, En (Fr.). lit. 'outside'. Instruction to emphasize melody or some other aspect of piece, So that it stands out from surroundings.

Demi-jeu (Fr.). Lit. 'half-play; i.e. play at half power on organ, harmonium, etc.

Demi-pause (Fr.). 'Half-rest', i.e. minim rest.

Demisemiquaver. Half a semiquave. or 1/32 of semibreve.

Denkmaler Der Tonkunst in Osterreich (Ger., Monuments of Music in Austria. The series of publications of old music analogous to Denkmaler Deutscher Tonkunst, incl. works by foreign composers written in Austria or found in Austrian libraries.

Density 21.5. The piece by Varese for solo platinum flute, which has this density.

Descant. The additional part sung (sometimes improvised) above a given melody, e.g. above a hymntune; descant recorder.

Deserts. The work by Varese for orch. and tape prob. the 1st ever to combine these resources.

Desk. An orchestral music-stand; in the strings of an orchestra each desk is shared by two players, so that first desk only is an instruction that the particular passage is to be played by the first two players only.

Deses (Ger.) D double flat.

Detache. The style of playing string instrument so that noticeable bow change is made on every note—though not necessarily so detached as to be staccato.

Deutscher Tanz (Ger.; It., danza tedesca), 'German dance'. Also known as Deutsch or Teutsch. In late 18th, early 19th cents., brisk dance in waltz time.

Deux (Fr.). Two; a deux indicates 2 separate paths merge, or single part divides into 2.

Development. The section of a movement (e.g. in Sonata-form) between the initial statement of themes and their final recapitulation, during which the themes are 'developed', i.e. expanded, modified, combined, broken up, etc.

Dhamar. A dhamar is also like a Holi. It is set only in the dhamar tal. The rhythm and the time measurements are the peculiarities in this type. Same piece or passage is taken again and again in different metres changing the rhythm and catching the "sam" of the tal. In North India, dhamars like the dhrupads are also very popular. Varieties of rhythm and fixed measure of the tal are its characteristics.

Dhannashri. This rag depicts a lady who is separated from her lover. She writes long loving letters to fill in the long and weary strenuous days, and praise for her lover's speedy return home.

Dholak. It is also a very popular instrument—a drum in the Punjab. No function is complete without playing on this.

Dhrupads. These Dhrupads are also known as Dhruvapads. This is a very old orthodox style of a composition. Dhruvapads were first introduced by Rajah Mansingh of Gwalior. Swami Haridas also is believed to have had his own style of rendering the Dhruvapads. Tansen became a great Dhrupad singer too.

This requires a good, well-trained voice and ability to perform. They start singing This in a very very slow tempo, in the Mandhara sthayi, then gradually Antra, Sanchari and Abhog are taken. There are three or four varieties of Dhrupads. Dhrupads are generally composed in 'ektal' choutal, etc. mainly. Still there are some expert "dhrupad" Singers in Rampur. "Sadra" is a king of fast dhrupad sung in Thaptal Trital.

Dhruva. It means Sthira, a fixed state. That is why the same is repeated again and again. These songs are standardized and are not to be altered.

Diabolus in Musica (Lat.). The lit. 'The devil in music' Term originated in Middle Ages we warning against use of Tritone, which was regarded as 'dangerous' progression.

Diapason. The 'basic' tone of the organ, 'open' or 'stopped' according to whether the ends of the pipes are clear or plugged, the 'open' being the louder. Normally of 8-Foot length: double diapason, of 16-foot length.

Diapason Normal (Fr.). A standard indication of pitch: A=435 Hz. The international standard now accepted is different: see Frequency.

Diaphony. The name sometimes given to simpler types of Organum.

Diapente (Gr.). The perfect fifth interval.

Diatonic. Refers to a given major or minor key (opposite of chromatic); so diatonic scale, any one of the major or minor scales; diatonic harmony, harmony made up predominantly from the resources of the prevailing key, without much use of notes outside its scale; similarly Diatonic, discord arriving from clashes within the key itself. Hence diatonicism, a pronounced use of diatonic harmony.

Diatonic Chord. The chord composed of notes proper to key.

Diatonic Harmony. Strictly harmony which employs only diatonic chords; more generally, harmony which is predominantly based on diatonic chords and their association.

Dichtung (Ger.). The poetry; symphonische Dichtung, symphonic poem.

Diction. The correct and clear enunciation in singing. (This is the recognized meaning in musical contexts.)

Didjeridoo, Didjeridu. Australian aboriginal wind instrument of trumpet type made out of A tree trunk 4-5 ft. long.

Dies Irae (Lat., Day of Wrath). A section of the Requiem Mass, the plain song tune of which is quoted e.g. in Berlioz's Fantastic symphony, Saint-Saens' Danse Macabre, and various works of Rakhmaninov including 'Rhapsody on a Theme of Paganini' for piano and orchestra.

Diese (Fr.). Sharp.

Diesis (Gr.) (1). In Pythagorean theory, difference between fourth and 2 'major' tones i.e. semitone slightly smaller than that of scale based on harmonic series. Also known as limma; (2) In Aristotelian theory, quarter-tone of Enharmonic tetrachord; (3) In modern acoustics, theoretical interval between B sharp and C, C sharp and D flat etc; great diesis is Interval between 4 minor thirds (e.g. E-G-B flat-D flat F flat) and octave (E-E); (4) (It.), sharp.

Diferncia (Sp). In 16th centuary, variation or Division.

Diminish

(1) To 'lessen' certain intervals;

(2) To subject a melody to Diminution.

Diminished. The term applied to a type of Interval regarded as a 'lessened' version of a certain Other interval. In practice this is a useful term only for—

(1) Diminished 5th, one semitone less than perfect 5th, and

(2) Diminished 7th, one semitone less than minor 7th.

Diminished Interval. The perfect or minor interval reduced by flattening upper note or sharpening lower, e.g. perfect fifth, C to G diminished fifth C to G flat, or C sharp to G; minor seventh, C to B flat; diminished seventh, C to B double flat, or C sharp to B flat. On keyboard instruments diminished intervals are indistinguishable from augmented or major interval below, e.g. diminished fifth, C to G flat sounds same as augmented fourth, C to F sharp; harmonic function to intervals, however, remains distinct.

Diminished Seventh Chord. The chord composed of 3 minor thirds, or diminished triad with diminished seventh superimposed, e.g. B-D-F-A flat.

Diminished Triad. The minor triad with fifth flattened, e.g. minor triad, C-E flat-G; diminished Triad, C-E flat-G flat. Triad on seventh note of major scale (e.g. in key of C major, B-D-F) is only diminished triad proper to key; all others require accidentals. In minor keys, same triad occurs if seventh note is sharpened, and triad on second note of scale is also diminished (e.g. in key of C minor, D-F-A flat).

Diminuendo (It.). Refers to 'diminishing the tone' is getting softer.

Diminution. The treatment of a melody in such a way as to decrease (usually halving) the time values of its notes (used e.g. in some fugures).

Direct. Sign rather like ornamental W, formerly used in manuscripts and printed music, (1) at End of line or page, positioned on staff to indicate in advance pitch of next note, (2) in middle of line, to draw attention to change of clef (Lat., custos).

Dirge. Vocal or instrumental composition intended for use at funerary rites.

Dirigent. (Ger.). Conductor.

Dis (Ger.). D sharp.

Discant. A developed form of the type of medieval part-writing called organum. The most Reliable medieval theorists describe it as essentially a homophonic, measured style.

Discord. Refers to combination of notes which incl. at least one dissonant interval. In popular use applied to music in which relationship between series of dissonances is not intelligible to listener.

Disis (Ger.). D double sharp.

Diskant (Ger.). Soprano, treble. Diskantmesse. Mass in which plain song, generally freely embroidered, appears not in tenor but in upper part.

Dissonance. Etymologically a jarring sound, or 'discord'. Term is incapable of precise definition, since ear is inevitable subjective. Ways in which dissonance can occur in music, however, remain constant:

(1) by introducing passing note which is dissonant with rest of chord,

(2) by tying over, or suspending, from one chord, note which is dissonant with next chord,

(3) an essential note of chord. Historically type.

(4) is result of other two, i.e. dissonances which a familiar as passing notes or suspensions come in time to be accepted without preparation.

Dital Harp. Another name for Harp-Guitar.

Div. Abbr. of Divisi or 'divided'.

Diversion. Same as Variation.

Divertimento (It., an amusement). A not-too-serious work, usually for a small instrumental Group, in several movements.

Divertissement (Fr., an amusement).

(1) A musical paraphrase on familiar tunes, or some similar light instrumental work;

(2) A danced entertainment of the type of Ballet (1), but being merely a suite of dances not unified by any fundamental idea or connecting story.

Divisi (It.). Divided—term used e.g. of the first violins or other string group of the orchestra When they temporarily split into two or more smaller bodies playing different parts.

Division Viol. Bass Viol slightly smaller than normal size, suitable for Divisions.

Divisions.

(1) An obsolete term for Variations because the splitting of the time-values of notes was formerly a common way of making variations;

(2) An obsolete term for long, agile vocal runs.

Dixieland. The style of 'classical' jazz derived from music that originated in New Orleans at start of 20th centuary. Simple and cheerful; usually performed by small groups.

Doctor of Music. The highest musical degree.

Dodecaphonic. A misapplied term: linguistically it should mean 'in 12 strands or parts', but It has been accepted as referring to the twelve- note method of composition.

Doh, in Tonic Sol-Fa. The spoken name for the first degree (tonic) of the scale, written d.

Doh. Eng. from of It., do (C).In Tonic Sol-Fa, first note (or tonic) of major scale.

Doigte (Fr.). The fingering.

Doice (It.). the sweet, gentle. Dolcissimo, very sweet.

Dolento (It.). sorrowful (ly).

Dolzflote (Ger.). Soft flute-like organ stop.

Dominant. The 5th note of the scale, in relation to the keynote: thus if the key is C (major or minor), the dominant is G. So dominant seventh, chord of the (minor) 7th on the dominant (in case G, B, D, F) resolving normally on the Tonic chord (in this case C major or minor).

Domra. Russian plucked instrument, usually three-stringed, with convex back like mandolin; Made in several sizes and used for folk music etc.

Doppelt so Schpell, (Ger.). Twice as fast.

Doppelschlag (Ger.). Turn (musical ornament).

Doppio (It.). The double; doppio movemento, at double the speed (of the preceding section).

Dorian Mode. The mode represented by the white keys of the piano beginning on D.

Dorian Mode.

(1) In ancient Greek music, descending scale E-D-C-B-A-G-F-E;

(2) From the Middle Ages onwards applied to ascending scale D-E-F-G-A-B-C-D.

'Dorian' Toccata and Fugue. The nickname for a certain Toccata and Fugue in D minor (not the familiar one) by Bach BWV 538; given because, although in fact in D minor, it was originally written without key-signature, as a work in the Dorian mode and ending on D would be.

Dot. Mark in musical notation:

(1) placed above note, indicating Staccato;

(2) placed after note, indicating that the time-value of the note is to be extended by half; similarly a double dot indicates that the time-value is to be extended by half as much again.

Double.

(1) (Eng.). Octave lower, e.g. double bassoon, built octave lower than bassoon.

(2) (Eng.). Prefixed to instrument, may also signify one that combines two instruments in one, e.g. double horn, which combines essential features of horn in F and horn in B flat alto.

Double (Fr.). A turn (musical ornament).

Double Bar. A double perpendicular line marking the end of a composition or of a major Division of it; usually but not always placed coincidentally with the single bar-line, and sometimes equipped with 'repeat' marks.

Double-bass. The largest and lowest bowed stringed instrument of the orchestra-also used in Jazz and dance bands (mainly pizzicato), and occasionally introduced into the military band for concerts; used occasionally in chamber music, very rarely solo. The standard modern instrument has 4 strings, and a compass from E just over an octave below the bass stave, upwards for nearly 2 octaves; but 5-string instruments, with an extra string sounding B Below bottom E, are also found. Is lowest member of violin family, but some players use underhand grip (as for viols).

Double Bassoon. The double-reed instrument, of wood or metal, built octave lower than Bassoon.

Double Concerto. The concerto for 2 solo instruments and orchestra.

Double Counterpoint. The name given to invertible counterpoint in 2 parts. Consists in adding to existing melody second melody which will fit equally well above or below first. In theory added melody can move up or down any interval to its new position, but in practice commonest intervals are those of octave, tenth and twelfth. It is not uncommon for 1st melody To move octave at same time, or even 2 octaves, in opposite direction, either to prevent crossing of parts or to make room for additional parts in between. Double counterpoint takes place frequently in fugues since Countersubject may be required to enter above subject in one place and below it in another.

Double-Croche (Fr.). Semi-quaver.

Double-flat. Indication of the lowering of the pitch of a note by 2 semitones. Its use necessitated by the 'grammar' of harmony, even though the resultant note, e.g. on the piano, will always have an alternative simpler name.

Double Flat. The sign bb indicating that pitch of note to which it is prefixed is to be lowered 2 semitones, e.g. on keyboard instrument B double flat will sound same as A.

Double Fugue

(1) Properly, Fugue in which new theme is introduced in course of piece and being itself treated fugally is finally combined with original subject, to which it forms countersubject;

(2) Name given to fugue in which subject and countersubject appear simultaneously at beginning and are regularly associated throughout piece.

Double-handed (of an instrumentalist). Refers to capable of playing 2 different instruments.

Double-Reed. 2 pieces of cane, lower, thicker ends being bound round metal tube, while upper ends, which have been very thin, practically meet, leaving, however, small aperture Through which player's breath is forced. This method of tone production is used in oboe, cor anglais, heckelphone, bassoon, double bassoon and sarrusophone.

Double-sharp. Refers to indication of the raising of the pitch of a note by 2 semitones. Its use is necessitated by the 'grammar' of harmony, even though the resultant note, e.g. on the piano, Will always have an alternative simpler name.

Double Stop. The chord of 2 notes played on bowed string instrument (e.g. violin) by using 2 adjacent strings. Term incl. chords where open string is used.

Double Tonguing. The means of achieving rapid articulation of successive notes (esp. repeated notes) on flute and brass instruments. Consists in alternately articulating consonants T and K. Not possible on reed instruments where mouthpiece is held inside mouth.

Double Touch. The system employed by some modern organ-builders, by which heavier pressure on keys can be used to bring into action new registrations, without necessity of changing-stops. In this way it is possible for solo and accompaniment to be played on same manual in 2 contrasted tone-colours. Common on cinema organs.

Double-whole-note. The note considered as a time-value.

Doucement (Fr.). Sweetly, gently.

Down-beat. Refers to the download movement of conductor's stick or hand, marking first beat of bar. Term also applied simply to first beat of bar.

Down-bow. The motion of the bow of a stringed instrument when pulled by the player the opposite (pushing) motion being an Up-bow.

Dramatic (soprano, tenor, etc.). Having powerful voice and a style suitable for forceful operatic roles.

Drame (Fr.). The drama; drame lyrique' lyric drama-term used.

Drame Lyrique (Fr.). Refers to one of French names for opera.

Dramma (It.). The drama; drama per musica (drama through music), term frequently used for 'opera' in the 17th and 18th centuries; drama giocoso, comic drama, i.e. (in musical contexts) comic opera which nevertheless has one or more non-comic characters-applied by Mozart to 'Don Giovanni'.

Dramma Per Musica (It.). The lit. 'drama by (or through music', i.e. opera. Term much used in Italy in 17th, 18th centuries.

Dringend (Ger.). Refers to pressing onwards, urgent.

Driving Note. The obs. term applied to suspended note or any note causing Syncopation.

Droite(e) (Fr.). The right, right hand; main droite or m.d., with the right hand (e.g. in piano Music).

Drone pipe(s). The sounding note(s) of fixed pitch continuing as a permanent bass on various forms of Bagpipe; hence, similar effect (drone bass) in other forms of music.

Drone. Lower pipes of bagpipe, each producing single persistent note.

Droit(e) (Fr.). Right. Main droite (m.d.), with the right hand (e.g. in keyboard music).

Drone Bass. Bass part which imitates drone of bagpipe by remaining on same note.

Drum. The percussion instrument of many varieties, all having a skin or other membrane which is stretched over a hollow space and struck-usually with a stick, but cp. Bongo.

Drum. This ancient tribal instrument, beats the time. The rhythmic sound produced there sometimes indicate every aspect of their daily life. The pangs of separation from the beloved, the pains of despised love, the joys of reunion, a marriage or a birth of a child, the agony of death, the aspiration of religion, invocation to God and all festivals. The effect of each sound conveys a different feeling.

Of course India has different kinds of drums in all sizes and shapes.

There are some two-faced drums, some large and fairly heavy and some small and light. Some are made of mud (earthen drums) and some made of wood. Only a particular kind of Wood can be used to make these. The wood is generally cut when the first rains fall and the drummer who makes the drum will offer some sacrifice to that particular tree, to the Rain God who is kind enough to give the rain, and the mother earth for protecting them—but for whose kindness he could not have had a good instrument.

There is still another superstition among them, that is, while they are fixing the hide on the already shaped wooden or earthen drums, they have to select such a day for this purpose, when the frogs are croaking loudly, so that the drums may give good and loud sound.

Usually the sides of the drums are made either with goatskins or any other hide or skin according to their own preferences. There is also a belief that the skin of a cow or a bullock which has been killed by a tiger gives the best sound. After the instrument is complete, he will invite all his friends and neighbours for a feast. They all dance together the whole night, when the new instrument is played for the first time.

Drum Kit. Set of drums and cymbals arranged so that they may all be played by one person. Drummer sits behind snare drum around which are arranged tenor drum, bass drum operated by foot pedal, and hi-hat cymbal operated by other foot. Crash cymbals have been fixed to Drums or supported on stands, and all are played by sticks, mallets or wire brushes. May Incl. other drums and accessories (e.g. temple blocks).

Due Corde (It.). The 'two strings':

(1) In violin music, indicates that passage playable on 1 string is to be played on 2, so producing undulating effect;

(2) In piano music, occasionally used to countermand una corda.

Dudelsack (Ger.). Bagpipe.

Duet. A combination of 2 performers (sometimes with accompaniment, as is usually implied e.g. by vocal duet), or a work for such a combination; piano duet, 2 performers on one piano.

Duettino (It.). A little duet.

Duetto (It.). The duent.

Dulcet. The dulciana of 4ft length and pitch.

Dulciana. The soft open metal diapason stop on organ. Usually of 8ft length and pitch, but can Be 4×16ft.

Dulcimer.

(1) Type of instrument (old, but still in use for traditional music e.g. in Eastern Europe) in which strings stretched over a soundboard are struck which hammers; the Hungarian kind, sometimes seen in the concert-hall, is the Cimbalom;

(2) Name given to an American 3-string folk instrument of Zither type ('Appalachian Dulcimer')—with strings plucked by player's right hand.

Dumbarton Oaks Concerto. The concerto in E flat major for 15 instruments by Stravinsky (1983), In style of modern concerto grosso.

Dumb or Dummy Keyboard. Silent keyboard (often portable), used by some pianists for finger practice.

Dumka. A layment of Ukrainian folk-origin, a movement in which slow and fast tempos alternate—term used by Dvorak, e.g. dumka movements in his string sextet and piano quintet.'Dumky Trio', is made up of 6 independent dumka movements in different keys.

Dumky Trio. Piano trio by Dvorak, op 96 (1891), consisting of 6 movts., each in form of Dumka.

Dump or Dompe. The 16th, 17th-centruies musical and literary term, prob. Denoting elegy or lament. Musical examples often carry name of person in title. All have been instrumental, and most have been constructed over simple Ground Bass.

Duo (It.). Two performers, or a work written for them; duo-pianist (U.S.), member of a duo playing on two pianos (not two people on one piano).

Duodecuple Scale (Lat., duodectm, 12). A scale of twelve notes, i.e. the ordinary European, scale considered as having twelve notes all of equal value, as in Twelve-Note music.

Duplet. A pair of note of equal time-value, written where the number of beats is not capable of simple division by 2—e.g. two notes occupying a bar of 3/8, (One of the notes may, of course, be replaced by a rest.)

Duple Time. Time in which the primary division is into 2 or 4—e.g.2/4, 4/4— as distinct particularly from Triple Time (primary division into 3). Note especially that 6/4 indicates a bar of three half-notes while 3/2 indicates a bar of three half-notes, giving different accents although both total six quarternotes.

Duplex Instruments. Instruments (esp. brass) that combine two instruments in one, e.g. double euphonium, which can play through wide euphonium bell or narrow saxtromba bell, and double horn.

Duplum (Lat.). The part immediately above tenor in 12th-centuary organum. Third part above these was called triplum. In 13th-centuary motet, duplum was called motetus.

Dur (Ger.). The major (as applied to key).

Duramente (It.). 'With hardness', i.e. sternly, harshly.

Durchfuhrung (Ger.). The lit. 'through-leading', i.e. development section of sonata movement. Also applied to exposition of fugue.

Durchgangsnote (Ger.). Passing Note.

Durchkomponiert (Ger., through-composed). The term used of a work, especially a song; composed in a continuous form, not repeating itself in successive stanzas—opposite of Strophic.

Dynamics. The gradations of loudness and softness in music.

E

E (Eng., Ger.: Fr., It., mi). Third note (or mediant) of scale of C major.

Ear Training. This term is same as Aural Training.

Echappee. Abbrev. of note echappee, i.e. 'escaped note'. Term used in theory of harmony to describe progression between 2 adjacent notes which first takes step in 'wrong' direction, then reverts to note orig. aimed at by interval of third.

Echalle. The scale, Gamme is more usual term.

Echo Attachment. An electronic device that adds artificial echo to sound of electric instrument. For higher quality echo, echo chamber is employed consisting of sealed chamber with loud- speaker, microphones and acoustic delay line.

Echo Organ. Refers to a manual (and the apparatus it controls) which is found on certain large organs, suitable for echo effects-having soft stops, and sometimes pipes at a distance from the main body of pipes.

Ecossiase (Fr.). Short for danse ecossaise, 'Scottish dance'. Quick dance in 2/4 time, popular in Britain and on Continent in late 18th, early 19th centuries.

Edinburgh Festival. The summer festival of music and drama held in Scotland, one largest in world.

Eighth-note (US). The quaver.

Einleitung (Ger.). Introduction, prelude, etc.

Eis (Ger.). E sharp.

Eisis (Get.). E double sharp.

Ektara. The simple Ektara was invented for the guidance and support of the village singer, who with his uncultivated voice feels the need for it. This Ektara was a mendicant's drone. It is made of a round stick usually of a bamboo. One end of this stick has a tuning peg and the other end has a hollow gourd resonator. It has an open string the ends of which are fastened to a nail fixed on the bamboo.

Electronde. An electronic instrument which is similar to Theremin, but incorporating mechanism to interrupt glissando and to control amplification. Tone is produced by utilizing differences between two frequencies.

Electrone. An electric organ, which is provided with stops and couplers like ordinary organ, but sound is produced by amplifying electrically generated vibrations.

Electric. The term used with reference to musical instruments in two senses:

(1) Where electricity has been used to facilitate the use of mechanical parts, e.g. electric action on a pipe-organ, not affecting the quality of the note produced;

(2) Where the use of amplification or other process determines or affects the quality of sound.

Electronic Instruments. There are three principal ways in which electricity is used to produce (as distinct from merely reproducing) musical sounds:

(1) By amplifying existing vibrations,

(2) By generating frequencies corresponding to vibrations of notes and converting them into sound, where system of intensifying or suppressing individual members of limited harmonic series makes possible the artificial representation of tone of large number of different instruments.

(3) By utilizing difference between two frequencies, where difference is controlled by movement of hand through air.

Electronic Music. Term applied not to every musical performance or experience involving electronic apparatus, but to a type of composition (increasingly widespread from mid-1950s) in which musical elements are assembled under the composer's direction on recorded tape, the playback of the tape then functioning as performance, no written score being necessary. (A score or diagram or other readable instruction may, however, be made.) The original sound-sources may be taken from a conventional instrument, a street-noise, or whatever, and treated by tape-manipulation (this use of 'real' sources being formerly termed Concrete Music), or may be themselves electronically produced under laboratory conditions. The process may be facilitated by voltage-controlled synthesizer (Synthesizer) and by computer. The eventual playback may be subject to modification under concert conditions.

Electrophonic. (word compounded from modern electric + Gk. phone 'sound' as in monophony, etc.). The term used to describe technically those instruments of which the notes are transmitted through electronic circuits ending in transducers (e.g. loudspeakers). They may be divided into:

(1) Electro-acoustic, in which the tone of a conventional instrument, or one slightly modified, is converted into electrical vibrations and then subjected to controlled amplification and modification, e.g. electric guitar (and bass guitar), electric violin, electric Piano;

(2) Electromechanical, those with electrostatic, electromagnetic, or photo-electric tone-generators.

(3) Electronic, those with electronic-tube tone-generators.

Elegie, Elegy. The term used for a song of lamentation, especially for the dead, or an instrumental work of similar intention or mood.

Eleventh. The interval of octave and fourth, e.g. from D below treble clef to G above treble clef.

Embouchure. The position and application of the lips to the mouthpiece of a wind instrument. (In French the word also means the mouthpiece itself).

Empfindung (Ger.). The term means 'feeling'. Mit Empfindung with feeling. Empfindung svoll, full of feeling.

Enchainez (Fr.). Means link (them) together—i.e. let the next movement follow its predecessor without a break.

Enclume (Fr.). Anvil.

Encore (Fr.). Again. Cry of audiences who want to hear more music than they paid for. If performer, complies additional music is called an 'encore'.

English guitar. Same as cittern.

English Horn. The term used for the woodwind instrument of oboe type, but standing a fifth lower than the oboe, and written as a Transposing Instrument a fifth higher than sounding; compass from the E below middle C upwards for about two and a half octaves. The Instrument seems to be called horn because of its original curved shape (different from the modern type) and English possibly because of its being known from England-Purcell in Dioclesian specifies a 'tenor hoboy'. i.e. 'tenor oboe', though this is apparently a difficult instrument.

English Suites Refers to the name given to set of 6 keyboard suites by Bach. On larger scale than French suites, and unlike latter they have preludes for the first movts. Origin of title is not clear.

Enharmonic

(1) In Greek music, enharmonic genus was oldest of 3 ways of sub-dividing terachord, other 2 being

diatomic and chromatic. Orig. seems to have consisted simply of major third with semitone below (e.g. A, F, E), but in quite early times, semitone was divided into 2 quarter-tones so that there were 4 notes, not 3:A, A, quarter-tone above E, and E. Existence of these small intervals (in use until Hellenistic times) shows close association between Greek and Oriental music.

(2) In modern acoustics, enharmonic diesis is interval between octave (e.g. C-C), i.e. 2/1 and 3 major third (C-E-G sharp-B sharp), i.e. 125/64. B is therefore flatter than C, and interval is 2÷125/64=128/ 125.On keyboard instruments, however B sharp and C are identical, and this has encouraged composers to use harmonic changes which explore this possibility. What for example , E sharp is substituted for C, this is known as enharmonic change, Enharmonic modulation is one which makes use of such a change to facilitate progress from one key to another.

Ensemble (Fr., together).

(1) The quality of teamwork in performance ('their ensemble was poor').

(2) An item in opera for several soloists, with or without chorus.

(3) A group of performers—the term implying a group of no fixed number, and not so numerous and regularly-constituted as to deserve the name of orchestra or choir.

Entracte. The music played between acts of play or opera.

Entree (Fr.). The term used mainly in 17th-centuries French music:

(1) Introduction piece in ballet or opera, for entry of characters on stage;

(2) Independent piece of instrumental music, similar in character to (1);

(3) Section of ballet or opera, equivalent of some 'scene' or even 'act'.

Entry. In fugue, 'entrance' of theme, not only at beginning but also on later appearances; also ,17th-centuries term for prelude.

Epidiapente (Gr.). Term which refers to 'Cannon at the fifth'

Episode A section in a piece of music considered to have a subordinate role; in particular,

(1) In a Rondo , a contrasting section between recurrences of the main theme;

(2) In a Fugue, a section occurring between entries of the subject.

Episodical form. Same as Rondo form.

Epithalmium. Marriage song.

Eponge (Fr.) The sponge; baguet tesd eponge the drum-sticks with sponge head.

Equale (Old Italian), 'equal'. As noun, piece for Equal Voices or instrument of same kind, esp. trombones.

Equali. Instrumental pieces for instruments of the same kind, especially funeral pieces for 4 tombstones.

Equal Temperament. The term used for tuning of keyboard instrument in such a way that all semitones are equal. This has the effect of putting all intervals except octave slightly out of tune. Advantage of system is that intervals have same values in all keys. Any other system of tuning favours some keys at expense of others and makes modulation difficult outside restricted range.

Equal Voices. Voices of same range (e.g. all basses) or same kind (e.g. all male).

Ernst (Ger.). Serious

Erzlaute (Ger.) Archlute.

Es (Ger.). E flat.

Escapemant. Refers to the mechanism in the piano which enables hammer to 'escape' after string has been struck, so leaving string free to vibrate, Double escapement, makes it possible to strike string second time without waiting for key to rise to normal position of rest.

Eses (Ger.). E double f.

Espressivo (It.). Expressively. Abbrev is espresso.

Essential Note. The note forming part of the chord, as opposed to passing note, suspension, appoggiatura etc.

Estinto (It.). So soft that music can hardly be heard.

Estro, Armonico, L'(It. Harmonious Inspiration). Set of 12 concertos op 3 , by Vivaldi, some of which were transcribed by Bach.

Estudiantina (Sp.). The peace in the light-hearted manner associated with students.

Ethnomusicology. This term deals with the study of different kinds of music to be found in any particular area, in-relation to their cultural or racial context.

Etouffer (Fr.). Means 'damp' (imperative). Indication to player to harp, cymbals etc. That sound must be immediately damped (opposite of laissez vibrer). So also sons etouffes, 'damped notes'.

Etudes Symphoniques (Fr., Symphonic Studies). Set of 12 variations for piano schumann, op 13 (1834, rev. 1852).

Etwas (Ger.). Somewhat, rather.

Eude (Fr.). Study.

Euphonium. Brass instrument (mainly used in the brass band and military band), equivalent to the tenor Tuba.

Eurhythmics. A system of expressing the rhythmical aspect of music by bodily moment, invented by Jacques-Dalcroze.

Evening and Tempest. The name given to one of a set of three symphonies by Haydn.

Exercise

(1) Vocal or instrumental study of no artistic value, e.g. a fine-finger exercise for piano;

(2) In the 18th-centuries, a short key-board work.

(3) The composition which candidates are obliged to write for certain university degrees in music.

Exposition

(1) Refers to that part of a Sonata-Form or similar movement in which the main themes are initially stated before they undergo Development;

(2) In a Fugue, the initial statement of the subject by all the 'voices' in turn.

Expressionism. The term borrowed from painting and applied to literature, drama and music—involving the expression of artist's state of mind by means of external symbol not necessarily in normal relation to each other.

Expression Marks. The indications which are provided by composer as aid to accurate interpretation of his text. They are concerned primarily with :

(1) Dynamics,

(2) Tempo,

(3) Mood.

Expressionism. The name original given to movement in visual arts. Term implies reaction against impressionism, which claimed objective representation of the outside world; expressionism on the other hand eschews everything but the highly subjective expression of inner emotions, often using distortion and symbolism.

Extemporize. Improvise.

Extension Organ. It is sometimes called unit organ : in which pipes are constructed to give more than one each note, thus saving space.

F

F. In Tonic Sol-Fa, 4th note (or subdominant) of major scale.

F. Abbr. of forte (It., loud) ; hence, as indications of increasingly greater loudness, ff, fff, etc.—sometimes in even greater aggregations.

F. The 4th note (or subdominant) of scale of C major (Eng., Ger., Fr., It. fa.). A abbrev f=forte (loud), ff= fortissimo (very loud), fp= forte piano (loud and immediately soft again), fz=forzando (lit.'forcing', i.e. accenting), mf=mezzo forte (moderately loud), pf=poco forte (moderately loud), sf or sfz=sforzando (same as forzando).

F clef originated as ornamental form of letters F and indicates note a fifth below middle C.

F Hole. The name given to a hole approximately in the shapes of an f, of which there are two cut in the belly of a violin, etc., for the sake of the sound.

Fa (Fr., It.). The note F; also fourth note of Guidonian hexachord.

Faburden, Fauxbourden. Term having various meanings, especially in church music—originally a method of improvising parallel harmony to plainsong, with the melody at the top; in modern usage the term signifies:

(1) A four-part harmonization of a hymn having the tune in the tenor, or

(2) A terrible part added above a hymn-tune i.e. a Descant. (The term literally means 'false-drone';

faburden is a good English form, but the French term is also used in English.)

Facile (Fr., It.). Easy. So facilia (It.), ease, fluency; also a simplified version, e.g. of a solo passage written for virtuoso performers and now brought within more modest capacities.

Fado (Port.). Type of Portuguese folk song, mainly urban and properly having a particular rhythm and binary form.

Fagott (Ger.). **Fagotto (It.),** Bassoon.

Fah. Anglicized form of Italian fa (F). In Tonic Sol-Fa, fourth note (or subdominant) of major scale.

Fa-La. The popular type of part-song current to late 16th century, early 17th century, known as balletto (It.) or Ballet (Eng.). Name derives from use of refrain using syllables 'fa la la'.

Fall. Cedence.

False-Relation (US, cross relation). The name given in classical harmony (i.e. late 18th-century, early 19th-century) to:

(1) Progression in which note in one part of first chord is followed by chromatic alteration of same note in another part of second chord.

(2) Simultaneous sounding in single chord of note and its chromatic alteration.

Falsetto (It.) Adult male voice which is used not in normal range but in higher register. If seriously cultivated, voice becomes male alto (or counter-tenor). Falsetto singing is used occasionally for notes which lie above normal range and sometimes also for comic effect. Compass can range up to E at top of treble clef.

Familiar Style (also It., stile familiare). Term probably originating in the 16th-century to describe vocal music in which the voices move uniformly together from one syllable to the next and from one note- value to the next—e.g. in a conventional hymn in four parts, without contrapuntal independence such as might be found in a madrigal.

Family. Term used to group instruments of similar nature and tone- quality—even if there are significant differences in shape (e.g. the saxophone family) or even if they do not all carry the same name (e.g. the 'violin-family' of violin, viola, cello, and double-bass.)

Fandango (Sp.). Spanish dance in triple time, probably of South American origin; accompanied normally by guitar, castanets,. etc.

Fanfare. This term means flourish for trumpets, or other instruments emulating character of trumpets. Fanfares are often used as ceremonial preludes, and are sometimes incorporated in extend compositions. In French form, term also applies to brass band.

Fandango. The lively Spanish dance in triple time, accompanied by guitar and castanets.

Fantasia. In general, piece in which composer follows his fancy rather than any conventional form, In particular:

(1) In 16th, 17th century, name was frequently used of composition for string or keyboard, in which composer, instead of adopting dance from or writing variations, lets imagination play freely in contrapuntal development of theme. Eng. term was 'fancy'.

(2) Work for keyboard or lute of improvisatory character.

(3) Extended work, freer in form than normal sonata;

(4) Work based on existing theme or themes;

(5) Development section of movt. in sonata form is sometimes known as 'free fantasia'.

Fantasiestruck. (Ger.). Same as Fantasia.

Fantasy. Term of various musical meanings, but nearly always associated with the idea of the 'free' play of the composer's imagination , as distinct from adherence to 'set' forms.

Farandole (Fr.). The dance of ancient origin still current in Province. Dancers advance in long chain preceded by player(s) on pipe and tabor. Usually in 6/8 times.

Farce.

(1) Orig. practice of interpolating Tropes into plainsong or polyphonic settings of liturgy;

(2) In 18th-centuary opera, comic scene introduced into serious work; Italian comic operas in one act were called farsa (c 1800).

Farewell Symphony. The nickname of Haydn's symphony no. 45, 1772 (Hob. I:45), in which the music of the last moment ends in such a way that the last players may leave their stands one after the other, only 2 violins eventually remaining. (Or perhaps Haydn's, as Continuo-player at harpsichord, remained?) This is said to have been a hint to Haydn's patron, Prince Esterhazy, that the orchestra deserved a holiday.

Farruca. The energetic Andaluasian dance.

Fausset (Fr.). Falsetto.

Fauxbourdon (Fr., It., folso bordone) lit. 'false-bass':

(1) In the 15th century the term was used to indicate simple form of 3-part harmony in which plainsong melody in treble is accompanied by 2 lower parts, one moving in parallel sixths, the other, supplied by singer , a 4th below melody. Origin and interrelation of fauxbourdon and English Faburden has been uncertain;

(2) Italian name folsobordone came to be applied to simple 4-parts harmonization of plainsong, polyphonic elaboration;

(3) In modern English hymnody , name fauxbourdon is often given to counterpart (or descant) for trebles superimposed on melody sung by congregation.

Feierlich (Ger.). Solemnly, exaltedly.

Feldmusik (Ger.) Lit. 'field-music' i.e. music to be played in open air by wind instruments; hence Feldpartie or Feldpartita, suite for open-air perf.

Feldpartie, Feldpartita (Ger.) 'field-suite' i.e. suite for open-air performance by a military band—cp. Partita.

Feminine. The term used in certain musical contexts to imply (unjustly?) relative weakness—so , e.g. the 'second subject' in Sonata-form is sometimes said to have feminine character as being less assertive than the 1st subject.

Feminine Cadence or Feminine Ending. The cadence, or ending, in which final chord is reached on weak beat of bar instead of more usual strong beat.

Fermata.(It.) Pause.

Fes (Ger.). F flat.

Fiato.(It.). 'breath'. Strumenti a fiato, wind instruments.

Fiddle. The conoquial term for violin or similar string instrument, esp. when used in folk music. Hence 'bass-fiddle' 'bull-fiddle' terms for double bass.

Fiddle Fugue. The nickname for an organ fugue in D minor by Bach (BWV 539) arranged from an earlier (1720) version for violin solo.

Fifara or **Fiffaro**.(It). 17th century name for transverse Flute.

Fife. Small flute still used , as for many centuries, in 'drums and fife' band. In modern form built tone lower than orchestral piccolo and has one or more keys.

Fifteenth. The organ stop of Diapason tone sounding 2 octaves above the note played.—i.e. 15 steps (of the diatomic scale) above, counting both the extreme notes.

Fifth. Interval reached by ascending 4 steps in diatomic scale. e.g. from C to G above; also called perfect fifth. Augmented fifth is fifth in which upper note is sharpened or lower note flattened. Diminished fifth is fifth of which upper is flattered or lower note sharpened.

'Fifths'Quarter. The nickname for Haydn's string quarter in D minor (no.2 of op. 76, 1797-8; Hob. III:76), because of the opening melodic leaps of a fifth. The minute movement is known as the 'witches, Minute'(Ger., Hexenmenuett) from its eerie character.

Figuration. The consistent use of particular melodic or harmonic Figure.

Figure. The short musical phrase—too short to be genuine 'theme'—but (achieving, through repetition) distinctive character in course of composition.

Figured Bass. A standardized notation for Continuo, practised especially in the 17th and 18th centuries, and also used today, e.g. in academic training and as a kind of harmonic shorthand. Figures with a bass-note indicate the distance above the bass-note of the other notes which are to be sounded. e.g. if the key is C major, and the bass-note is C, the figure 5 would indicate G, and 5 would indicate G; but the choice of the particular octave in which this G-G is to be placed is left to the musicianship of the performer. Various abbreviations and other conventions are also used. (The 'Chord-symbols' used in modern pop music, though similar in being a kind of shorthand, are not the same. They are named after the chords-major, minor, augmented, etc. irrespective of which note of these chords come in the bass; figured-bass symbols are invariably relative to a particular bass note.)

Figured Chorale. The setting of chlorate melody for organ, in which particular figuration is employed throughout.

Filar La Voice. The lit. 'to draw out the voice', i.e. sustain note, in one long drawn-out breath, with or without crescendo and decrescendo.

Fin (Fr.) End.

Final (1, Eng.). The note on which the modal scale ends analogous to the keynote of the major or minor scale; (2, Fr.)=Finale.

Finale.

(1) The last movement of a work in several movements;

(2) An ensemble ending an act of an opera—so first finale, second finale, etc., referring to Acts I, II, etc.

Fine (It.) The end —term sometime occurring in the middle of the music as notated, in conjunction with some instruction at the end of the music-type to go back to on earlier point out and proceed from there to the point where fine occurs.

Finger-board. The long strip of wood on string instrument on which fingers of left hand press down string at any chosen point and so shorten their vibrating length and raise pitch.

Finger Cymbals. The pair of tiny cymbals strapped to thumb and finger; they give high bell more of definite pitch.

Fingering

(1) The use of fingers in playing an instrument.

(2) The indication of which fingers are to be used for which notes-so (in piano-playing) continental fingering, numbering the thumbs as 1 and the

other fingers as 2-5, as opposed to (obsolete) English fingering, in which the thumb was signified by + and the other fingers as 1-4.

Fipple. The obstructive block of wood which canalifies the air in the instrumental species called the fipple flute-of which the chief example is the Recorder.

First. The term implying in an orchestra (e.g. first trombone) a position of leadership as well as (usually) a part higher in pitch; but in a choir (e.g. first basses) implying only a higher-pitched part, not leadership.

First-Movement Form. The term sometimes used for Sonata-form.

Fis (Ger.). F sharp.

Fisarmonica (It.). Accordion.

Fisi (Ger.). F double sharp.

Five-three Chord. The basic , or common, triad. In figured bass denoted by figures 5/3, referring to third and the fifth above root, e.g. C-E-G.

Flageolet. The obsolete high 6 holed wind instrument (similar to recorder but with different arrangement of fingers and thumb- holes), Used e.g. in Handle's 'Rinaldo, : double flageolet, instrument of two such pipes side by side, often seen in 'pastoral' illustrations. The terms flageolet-notes (Eng.) , Flageolets (Fr.), Flageolette (Ger.), meaning Harmonics on a stringed instrument, refer to the supposed resemblance of these thin-sounding notes to those of that flageolet.

Flageolet-notes. Harmonics on string instruments.

Flam. The drum stroke used to mark accent. Consists of two notes played very closely together.

Flamenco or Cante Flamenco. The species of Spanish song, from Andalusia, performed with guitar accompaniment; often accompanies dance. Various subspecies named after different areas of Andalusia including malaguena, sevillana. Mood of music is often (though not necessarily) said. Solo guitarists often play in 'flamenco style' as opposed to classical style.

Flat

(1) The sign b indicating that note to which it is prefixed is to be lowered by one semitone. Holds good for rest of bar, unless contradicted. If forms part of Key Signature, holds good, unless contradicted until there is a new key signature which omits it.

(2) In French and Italian, flattened notes are referred to by name of note followed by word for flat; in German , suffix '-s' or '-es' is added to name of note, e.g. E Flat=Fr. mi bemol, Ger. Es, It. mi bemolle. Exception to rule is that Ger. B (without any suffix) = B flat (B natural is represented by H; B double flat is Bes);

(3) Applied to an interval = minor, e.g. flat 7th= minor 7th, flat 3rd= minor 3rd. This use of word, though not obsolute, is Old-fashioned;

(4) The 'flat key' is now one which has one or more flats in the key signature, e.g. F (1 flat), B flat (2 flats), E flat (3 flats), etc. 'Flat-key' formerly meant minor key, just as 'flat 3rd' meant minor 3rd;

(5) An instrument or voice is flat if the notes produced are lower than normal pitch. A single note can also be flat , as a result of faulty tuning or careless performance.

Flat-Twenty-first. In a mixture stop on the organ, a rank sounding three octaves less one tone above the note struck.

Flatterzunge (Ger.). The flutter-tongue.

Flautando or **Flautato** (It.). The term means 'playing like a flute'. Direction to string players :

(1) To play harmonics,

(2) To play gently near end of finger board.

Flaut (Flute) (In the widest sense). Since the period of Haydn this has meant the ordinary side-blown Flute, i.e. the transverse flute (flauto traverso); its small size is the flauto piccolo, or little flute-commonly called Piccolo. However, in preceding periods flauto alone may indicate the Recorder or other end-blown flute, Bach for instance writing flauto traverso in full (or just traverso) when he wants not the recorder but the side-blown flute; similarly flauto piccolo in Bach (the word traverso omitted) is thought to mean a flageolet, the piccolo of modern usage having not yet been in vented.

Flautone (It.). Bass flute.

Flebile (It.). Tearful, planitive, mournful.

Flexatone. The simple instrument consisting of steel blade and small clapper mounted on flexible strip. On shaking, clapper, strikes blade to produce bell sound; pitch gets varied by pressing blade.

Flicorno. The name of a family of a brass instruments similar to sax-horn family, used in Italian military bands.

Fiessend (Ger.). Flowing.

Florid. The term descriptive of melody that is full of Ornaments— whether such are written in by composer or, as common.

Flote (Ger.). Flute, Kleine Flote, Piccolo.

Flourish

(1) Panfare;

(2) Decorative musical figure, either written or improvised.

Flue-pipe. An organ pipe into which the air is made to enter directly, as in to a flute or recorder (not striking a vibrant tongue or Reed, as in a red-pipe).

Flugel. A grand piano i.e. a wing-shaped.

Flugelhorn (Ger.)

(1) Usually anglicized as 'flugelhorn', soprano saxhorn in B flat , similar in shape to bugle, but with three pistons. Has same compass as B flat cornet, but fuller tone. Used in brass bands and jazz;

(2) In general, German equivalent of Saxhorn family.

Flute

(1) Beaked flute or English flute (French, flute a bec, flute douce; Ger., Blackflote; It flauto dolce, flauto d 'eco), now known exclusively as recorder.

(2) Transverse or German flute now known simply of flute. 'Woodwind' instrument, generally made of either wood or silver. One end of tube is stopped, and sound is produced by blowing across aperture cut inside at that end; pitch is controlled by finger-operated key system. Compass is normally from middle C to three octaves above, though sometimes has extra semitones at bottom. In addition to normal-sized flute there are also (a) Piccolo, built octave higher, (b) bass flute or alto flute, built 4th lower. Flute d'amour built minor 3rd lower, is obsolete. Flutes built minor 3rd or semitone above normal pitch were at one time used in military bands and treated as transposing instruments. Though of great antiquity, flute did not come into general use of chamber and orchestral music till early 18th centuary. (Note. that at this time flauto=recorder, flauto traverso or traverso= transverse flute).

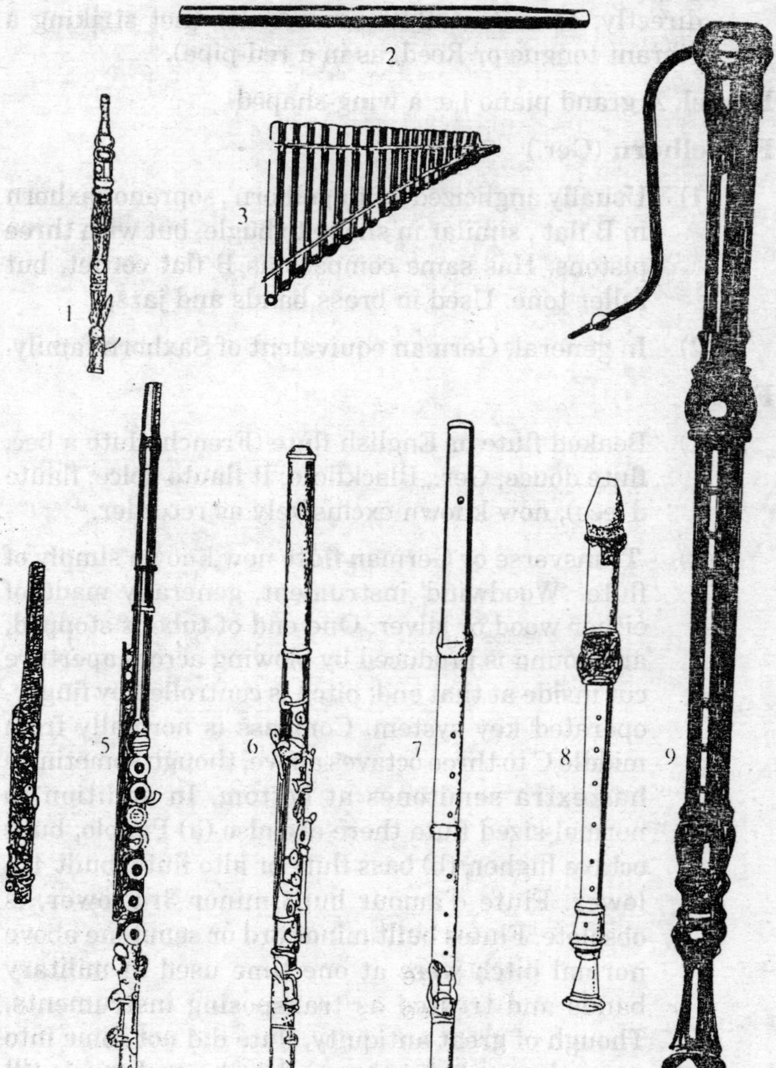

Flute

(1) Keyed Flageolet, (2) File, (3) Panpipes, (4) Piccolo, (5) Metal flute, (6) Wooden flute, (7) 18th-centuary. flute, (8) Alto recorder, and (9) Bass recorder.

Flute-a-bec (Fr., beaked flute) = Rrecorder.

Flutist. The Player of the flute.

Flutrer Tongue. The method of tone productions sometimes used in wind instruments: consists of rolling tongue as if saying drr. Result, if applied to single note, is rapid tremolo.

Folia, La (Sp., also La follia, It.) The name originally of a dance ('The Folly') of Portuguese origin, and hence the name of a particular tune used for the dance.

Follies d'Espagne. Musical form in dance rhythm and derived from Folia conventions. Basic tune was used as subject for variations by many composers most notably Corelli in violin sonata, op 5 No.12 (1700).

Folk-music, Song Tune. Terms implying that the work concerned has been transmitted actually among 'the people' from one generation to the next, and can be ascribed to no particular composer. As this definition suggest:

(1) a folk song must be, or have been, 'popular', but not every 'popular' song is a folk-song.

(2) folk-song flourishes among a primitive' population, where music does not generally take a written form;

(3) because of aural transmission. a folk-song is likely to exist in several differing version. Folk-song, although 'national' in character, has tended to show wide international similarities: in particular it has preserved the Modes longer than normal 'composed' music.

Folk-Song. The term used implying song of no known authorship which has been preserved in a community by oral tradition. Folk song have been introduced into serious music or used as theme for variations.

Foot. In organ pipes, measure of pitch: 2ft pipe sounds middle C, and 4ft, 8ft, 16ft, and 32ft pipes relatively sound C octave lower than pipe before.

Foriana, Furlana.

(1) The lively dance in 6/8 or time, originating in Friulu, NE Italy;

(2) In the late 16th-cent, name ballo furlano applied to dance in 4/4 time and moderate tempo.

Form. The layout of a piece of music which is considered as a succession of sections. A simple song may thus be said to have a form consisting of, say, one line, the first line, the first line repeated, then another line; while a more involved piece may be said to have form corresponding to one of various basic types e.g. Binary, Ternary, Fugue, Passacaglia, Sonata-Form, Variations; or such a piece may be said to be 'free' in form. i.e., unrelated to such a 'set' type.

Formalism. A supposed fault in composition for which Russian composers have been denounced by Soviet officialdom at various times in 1948; the apparent implication is that the music concerned has been over-intellectually conceived, with undue emphasis on 'form' as distinct (supposedly) from 'content'. There usually seems an added implications that the music is over-discordant and uncritically pursues modernity for its own sake.

Formes Fixes.(Fr.). The collective name for ballade, virelai and rondeau, 3 main forms of late medieval French poetry and music.

Forte, Fortissimo (It.). Refers to loud, very loud (abbr. f, ff; quite commonly fff and even greater aggregations are used to indicate still greater loudness).

Fortepiano. An early Italian name meaning the same as Pianoforce. Its use in English to denote the late 18th-centuary Piano is arbitrary and affected. (Fortepiano is, however, the standard Russian word for the normal instrument).

Fortissimo (It.). Very loud; usually abbrev. to ff.

Fortspinnung (Ger.). The term means continuation'. Term for process of continuation` or development of continuation or development of musical material in symphonies, etc. as opposed to symmetrical repetition of that material.

Forty-Eight. The common name for Bach's The Well-tempered Clavier.

Forza (It.). The 'force'. Can forza, emphatically, vigorously.

Forzando (It.). The 'forcing', i.e. strongly accented. Usually abbrev. to fz.

Foundation Stops. On organ, all stops except Mutation Stops.

Foundation Tone. The tone of more dignified stops, e.g. diapasons.

Four Temperaments. The:

(1) Title of symphony no. 2.1902, by C. Nielsen (Dan., De fire temperamenter), each of the 'temperaments' having one movement;

(2) Title of Hindemith's Theme and Variations for piano and strings, 1940, each 'temperament' taking charge on one variation, (The reference has been to the 'temperaments' thought in medieval times to be the dominant factor in a man's character—choleric phlegmatic, melancholic, sanguine.)

Fourniture (Fr.). Furniture (Organ stop).

Fourth. Refers to the interval reached by ascending 3 steps diatonic scale, e.g. G to C above; also called perfect fourth. In Harmonic Series, interval between third and fourth notes of series, thus having ratio 4/3.

Following terms are in use: augmented fourth, fourth in which upper note is sharpened or lower note flattened; diminished fourth, fourth in which upper note is flattened or lower note sharpened.

Fourth Chord. The chord consisting of superimposed fourths, or of fourths in combination with other intervals.

Foxtrot. Dance of US origin in duple times; first because popular 1912. Severa variants appeared, and word came to lose limited application to particular dance. Two main types—fast and slow.

Franco De Colonia or Franco of Cologne (fl 13th-cent.), theorist. Systematized notation of mensural music in treatise Ars cantus mensurabilis.

Free Fantasia. The name sometimes given to the Development section of a movement, e.g. in Sonata-form.

French Sixth. Type of 'augmented sixth' chord distinguished by the intermediate intervals of the chord—e.g. (reading upwards) Db, F, G, B.

French Harp (US) The mouth organ.

French Suites. The set of 6 keyboard suites by Bach (c 1722).Some say they were so-called because of supposedly characteristic French style. On smaller scale than English Suites.

Frequency. The term in acoustics for the number of complete vibrations undergone by an air-column or a resonating body in one second. The unit of measurement (one cycle per second) is the Hertz, abbreviated as Hz. As frequency increases, the pitch of the note sounded is raised, so pitch can be defined by frequency; by international agreements, 1939, the A commonly used for tuning (i.e. that above middle C) is fixed at 440 Hz.

Fret. The name given to each of the strips of wood or metal fixed on the fingerboard of, e.g. guitar, viols, lute (but not the violin family). The player presses his fingers against a fret to shorten the length of strings vibrating. So fretted instruments, those fitted with frets.

Frog.(US). The nut of violin or violin bow.

'Frog' Quartet (Ger., Froschquartett). The nickname given to Haydn's string quartet in D major, op 50, no. 6 supposedly because of 'croaking' theme in finale.

From My Life (Cz. Z meho zivota). Title of Smentna's string quartet no 1 in E minor(1876).

Frottola (It.), lit 'little mixture'. Type of strophic song of popular character current in aristocratic circles in late 15th, early 16th centuary. Italy. Foreruner of Madrical.

Fugato (It.) Term applied to section of composition which is treated fugally, though composition as whole is not fugue.

Fughetta (It.). The short fugue.

Fugue. A type of contrapuntal composition for a given number of parts or 'voices'(so called, whether the work is vocal or instrumental). Hence fugue in three voices, a four-part fugue, etc. The essential feature of a fugue is the entries of all the voices successively in Imitation of each other. The opening entry is in the tonic key and is called the subject; the imitative entry of the next voice, in the dominant, is called the answer; similarly with the entries of subsequent voices (if any) alternately. Commonly there are several complete entries of all voices (with the order changed) in the course of fugue; the complete entries are separated by episodes. Commonly also each voice having announced the subject or answer passes to another fixed thematic element called the counter subject—the counter-subject being heard in the first voice simultaneously with the answer in the second voice, etc. But the great masters of fugue such as Bach do not confine the fugue to a strict pattern, though time-wasting academic theorists have done so.

Full Anthem. The Anthem in which voices supply all necessary harmony, without need for independent accompaniment, in contrast to Verse Anthem.

Full Orchestra. An orchestra of the 4 usual sections (strings, woodwind, brass, percussion) and of normal concert-hall strength.

Full Organ. The direction that the organ should be played at full strength. Owing to the construction of the instrument and of the human ear, this does not necessarily imply the use of all the stops.

Full Score. Orchestral Score, in which part for each instrument appears on separate stave,(usually) arranged in conventional orders.

Fundamental. First or lowest, note or Harmonic series.

Fundamental Bass. The term employed by Rameau to indicate 'root' any chord, or 'roots' of series of chords. Any 2 chords composed of same notes, is whatever vertical order, are considered to have same fundamental base. Foundation of theory on Inversions.

Fundamental, Fundamental Note. The primary or 'parent' note of the Harmonic Series.

Funebre, Funebre (It.,Fr.). Of a funeral. So marcia funebre, marche funebre, funeral march.

Fuoco (It.). Fire; can fuoco, with fire.

Furiant (Cz.). The quickest Czech dance with changing rhythms—thought some of Dvorak's movements so entitled do not change in rhythm. (The word is not concerned with 'fury').

Futurism (It., futurismo). The movement started by Italian writer F.T. Marinetti in 1911. First concert of Futuristic music given by him and composer Luigi Rossolo in Milan (1914), consisting of 'networks of voices' employing thunders, whistlers, etc; caused riot. Euturist music defined by Marinetti as 'synthetic expression of great economic, erotic, heroic, aviational, mechanical dynamism'.

Fz. The less frequent encountered equivalent of sf.

G

G. Fifth note (or dominant of scale of C major). As abbrev. m.g.== main gauche (left hand), G.P.==General Pause (rest for complete orchestra).

G clef, now invariably placed on 2nd line of stave, has been treble clef, making G above middle C.

Gagaku (Jap.). The orchestral music which is traditionally associated (since the 8th century) with the Japanese court, using wind, strings and percussion.

Gaillard (Fr.) = Galliard.

Galanterian (Ger.). The name given in 18th cent. to dances in suite which are added optionally to regular allemande, courante, sarabande, and gigue. Normally placed between sarabande and gigue.

Galantieren, Galanteries (Ger., Fr.,). In the classical suite, those numbers (e.g. minuet, polonaise) whose inclusion was optional, not obligatory.

Galliard. The term for the lively dance at least as old as the 15th cent., usually but not always in 3/2 time; often contrasted with, and sometimes built from the same musical material as a pavan (which is slower).

Galpo. A 19th century ballroom dance in quick 2/4 time. Originated in Germany.

Galoubet (Fr.). The 3-hole whistle flute, which is played with left hand while right hand beats tabor (Tambourin).

Gamba. Abbrev. of Vipla Da Gamba. Also organ stop imitating that instrument.

Gamelan Orchestra. Indonesian instrument ensemble. It is principally composed of xylophones, marimbas, gongs and drums. Music is based on simples 5-note scales but highly sophisticated in texture and rhythmically very complex.

Gamme (Fr.) Scale.

Gamut

(1) The compass, range (also metaphorically);

(2) (various obsolete senses) the G at the bottom of the bass clef; the written system of Hexachords; the musical scale (like French gamme).

Ganzetaktnote (Ger.). The whole-note, semibreve—literally meaning a note lasting a whole bar or measure.

Ganzton (Ger.) Whole-tone.

Gapped (of a scale). Having some intervals of more than a tone's distance, unlike the normal major or minor scales; e.g. the pentatonic scale.

Gapped Scale. The scale with some intervals larger than whole tone, e.g. pentatonic scale.

Garbato (It.). Graceful.

Gastein Symphony. The term used for supposed symphony of Schubert, now lost, said to have been written in Gastein (Austria). Some think sonata in C for piano duet is arrangement of it.

Gavotte. The term used for the old dance in 4/4 time beginning on the third beat of the bar; sometimes (but not always) a constituent of the baroque suite, and occasionally revived in modern times.

Gebrauchmusik (Ger.). Utility Music.

Gedackt, Gedact. The end-stopped type of organ pipe of soft tone. (The term means 'covered'; in modern German, gedeckt).

Geetams. After the necessary janta (double and treble) swaras and the alankarams, the pupil is taught small swarajatis (lakshana geetams which give all the qualities and the features of that particular raga), then the little songs called geetam in all suddha and vikrita swara-ragas,etc. After the pupil is properly established and has acquired the fundamental knowledge of music, then only the more difficult and scholarly compositions are taken up.

Gerge (Ger.). The fiddle, violin.

Geistlich(Ger.) The religious, sacred , Geistilche Lieder, the sacred songs.

Generalpause (Ger.). The general pause, rest of one or more bars for complete orchestra. Indicated by abbrev. G.P.

German Flute. The obsolete name for the ordinary (cross-blown) flute as distinct from the Recorder, formerly known as the 'English-Flute'.

Ges (Ger.). G flat.

Gesang (Ger.). Song, humm. So Lobgesang (Mendelssohn)=Hymn of praise.

Gesangvoll (Ger.). Songful—same as cantabile.

Geschwind (Ger.). Quick.

Geses (Ger.). G double flat.

Gestopft (Ger.). Stopped (notes on the horn).

Geteilt (Ger.,in older spelling getheilt). Divided.

Getragen (Ger.). Slow and sustained—same as sostenuto.

Gharanas. In the Hindustani system of music we find that the different Gharanas ('traditional' ways of presentation) have different styles. The same raga may be presented by each gharana-singer slightly differently, the presentation of the one from the other will vary, and may sound quite peculiar to the other. The most popular of all these Gharanas are Gwalior style, Kirana style, Agra and Delhi styles. Each has its own style of presentation.

Now let us just study a few outstanding characteristics of the different styles.

(1) Kirana Ghar. Abdul Karim Khan, one of our later musicians of eminence, used to follow the Kirana Ghar, which was also one of the popular gharanas with a good style.

The Gwalior, Agra and Delhi Gharanas have come to be recognized as the pioneers of the khyal, style, who also produced eminent gayaks.

(2) Gwalior. A clear-cut presentation of the first part, Sthai and then the Antra. The important portions of the song with proper combination of the words and swaras. A neat presentation, with 'bolalaps', beautiful sequences of 'tan', gradual increase of the speed, words woven out into quick 'tan'.

Then after the vilambit is over, a skilled singer would clearly take up the fast khyal and take up his own creative extempore elaborations, rapid 'tans' beautifully intricated, delicate embellishments, which give scope to express his own talent in this art. Varied and straight, full-throated speedy passages of swaras, effectively produced add to the charm of the khyal, and these are much appreciated.

A majority of the musicians now follow this rule, as they consider this style as the most authentic of all gharanas for khyal singing.

(3) Agra. The Agra style was known for its simplicity, dignity and restraint and virtues, combined with also bits of romantic expression in feeling and accent. This produced an outlook of a romantic interpretation.

Many noted Ustads like Faiyaz Khan belonged to this Agra Gharana.

(4) Delhi. The Delhi Gharana which was never so very popular and especially after the demise of its great pioneer originator Tanras Khan and a few of his

descendants, who were only individually great, is on the decline (except for the noted Shri Chand Khan) and is almost fading away.

Thus the gharanas in the Hindustani music have played a vital role in the development of style and technique.

Ghazals. These are simple melodies.. They are also love lyric, and resemble the 'dadras' which are also another form of love songs prevalent in the Hindustani music. These are somewhat placed between the thumris and tappas, and have become very popular.

'Giant' Fugue. The nickname of chorale prelude for organ by Bach. from Clavierubung, part 3—so called because of recurrence on pedals of imposing figure symbolising unshakeable faith.

Gigue (Fr.) = Jig.

Gigue

(1) (Fr.) Medieval name for bowed sting instrument;

(2) Lively dance (It., giga).

'Gigue' Fugue or 'Jig' Fugue. Refers to the nickname given to fugue in G for 2 manuals and pedal in 12/8 time, generally regarded as early work of Bach.

Gigues (Fr.). First of Debussy's Images for orchestra.

Giocoso (It.). Merry, playful, humorous.

Gis, Gisis (Ger.). G sharp, G double-sharp.

Gittam. The medieval English name for 4-stringed instrument of guitar family, played with plectrum. In Tudor and Stuart times, term used loosely to refer to more than one kind of instrument, incl. Spanish guitar. Not necessarily identical with Cittern.

Glee. The simple part-song, generally for male voices.

Glissando (It.). Execution of rapid continuous movement up or down scale. Glissando is often abbrev. gliss or indicated by oblique stroke (straight or wavy) between highest and lowest notes.

Glocke, (Ger.,pl. Glocken). Bell.

Glockenspiel. The percussion instrument (various sizes) consisting of series of steel plates of different sizes, arranged like key-board of piano so as to provide complete chromatic compass. Steel plates are struck with wooden hammers held in hands, though at one time instrument was fitted with keyboard (like Celeste). German name has become virtually international.

Glogauer Liederbuch (Ger.). 15th-century. German collection of songs and dances, arranged for vocal or instrumental ensemble.

Glusto. Strict, just, proper; hence such expressions as allegro giusto, meaning either:

(1) Allegro with a special attention to keeping a strict beat, or

(2) A moderate (neither too fast nor too slow) allegro.

Glass Harmonica. The obsolete instrument consisting of glass vessels of various sizes, rubbed with dampened finger (or operated mechanically). Also called the 'musical glasses' invented by Benjamin Franklin, 1763.

Glee. The short choral composition, properly in several sections and for unaccompanied male voices.

Glissando (mock-It. from Fr. glisser, to side). The term used for the sliding up and down the scale, i.e. making a quick uninterrupted passage up or down the scale, e.g. on the piano, harp, xylophone, trombone. The effect of Portamento on stringed instruments has not been the same, because it implies only the smooth linking of two notes, not the deliberate sounding of the notes between.

Glocke (n) (Ger). Bell(s)-referring in the orchestral scores, to tubular bells.

Glockenspiel (Ger. play of the bells). The percussion instrument of tuned metal bars giving small bell-like sound: played with keyboard or (more usually) small hammers held in hand. (The term also used for chime of real bells played mechanically by hand, i.e. a carillon.)

Gloria (Let.)

(1) Initial word of 'Gloria in excelsis Deo' (Glory to God in the highest), second part of Ordinary of Mass;

(2) Gloria Patri (or doxology) sung at the end of psalm or canticle.

God Save the King (Queen). British national anthem; author and composer unknown, though a keyboard piece by Bull (in the minor key) has some relationship to the tune. Generally adopted in the mid-18th century. (Tune also set to various other words— e.g. U.S., 'My Country, 'tis of Thee',1831.)

Gong. The circular percussion instrument of bronze, made in various sizes, usually with a turned-down rim; sometimes of definite and sometimes of indefinite pitch. (This is a broad, ethno-musicological definition, but in modern orchestral usage there is a tendency to reserve gong for various-sized instruments with definite pitch and Tam-tam for those with indefinite.)

Gopak. Russian folk-dance in quick 2/4 time. (In English sometimes also written as hopak.)

Gorgheggio (It.). In singing, term used of fast, extended passage where vowel is continued over many notes.

Goswami Tulsidas. We all know how the great sagas of our holy land have delivered the divine message for the spiritual advancement among the masses.

We find from the texts, how the saint poet musician of 1600 century A.D. the author of sacred epic Ramayana, had introduced the whole life and deeds of

Sri Rama, revealing the mysteries of the Universe, in simple lucid spoken Hindi.

Tulsidas was born of a very ordinary Brahmin parents. It is believed that the child's horoscope was found unlucky, and the parents were advised to throw the infant outside to the mercy of God and nature to live or die. Providential, however, it was, that the boy who was destined to become one of the leading personages of this pious land, was to have been picked up from wayside, by the mendicant who happened to pass that way, and thus rescued.

When God had ordained him to be His messenger and a prophet of repute, how cold his fate be otherwise?

Tulsidas grew up as a child of travelling mendicant, listening to stories connected with gods, with rapt attention.

His adopted parents lived in Chitrakoot for some time and in Rajapur and Bhundelkand for the rest of the time.

Tulsidas spent most of his life, living at the holy city of Varanasi-Banaras.

Actually, his literary talents only blossomed after his fortieth year, and lasted to about forty years or more.

He lived to see more than a hundred autumns, 1574 A.D. to 1683 A.D.

He was not only a writer of great repute, but was also a great lover and composer of music. Tulsidas composed many beautiful bhajans in praise of Lord Rama, expressing the truth and sentiments of the supreme bliss and immortality through his philosophical songs.

Gothic Music. The term applied to music in N Europe contemporary with Gothic architecture (c 13th- early 15th cents).

Grace-note. The note considered additional to the melody, inserted as an Ornament.

Gradevole (It.). Pleasing.

Gradual (Lat., graduale)

(1) The responsorial chant, a part of Proper of RC Mass;

(2) Orig. book containing graduals, hence book containing all music of Mass to be sung by choir.

Gran Cassa (It.) =Bass Drum.

Grand Chour (Fr.) =Full Organ.

Grand Duo. The name given to Schubert's sonata in C for piano duet. Some think it is arrangement of lost Gastein Symphony.

Grand Jeu (Fr.). Full organ.

Grand Opera. Term that arose in France in 19th centuary to distinguish serious operas set to music throughout from opera-comique, which had dialogue. Term came to be used not simply of form but of lavish scale of performances.

Graphic Notation. The term describing certain newer (post-1950) types of musical notation, especially those which pictorialize the action required of the performer, or which represent duration by comparative length of printing lines and other visual symbol.

Grave (It., heavy, grave). In slow tempo.

Great. The usual abbreviation for Great Organ.

Great Organ (or simply Great). The chief and most powerful division of an organ (a manual and equipment controlled by it). No connection with Great Organ Mass.

Greensleeves. The old English tune mentioned by Shakespeare and found with several sets of words and in several old musical arrangements.

Gregorian Chant. The tune referring to large collection of ancient monophonic melodies, preserved, and until recently widely performed, within RC church. Most chants belong either to Mass or Office.

Gregorian Tone. The name given to each of 8 melodies of Gregorian chant (each in a different Mode) prescribed by Roman Catholic Church for the psalms. Tonus Peregrinus is additional to these.

Griffbrett (Ger.). The lit. 'grip board', i.e. finger-board of voilin etc.

Grosse Caisse (Fr.) =Bass Drum.

Grosse Fuge (Ger.) =Great Fugue.

Grosse Trommel (Ger.) =Bass Drum.

Grosses Orchester (Ger.) =Full Orchestra.

Grouad. The term sometimes used for Ground Bass.

Ground Bass. The bass line constantly repeated throughout composition, forming foundation tor varied melodic or contrapuntal treatment.

Gruppetto (It.) =Turn (type of ornament).

Gruppo or Gruppetto (It.).Generic term for various ornaments consisting of one or more decorative notes with melody note, in particular:

(1) Shake or Trill employing both upper and lower accessory notes:

(2) Turn (represented by diminutive gruppetto).

Guiro. The scaper consisting of touched gourd, played by scraping scraping stick our notches.

Guitar. The plucked, fretted string instrument : it exists in various types of which the principal one came to other European countries from Spain and is therefore sometimes called 'Spanish guitar': now normally with six strings, with compass E below the bass stave upwards for more than three octaves. This type (now also called 'classical guitar') enjoyed revival in the 20th century celling forth concertos by Villa-Lobos and others; it is also (rarely) used in chamber music (e.g. Schoenberg, 'Serenade'). The electric guitar and four-stringed electric bass guitar are chiefly used in pop music, etc.; in pop circles acoustic guitar (primarily meaning non-electric) customarily demands a bulkier instrument than the spanish guitar. Related instruments include Balalaika, Bandurria Cittern and Gittern.

Guitar

(1) Ornate 17th century Italian guitar

(2) Bandurria

(3) Ciltern

(4) Banjo

(5) Guitar

Guitare d' amour. Alternative name for Arpeggione.

Gusla. Ancient Slovanic one-strong bowed instrument, distinct from the following.

Gusli. Russian instrument of zither type used in folk-music; 'played' by Sadko in Rimsky-Korsakov's opera of that name, the effect being simulated in the orchestra.

Gymel (from Lat. cantus gemellus, 'twin song'). The term first occurring in 15th century to denote characteristically English style of singing in 2 parts with same range. Practice goes back to 13th century, earlier examples making liberal use of parallel thirds.

H

H. German note-symbol.

H (Ger.). B natural.

Habanera. Cuban dance with singing, introduced into Spain. The word comes from Habana (i.e. Havana), Cuba; whence the French equivalent term, havanaise. The spelling habanera is mistaken.

Hairpins. The colloquial name for the signs < and > indicating respectively crescendo and diminuendo.

Halb, Halbe (Ger.) Half. Halbe, Halbe Note, or Halbetaknote, minim. Halbe Pause, minim rest. Halbschluss, half cadence. Halbsopran, mezzo-soprano. Halbtenor, baritone. Halbton, semitone.

Half-close = Imperfect Cadence.

Half-note. The note considered as a time-value. This term is standard N. American usage and, as mathematically corresponding to the element of time-signature represented by /2, should clearly be preferred to minim, still surviving in British use.

Half Step (US). The semitone.

Halfte, Die (Ger., the half). The direction indicating that a passage is to be played by only half the normal number of instruments, e.g. half the first violins.

Half Tone (US). Semitone.

Hallelujah. Basically, Biblical word for joyous praise of God. In chant it is spelt Alleluia.

Hallelujah Chorus. The chorus consisting mostly of the one repeated word, 'Hallelujah', at the end of Part II of Handel's 'Messiah'. (This is what the term now refers to, though other works have similar choruses).

'Hallelujah' Concerto. The nickname for Handel's organ concerto into B (ho. 3 of his second set, published 1740), because it contains a phrase also occurring in the 'Hallelujah Chorus'.

Halling. The popular Norwegian dance, moderately fast in tempo and generally 2/4 time. Performed by men with much dramatic action incl. leaps in air. Properly accompanied by Hardanger Fiddle.

Hammerklavier (Ger.). The obsolete German name for piano. Habit of referring to Beethoven's piano sonata op 106 in B flat as "the 'Hammerklavier' sonata" is pointless as Beethoven also used word in titles of other piano sonatas.

Hammond Organ. The type of Electronic organ, usually with 2 manuals and pedal keyboard.

Handel Variations. The set of 20 variations of fugue for piano by Brahms, op 24 (1961). Work is based on Air from Handel's harpsichord suite in B flat.

Hand-horn. The 'natural' Horn (i.e. without valves) : incapable of a continuous scale, it could produce only the notes of the harmonic series, plus a few other obtained by putting the hand in the bell.

Hardanger Fiddle. Norwegian folk violin, with 4 sympathetic strings in addition to normal 4.

Harm. The direction to stringed instruments that certain notes are to be played in 'harmonics'.

Harmonic (adjective)

(1) Relating to harmony; hence the Harmonic minor scale used in harmonizing; hence also the

Harmonic Series being the series of tones (harmonic tones) from which the system of harmony has historically sprung;

(2) Relating to Harmonic Series itself; hence e.g. the harmonic flute stop on an organ, producing 4-Foot tone from 8-Foot pipe pierced at half-length—i.e. using the second tone of the Harmonic Series.

Harmonic (noun). =Harmonic tone i.e. one of the tones of Harmonic Series. The lowest such tone, or 'fundamental', is called the first harmonic, the next lowest and second harmonic, etc. But in such phrases as 'playing in harmonics' on stringed instruments, the allution is to harmonics with the exclusion of the first—since the first is the 'normal' sound requiring no special directions. To obtain these harmonics other than the first, it is necessary to set the string vibration not as a whole length but in fractional parts of its length. A violinist, etc., does this by placing a finger lightly at a given point of vibrating string: when the string is an open string (i.e. not otherwise fingered) then the result is called a natural harmonic, but when the string is a stopped string (one finger used for stopping and another finger for 'lightly placing') then the result is an artificial harmonic. The harmonics obtainable on harp (also by 'lightly placing' the finger on vibrating string) are in the sense 'natural' harmonics.

Harmonic Series. The set of tones (called harmonic tones or simply harmonics) produced by a vibrating string on air-column, according to whether this is vibrating as a unit through its whole length or in aliquot parts (1/2, 1/3, 1/4 etc.). Vibration of the whole length gives the lowest ('fundamental') tone, or 'first harmonic'. The other tones, or 'upper partials', i.e. the second, third, fourth and higher harmonics, are at fixed intervals above the fundamental—an octave above it, then a perfect fifth above that, and so on, decreasingly, ad infinitum. E g. if the fundamental is the C in the base stave, the series will begins as follows:

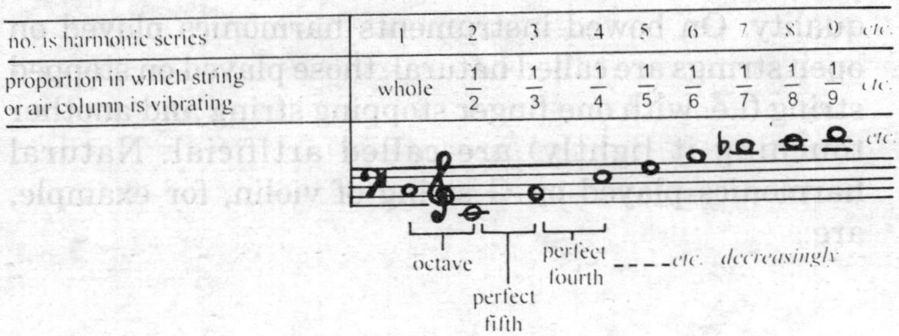

(Not all of these, however, correspond exactly to the notes as turned in modern scales).

Harmonica. The name given to various types of musical instruments—especially, today, to the instrument also called 'mouth organ', i.e. small wind-instrument with metal reeds (one to each note), made in various sizes, most often with range upwards from about middle C, the superior models having chromatic compass. The instrument has mainly been used informally, e.g. by children, but works by e.g. Milhaud and Vaughan Williams have been written for Larry Adler, its most notable exponent. (Cp. Reed Organ.) The name was also given to an instrument consisting of musically tuned glasses (now obsolete).

Harmonic Analysis. Refers to the study of chords of harmonies, of piece of music, both individually and in succession.

Harmonic Flute. The organ stop. Hole is bored mid-way in open cylindrical metal pipe, making predominant pitch the first harmonic, or octave (4ft pitch).

Harmonic Piccolo. The organ stop similar to harmonic flute, but sounding octave higher (2ft pitch).

Harmonics. The sounds produced on string instrument or harp by touching string lightly at one of its nodes, i.e.

exact fractional points. They correspond to upper partials (overtones) of string, and have soft, flute-like quality. On bowed instruments harmonics played on open strings are called natural, those played on stopped string (i.e. with one finger stopping string and another touching it lightly) are called artificial. Natural harmonics played on G string of violin, for example, are:

Black notes indicate at what point string is touched.

Harmonics are indicated by writing either small circle over the sound to be produced or diamond-shaped note corresponding to be touched.

Harmonic Series. The composite series of notes produced by vibrating substance of air column. If the principal note (or 'fundamental') is C below bass clief, first 16 notes of series well be:

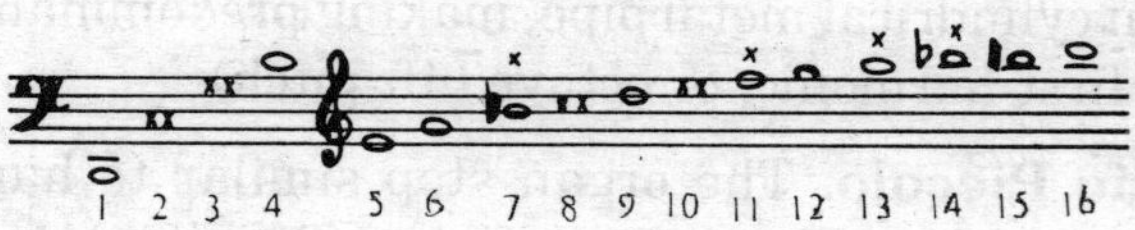

Of these nos. 7, 11, 13 and 14 are not in tune with normal scale. Nos. 12-16 (and upwards) are called 'overtones' or 'upper partials'. Actual sound of overtones is faint. Their effect in practice is to enrich sound of principal note. Individual tone-quality of instruments results from presence or absence of particular overtones, and from their relative intensity.

Harmonie (Fr.)

(1) Harmony.

(2) Wind band (not a purely brass band, which in Fr. is fanfare). Also in German, in both tenses.

Harmoniemusik (Ger.). The music for wind instruments.

Harmonium. The small portable instrument of Reed-organ family, in which pedals actuate a bellows which drives air through the reeds. Mainly used as a substitute in humble circumstances for the organ as an accompaniment to hymns, etc., very occasionally elsewhere.

Harmony. The simultaneous sounding of notes in a way that is musically significant. (Counter point is concerned with the simultaneous combinations of melodies, not individual notes; but counterpoint and harmony represent overlapping types of relationships between notes, and a composer considers both relationships together.).

Harp. The plucked stringed instrument of ancient origin, of which the chief modern development (double-action harp, from early 19th century) now has a compass from B below the bass clef upwards for nearly 7 octaves. It is much used in orchestral music, less in chamber music, solos, and accompaniment of voices.

1

2

Harp

(1) Small 14th and 15th century Irish harp, with a thick, solid soundbox, heavy neck, curved fore-pillar and brass strings.

(2) Early 19th century English pedal harp, a drawing-room instrument.

Harpsichord. The keyboard instrument of horizontal harp of trapezoid shape in which strings are plucked by quill or leather tongue attached to jack, upright piece of wood set in motion by inner end of key. In developed form, had one or (exceptionally 3) keyboards (2nd being used either for ease of transposing or contrast of tone), and upto 4 stops, for 8ft and 4ft pitch and for producing special effects e.g. lute.

Harp Stop. A contrivance on a harpsichord damping the strings so that the resulting tone resembles the rather thin tone of a harp.

Hausmusik (Ger.). 'House music', i.e. music for domestic rather than public performance.

Hawaiian Guitar. The style of guitar playing in which steel bar is used to stop strings instead of fingers. In this way, pitch is made to slide between notes.

'Haydn' Quartets. The name was given to Mozart's string quartets nos. 14-19, so called because dedicated to Haydn.

Head Voice. The 'register' of voice which gives the feeling to the singer of vibrating in head—i.e. the higher register, contrasted with Chest Voice.

Heckelclarina (Ger.). The wooden instrument of saxophone type in B flat. Has single reed. Compass is same as soprano saxophone.

Heckelphone. The double reed instrument corresponding to French baritone oboe, with range octave below oboe.

Heckelphone-clarinet. The wooden instrument of saxophone type designed for use in military bands. Has single reed. Compass is same as alto saxophone.

Heel. End of bow of string instrument held by hand.

Helicon, form of tuba passing round the player's body, e.g. the Sausaphone. The name is from its helical (i.e. spiral) shape, not from the ancient Mt Helicon, sacred to the Muses.

Hemidemisemiquaver. The quarter of a semiquaver, or 1/64 of semi-breve. Single hemidemisemiquaver is written:

Group of four

hemidemisemiquaver rest

Hemiolia, Hemiolia (the former term is commoner, the latter more correct, from Gk., one-and-a-half). Term implying the ratio 3:2. In current usage it mainly refers to rhythmic change resulting when a pulse of 2×3 is temporarily replaced by 3×2 or vice versa.

Heptachord (Gr., seven string). The scale of 7 notes, e.g. modern major or minor scale.

Hermeneutics. The term usually meaning interpretation of Scriptures, applied by Hermann Kretzschmar (1848-1924) to his method of interpreting musical motifs as expression of human feeling. Method places greater emphasis than 18th-century. Affektenleher on scientific approach to intervals, rhythms etc.

Heroic Tenor. The tenor capable of 'heavy' dramatic roles in opera, especially (as translation of Ger. Heldentenor) in Wagner.

Hervogehoben (Ger.). Emphasized.

Heterophony (Gr.). The 'difference of sounds', i.e. simultaneous playing by 2 or more performers in differently treated forms of same melody. Principle may have been used in Greek music, and is basis of ensemble playing in China, Japan, Java and Bali.

Hexachord (Gr., six string). The scale of 6 notes, adopted by Guido d' Arezzo and incorporated in medieval musical theory.

There were 3 hexachords:

(1) Hexachordum drum (hard hexachord: G, A, B, C, D, E;

(2) Hexachordum naturale (natural hexachord): C, D, E, F, G, A;

(3) Hexachordum molle (soft hexachord): F, G, A, B flat, C, D.

Each hexachord had same succession of intervals: 2 tones, semitones and 2 tones. Range of notes in ordinary use was divided into 7 overlapping hexachords (from G at bottom of bass clef to E top of treble clef). Application of syllabus notes of hexachords was called Solmization.

Hexenmenuett. (Ger., Witch Minuet. The nickname given to minuet in Haydn's Quintenqurtett because of its cerie character.

Hindola. Hindola literally means a swing.

This raga is connected to the jhoola festival in the month of savan, approximately about August.

The picture as depicted is, Lord Krishna, seated on the swing with his female companions swinging and singing to him. He is humorous and witty, cutting jokes at them, courting many women without being true to any one of them. He is the boundless wonder and delight of all the Gopis.

This is a majestic and at the same time a fine suited raga throwing the lusture of its charming attraction on all those who listen to this.

This is a seasonal morning raga.

Hi-hat Cymbal or Choke Cymbal. The pair of cymbals mounted face to face on stand. Lomer one is fixed but upper can be moved by foot pedal and made to strike lower one. Essential part of drum kit.

Hocket. Breaking of melody into single notes or very short phrases by means of rest. Most often used in 2 parts at a time, so that one sings while the other has rest. In some cases may be based on single melody which is shared by two voices. Also used in instrumental music.

Hocket (Fr., 'hoquet' hiccup). In medieval church music, the insertion of rest into vocal parts, even in the middle of words—often for expressive purposes.

Hoe down. An American folk-dance included in Copland's ballet, Rodeo.

Hotstetter. See Hoffstetter.

Hohflote (Ger., hollow-sounding flute) type of 8-Foot organ stop in wood or metal.

Holzblaser (Ger.). Woodwind players.

Holzblasinstrumente (Ger.) Woodwind.

Homophony. Term applied to music in which one takes melody and other parts accompany it. Opposite to polyphony, in which all parts play more or less equal part in overall effect. Term also used to describe Homo Rhythmic style.

Homorhythmic. The term applied to polyphonic music in which all parts more in same rhythm.

Hondo (Sp., deep). The term used in the expression cante hondo (deep song), type of sad Andalusian song characteristically using some intervals smaller than semitone.

Horn

(1) Type of wind-instrument descended from primitive use of animal's horn for blowing through. The term now applies especially to the coiled brass orchestral instrument which was developed (particularly in France, whence the name French horn) from the earlier hunting horn and hand-horn. This earlier instrument, without valves or keys, yielded to the player only the notes of the Harmonic Series, like a bugle, plus a few obtainable by the insertion of the hand in the bell of the instrument. The particular harmonic series sounded depended on the length of the instrument's tube.

(2) Term used colloquially in the brass band to mean not the above instrument (not used in brass band) but the tenor Saxhorn; and used as jazz slang to mean trumpet, a trombone, even a saxophone.

Hornpipe

(1) The wind instrument with single reed and horn attached to each end, played in Celtic countries.

(2) By beginning of 16th century applied to dance in triple time. About mid 18th century, rhythm changed to 4/4, and it acquired association with sailors.

Humoreske, Humoresque. Type of instrumental composition supposedly of a wayward or capricious nature—term used e.g. by Schumann and Dvorak.

Hunting-horn. Instrument used to give signals while hunting, from which evolved the orchestral Horn.

Hurdy-Gurdy. Term applied wrongly to an instrument worked by turning handles (e.g. Barrel-organ, Street Piano) and correctly only to one such instrument, a kind of portable, mechanical viol called a French vielle. One hand turns a handle actuating a rosined wheel which acts as a bow; the other hand stops the strings not directly (as on a violin) but by the means of tiny piano-like keyboard. In addition there are one or two freely vibrating strings, giving a Drone bass. Mozart and others wrote for this instrument.

Hymn. A song of the praise of deity, saint etc.; especially (in Protestant churches) such as has words specially written, not taken directly from Bible, and is sung congregationally. Also an extended composition towards supposedly of a hymn-like nature or an instrumental composition suggesting a vocal hymn.

Hymen. The large-scale electronic work by Stockhausen inspired by national anthems of the world. Exists in several versions, either as tape composition or mixing tape with instrumental ensemble or orchestra.

I

I. Abbr. for International (e.g. I.S.C.M., International Society for Contemporary Music).

Idee Fixe (Fr., fixed idea). Term used by Berlioz for motto theme, i.e. recurring theme in a piece of music. Most famous example is in Berlioz's Symphonie Fantastique.

Idiophone. Any instrument in which solid mass of material (often whole instrument) vibrates to make sound. There are 4 classes:

(1) struck idiophones (e.g. bells, xylophone),

(2) shaken idiophones (e.g. rattles),

(3) plucked idiophones (e.g. jew's harp),

(4) rubbed idiophones (e.g. glass harmonica).

Idyll. The literary term for peaceful, pastoral work—transferred to music.

Illustrative Music. The music describing, evoking, or otherwise alluding to a non-musical source, e.g. a poem novel, plat, picture, landscape, or an explicit emotional experience. (The more usual, but confusing, term for this is 'programme music'.)

Imitation. A composers' device in part-writing: one voice repeats (if not literally, then at least recognizably) a figure previously stated by another voice. Canon and Fugue use imitation according to strict and regular patterns.

Imperfect Consonance. Intervals of third and sixth.

Impressionism. Term borrowed from painting and used to

describe the work e.g. if Debussy and Ravel in so far as they seem to interpret their titles not in a narrative or dramatic way (like the Romantics) but as though an observer were recording the impression on him at a given point.

Impromptu. Title applied to early romantic composers to short piece for piano with something of character of extemporization, or air of delicacy or causalness.

Improvisation. The art of spontaneous composition, variation or ornamentation. Chief form are improvisation of one or more counterpoints on given theme or Cantus Firmus, of variations on given theme or harmonic framework, of ornamentation which embellishes given melody, and of part of movements, e.g. Cadenza, or of complete movements or set of movements on original given themes.

Improvise (or 'extemporize'). To perform according to spontaneous fancy, not from memory or from written copy—though often a performer improvises 'on' (i.e. round about) a given tune. Hence improvisation: this term is sometimes also used as title of actual written-down piece presumably intended to convey the roving spirit of genuine improvisation.

In. Term having various musical usages including:

(1) indication of a conductor's beat—so e.g. in 2, meaning that two beats will actually be given to each bar, although the composer may have indicated two or four or six, etc;

(2) Indication of the division of forces in an orchestra—so e.g. in 4, applied to violas, would indicate that the viola-players are to be divided into four sections each playing a different part;

(3) Indication of key, e.g. symphony in C minor;

(4) Indication of (a) the basic key in which wind instrument is pitched, and sometimes also of

(b) the transposition it consequently requires (Transposing Instrument).

Incidental Music. The strictly speaking music for performance for during action of play. Commonly used to include overtures and interludes.

Indeterminacy. Mode of composition, which either employs elements of chance (Aleatory Music) or leaves decisions to performers.

Inflection. Inflected note is note with Accidental placed before it.

Incipit. The first few bars of a musical work, used e.g. in bibliographical compilation to identify which work is being referred to.

Innig (Ger). Hearfelt, suggesting quietly intense manner of performance.

Instrument, Musical. An object (other then the organs of body) used for the production of musical sound by the application of mechanical energy—or, as in Electrophonic instruments, by the application of electrical impulses. Non-electrophonic instruments are classified scientifically as Aerophones, Chordophones, Idiophones and Membranophones, but the usual practical classification is into wind, string, and percussion.

Instrumentation. The writing of music for particular instruments—term used particularly with reference to a composer's necessary knowledge of what is practicable, and what sounds well, on different instruments.

Instruments. Instruments used in Western music may for general purposes be divided into 5 types:

(1) Woodwind : recorder, transverse flute, and instruments using single or double reed, even if sometimes made of metal, e.g. oboe, clarinet, bassoon, saxophone;

(2) Brass: trumpet, cornet, bugle, French horn, trombone, and other lip-read instruments;

(3) Percussion: drum, cymbal, triangle etc;

(4) Keyboard: harpsichord, virginal, clavichord, pianoforte, organ, celesta;

(5) String: viol and violin families, harp, lute, guitar.

Alternative classification on acoustical principles divides instruments into 5 main categories:

(1) Idiophones: instruments made of naturally sonorous material;

(2) Membranophones: instruments using stretched membrane;

(3) Aerophones: woodwind, brass, and those instruments using free reed;

(4) Chordophones: instruments using strings;

(5) Electrophones: e.g. etherophone and electronic organ.

Interlude. The piece of music inserted between other pieces (e.g. organ passage between the verses of a hymn) or between non-musical events, e.g. between the acts of play.

Intermede (Fr.). Intermezzo.

Intermezzo. The play with music, performed between acts of drama and opera.

Interpretation. Activity of performer in communicating intentions of composer, esp. those not given explicitly by notation.

Interval. The 'distance' between two notes, insofar as one of them is higher or lower than other. Thus the interval from C to G above it is a 'fifth', to the A above it is a 'sixth', etc. The names 'fifth', 'sixth', etc., are themselves further defined. Intervals above the octave ('eighth') are called compound intervals, being 'compounded' of so many octaves plus a smaller interval. Thus the interval from C to next G above it but one (twelve notes, counting the extremes) is called twelfth and is a compound interval made of an octave (C-C) and a fifth (C-G).

Intonation.

(1) judgement of pitch by performer;

(2) opening song of plain song melody.

Intonation. Tuning (or pitch), thus a singer's or violinist's intonation is praised if the notes are placed with high a degree of precision.

Introduction. The section (usually in slow time) often found at start of symphony, string quartet, sonata or overture; usually written for both structural and dramatic reasons.

Inversion

(1) Of Interval: intervals inverted when lower note is sounded above upper note, e.g.:

Inversion:

Number of interval when inverted is found by subtracting it from nine e.g. inversion of fifths fourth. Qualifying term of perfect interval is unchanged by inversion, e.g. inversion of perfect fifth is perfect fourth. Major interval when inverted becomes minor, diminished becomes augmented and vice versa;

(2) Of melody: melody is inverted when interval through which it proceeds are replaced by their inversions (also called contrary motion, and per arsin et thesin). Where statement overlaps inversion, results in imitation by contrary motion, also called canon by inversion or 'mirror' canon;

(3) Of chord;

(4) Of counterpoint.

Invert. To turn upside down, thus;

(1) A chord not in its 'root position' is said to be in one or other inversion.

(2) Two melodies in counterpoint may be mutually inverted by the upper becoming the lower and vice versa (counterpoint capable of making sense under this treatment is called invertible counterpoint and forms the stuff of, e.g., Fugue);

(3) A single melody may be inverted by being performed 'upside down', i.e. with all its successive intervals applied in the opposite direction.

Ionian Mode. The mode which may be represented by white keys of the piano from C to C.

Isorhythmic (from Gk, equal-rhythmed). Term applied to certain medieval motets, e.g. by Machaut, of which the rhythms are repeated according to a strict scheme not corresponding to repetition in the melody.

Istesso Tempo, I' (It.). At the same tempo, i.e. preserving the same pace although the unit of beat may have changed—say from 2/4 to 6/8, in which case the old and the new would have the same duration.

Istesso Tempo, I' (It.), 'in the same time'. Indication that beat is to remain same even though time-signatures changes.

Italian Overtures. The type of overture. Characterized by 3-movement layout: quick/slow/quick. Precursor or classical symphony.

Italian Sixth. To type of 'augmented sixth' chord distinguished by having a major third (and no other note) between the notes forming the sixth. The reason for the names is not known.

J

Jack. The vertical strip of wood which is carrying the plectrum that plucks the strings of a harpsichord, virginals, etc; as the fingerkey is depressed, the jack moves up and string is plucked.

Jam Session. Informal improvised performance by jazz musicians.

Janissary Music. The term for the effect produced by using triangle, cymbals, and bass drum.

Javalis. These are also more or less of the same type and category of the padams. But the difference is that javalis are of human love and human desires. Pining for the love of man full of human and wordly desires and motives, you cannot find any inner hidden meaning, except what it conveys outwardly which is brisk and lively and most enjoyable.

Like the ghazals in North, this also treats of light love and is of catchy nature.

These Javalis are the offshoots of the recent years only, in popular and attractive tunes. They are composed in common ragas mostly borrowed from Hindustani music, in very ordinary colloquial Telugu language.

These love songs contains light-classical type of music and are sung in Nayaka-Nayaki and Sakhi Bhavas.

Girls belonging to respectable families were not allowed to learn and sing these Javalis. Now these have become quite popular and are much appreciated. The feature of Javali also is the same as any other composition, having pallavi, anupallavi, and choronam etc. in it.

There are many composers of 19th century who have composed Javalis, mostly in Telgu language and some in Kannada and Tamil language too.

Patnam Subramanya Iyer, Dharmapuri Subbaramier, Venkatagiriappa of Bellary Raja Rao and a few other have composed Javalis.

Jazz. Style of music matched by various degree of improvisation, intensely rhythmic playing and by individual approach to instrument tone and rhythmic articulation. Most groups consist of rhythmic section of drums, double bass or bass guitar, and piano and guitar (usually amplified) to produce rhythmic springboard for other instrument: usually called horns, these are mostly wind instruments, esp. trumpet, trombone and saxophone.

Jew's Harp. The primitive instrument held in the mouth, having a strip of metal 'twanged' (i.e. set vibrating) by the finger, the player eliciting different notes by altering the shape of the cavity of the mouth.

Jew's Harp. The simple instrument consisting of a metal frame to which strip of metal is fixed. Frame is placed loosely between teeth and strip is twanged. Produces several harmonics, which can be made to resonate individually in mouth cavity.

Jig. Types of dance usually in 6/8 or 12/8 time; and often constituting the last movement of 18th-century suite, in which it was usually built in Binary form.

Jingling Johnny. The obsolete military-band percussion instrument shaped like a tree or pavilion (hence other name, Chinese pavilion) and hung with bells which were shaken.

Jongleur. The medieval minstrel and entertainer. Term carried peorative connotation.

Jota. Spanish dance from Aragon in moderately fast 3/4 time accompanied by castanets.

Just Intonation. The adoption in performance of the 'natural' non-tempered scale. This is theoretically possible on voices, bowed-string instruments, etc., in which the pitch of the notes is not mechanically fixed.

K

K. Abbreviation:

(1) of Kochel (in numbering Mozart's works), and

(2) of Kirkpatrick (in numbering D. Scarlatti's).

Kabir Das. Kabir Das was a contemporary of Meera. He was also born in the 15th century A.D. in the holy city of Banaras, on the banks of the river Ganga.

He was born of a Mohammadan weaver couple and was brought up in the most oridinary way.

Kabir from his childhood showed tendency to devotion of a very high order.

Due to his Samskaras of previous life, he began to sing philosophical songs and talked of cosmic consciousness and self-realisation only, much astonishingly.

He collected innumerable disciples and followers of all sects and creeds. He never called God by any particular name like Rama, Krishna, Allah or Jesus. His preaching was all-pervading universal, supreme force and not the praises of God.

To him, God in any one form never existed. It is just an unperceivable divine force of no form or shape.

He became very popular on account of his very simple and easy, heart-penetrating songs he composed. His language was simple and full of meaning.

It is felt as though Kabir lived all his life in Banaras and only left for Ratangiri not very far from Banaras to die in his later years. His tomb could be seen at Ratangiri. The street where he lived in Banaras is known as Kabir Chaura after his name.

Kallinath. Kallinath belonged to roughly about 1475 to 1533 and was known as a great versatile genius. He wrote the book Kalanidhi as a 'vyakhyan' interpretation to Rama Matya's Swara Melakalanidhi and Sarngdeva's Sangeeta Ratnakara.

Kammer (Ger.). Chamber.

Kammerton

(1) Pitch of orchestral instruments in 17th, 18th centuries, in Germany, substantially lower than Chorton, to which older organs were tuned;

(2) in modern Germany=standard pitch (Fr., diapason normal), according to which A in the middle of treble clef is established at 440 cycles per second.

Kapelimeister. Lit.'master of the chapel', i.e. director of music to monarch, prince, bishop or nobleman. Term Kapelimeister-musik is used contemptuously by German writers to describe music which is correct but lacking in invention.

Kazoo. The children's musical instrument into which one hums to produce an effect rather superior to that comb-and-paper.

Kb. Abbr. for Ger. Kontrabass, i.e. double-bass.

Keen (Ir , Caoine). An Irish funeral song accompanied by wailing; to wail thus.

Kettledrum. The cauldron-shaped drum originally from the Orient, and originally smaller and more delicate-sounding than now; in modern form, tuned to definite pitch, normally by handles on the rim. The drum rests on a stand, the skin facing upwards; the tone-quality may be varied according to the drumsticks used and point of impact. A cloth on the drum may be used to give the effect of a mute. Mechanically tuned drums, using pedals, and commonly called pedal drums, have also come into wide use in the 20th century; they

(1) make tuning quicker, allowing rapid changes in the middle of a movement, and

(2) allow the use of glissando (drum struck, then pedal depressed—e.g. in Bartok's Concerto for Orchestra). The Kettledrum is standard also in the mounted military band—one slung each side of a horse.

Key

(1) A lever, e.g. on piano, organ, or a woodwind instrument, depressed by finger or foot to produce a note.

(2) A classification of notes of a scale, the most important note being called the key-note and the other functioning in relation to it. If the keynote is C, then the key may be either C major or C minor, according to whether the major or minor scale is used basically in the music concerned (major); notes outside the 'basic' scale are said to be foreign to the key. The sharps and flats appertaining to the key used get displayed in a key-signature; other sharps, flats, and naturals occurring 'casually' in the music are written as accidentals.

Keyboard. A continuous arrangement of keys:

(1) either for the finger, as on the piano, or for the feet, as on the 'pedal keyboard' of an origin. So also keyboard of light, instrument throwing colours on a screen in Skryabin's 'prometheus'. The term keyboard is also used as a general term for a 'keyboard instrument'—especially in such contexts as 'Bach's keyboard works' where the works may be suitable for more then one type of keyed instrument.

Keyboard Music. The generic term for all music written for keyboard instruments, esp. music upto and including times of Bach and Handel, much of which was not designed specifically for any particular keyboard instrument.

Key Bugle. The bugle with holes pierced in tube and controlled by keys. Also called Kent-bugle.

Key Note. Same as tonic.

Key-signatures. The indication in written music of the number of sharps and flats in the prevailing keys, such indication normally being placed at beginning of each lines of music (or at any point when key-signature is changed).

Khorovod (Rus.). Type of traditional Russian round dance with singing; one of the sections (based on Russian folk-tunes) of Stravinsky's 'the firebird' is so named.

Khyals. A Khyal has really originated from Persians. It has its own peculiarities. This style has first been handed down to us by Amir Khusro. Amir Khusro was a renowned Persian musician poet, during the time of Allaudin Khilji. He was the first man who introduced Persian culture and tried to mix both the systems of music, i.e. Indian and Persian systems of music. He brought new ragas and taught them to our people, which are till today very popular. Some of the new ragas Amir Khusro had introduced were—Yaman, Sarparda Zilaph, and other similar ragas.

Also Adaranga and Sadaranga, the court musicians under the patronage of Muhammad Shah, the then Sultan and Hussain, were considered as the originators of this Khyal Style (12 6-1316). Whatever it is, a khyal has now become the standard for the classical music. The beauty in this style is, you can expand it to any length of time, giving various kalas (patterns). These khyals are of two kinds—the vilambit which is sung very very slow (slow tempo) and which is usually composed and set to ektal, Adachoutal, Tilwada, Deepchandi, etc., and the 'dhrut', that is fast khyal, which is sung in a fast tempo, with good elaboration of taans in different patterns. Fast khyal is usually set in "trital", jhap tap or ektal.

A skilful musician will render the 'Sthai' and 'Antra' with dignity, grace, emotional zeal, and playfulness and carry his listeners with him to the end of a beautifully patterned conclusion most flexible and in bewitching manner.

There is a saying that Gwalior was once upon a time the seat of music, and the reason for this, according to stories, is that the music used to ring through the walls and humming of the breeze. That is how everyone there became music-minded. The kings and subjects were absorbed and drowned in music, as is the case with music. But gradually the keen desire for music faded away till the time when Pt. Bhatkhande appeared at this critical stage to revive this dying art, for which he strove hard with his selfless, dedicated zeal. He brought back the perishing and almost dying 'vidya' back into its full splendour.

He has introduced his own style of Gayaki of Khyals, on the same basis with a few minor alternations here and there, and it is now in practice and has almost become a standardized style known as 'Bhatkhande style'.

Kielflugel (Gr.). Harpsichord.

Kindertotenlieder (Ger. Songs on death of children). Cycle of 5 songs with orchestral accompaniment by Mahler, words by F. Ruckert.

'King of Prussia' Quartets. An alternative name for Mozart's set of Prussian quartets.

Kirtana. A Kirtana is older and more devotional in character with simple rhythms. The music in this variety is like a support and the sahitya plays an important upper hand. The part played by music in this is of a minor nature and this can easily be learnt by any pupil. In this, charanas are all sung in the same dhatu. These kirtans can be sung even by an average trained person. These are all standardized and fixed in raga, tala, Sangathis, etc. and do not have any scope for development.

Kit. The miniature violin, formerly used by dancing-masters. Made either in ordinary shape of violin or long and narrow like REBEC (earlier form).

Kitchen Department. Humorous term for the percussion section of an orchestra.

Kithara. The lyre of ancient Greece, later adopted by Romans. Had square box resonator and up to 11 gut strings. Used as accompaniment to voice and as solo instrument.

Klang (Ger.). Sound, sonority.

Klangfarbenmelodie. (Ger.). Term coined by Schoenberg in Harmonielehre (1911) to describe form of composition in which varying tone colours are applied to single level or pitch, or to different pitches, thus establishing timbre as important structural element.

Klappenhorn. Key bugle.

Klarinette (Ger.). Clarinet.

Klaviatur (Ger.). The keyboard.

Klavier (Ger., also Clavier).

(1) keyboard;

(2) keyboard instruments with strings, i.e., clavichord, harpsichord or piano;

(3) Specifically, in modern German, piano.

Klavierauszug (Ger.). A piano 'reduction' – i.e., the score of an orchestral or similar work arranged for piano.

Klein (Ger.). Little; kleine Flote (little flute), piccolo; kleine Trommel (little drum), side drum.

Knarre (Ger). Rattle.

Kneifena (Ger.). The plucking, i.e., pizzicato.

Kniegeige (Ger.). Viola da gamba.

Kollatam. A folk dance of Andhra. A group of women play with two little decorated sticks each in their hands, beating the rhythm, singing and turning round and round in a very impressive manner.

The Haridas Patalu are sung by a group of men folk, supposed to be pilgrims, who at each halt they make, collect together and dance singing with it, clapping their hands-in a way as to plead and pray, to the deities to make their Yatra (pilgrimage) a success. They keep a wick-oil-lamp in the centre and dance to the rhythm turning round and round with ecstasy full of faith. Their typical village type of dresses with turbans on their heads and Dhotis (loin-cloth) drawn and tucked upwards in very interesting and picturesque to watch.

Then there are Telugu 'Daruvu songs', which are meant mostly for dance drama, narrating some historical instances. These take us deep into nature and reveal the feelings, and circumstances of the people and some of the scenes of the past.

Kontrabass (Ger.). Double bass. Also used as prefix to denote instruments octave lower than normal bass members of family, e.g., Kontrabassposaune, double bass trombone.

Kontrafagott (Ger.). Double-bassoon.

Kontretanz (Ger.). Country dance.

Konzert (Ger.).

(1) Concert

(2) Concerto

Konzertmeister (Ger.). The principal 1st violin in orchestra.

Konzertmeister (Ger). The leader of an orchestra; (U.S.), concertmaster.

Kornett (Ger.). Modern cornet.

Koto. A Japanese plucked stringed instrument of the zither type, usually with 13 strings, placed horizontally and played by three plectrums worn on thumb and two fingers.

Kraftig (Ger.). Vigorously.

Krakowiak. Polish dance (named after city of Cracow) in lively 2/4 time with syncopated accents.

Kerbsgang (Ger.). Term for composition that sounds the same when played forwards or backwards.

Kriti. Next in order of importance of all the Karnataka musical forms comes the Kriti. Every composer of some eminence will attempt to compose some Kritis He will not be satisfied without making his trial on this composition. A kriti gives ample scope to display and express his creative ability and to pour out his heart's ideas and thoughts through music with the pure colourful bhavas of the mind and its rich varied styles. These contain themes mostly drenched in devotion and diving ecstasy of love, and are sung and developed nicely with spicy kalpana swaras and pallavi.

Many people get confused with Kritis and Kittanams. Actually there is very little difference. Kriti has originated from kirtanams only. A Kriti is that which is sung chiefly giving more emphasis on music and less on sahitya. A kriti has its own individuality, the melodic beauty, construction of Sangatis according to the meaning, the feeling of aesthetic fullness, etc., have all their originality and are brought to the climax with the peak sangatis, which are built up.

A kriti composition is that even when it is just played on any instrument, seems to speak in its own musical language without losing its charm, or the beauty of expression and its original effect. In fact, it enhances its enchanting appeal and gives greater joy to the listener. A Kriti is the outpouring of a composer's inspiration which comes spontaneously as a product of conscious effort, full of literary and technical designs. The sahitya is usually of a sacred character theme containing mostly, a highly spiritual thought and a dignified set of words and sequences.

Thyagaraja, the noted musician composer's musical compositions of kritis, stand apart from the rest of their king. He has poured forth this language of music abundantly, passing his musical thoughts, keeping the purity of the rage, tala, tampo, style and the bhave, giving the enchanting power of universal appeal and echo, in the heart of every being overstepping all bounds. Thyagaraja added the crystallized sequences of sangatis in varied rich pleasant colours of a descriptive nature.

A Kriti "ganakrama" (procedure) usually consists of three divisions:

(1) Pallavi,

(2) Anupallavi,

(3) Charana, and some kritis contain chittaswaras in the concluding part. But it is not essential to have chittaswaras (ending swaras) in every kriti.

Chittaswaras are the standardized kalpana swaras. Some kritis also have swara sahityas, that is, the swara's part sung first and then the sahitya specially made to suit that swara passage. For example, vachamagocharundani in rag Athana contains some very goon "swara sahityas". These standardized Sangatis and swara sahityas emphasize the emotional and delicate aspect of the bhava and the meaning it contains, enhancing the beauty of the raga thereby.

Muthuswami Dixitar had composed all kinds of kritis in all categories.

If a singer tries to contemplate on a Sangati of his own, it will not only fit in properly, but even may sound awkward and unpleasant to hear. In Karnataka music a kriti is most popular of all the forms and is considered as the highest standard for classical music, and there can be no concerts without kritis. The stylish rendering with the beautifully patterned kalpana swaras can really make the audience spellbound carrying the listener to celestial heights.

The beauty of a kriti is, that it arouses a feeling of expectancy in the listener's minds making them eagerly await the next complicated sangati and so on. So, we know that it is essential for a kriti to have pallavi, anupallavi and charana and in some cases, more than two or three charanas. But it is very rare. There are some simple kritis not having even a single charana. But these are extraordinary and rare ones. Usually at the end of the kriti the 'mudra' of the composer (signature) is taken.

Kreutzer Sonata. The nickname for Beethoven's sonata in A (1803) for violin and piano, dedicated to Rodolphe Kreutzer.

Kreqz (Ger.). Sharp (lit. 'Cross'—earlier form of sign).

Kreuzflote (Ger.). Transverse Flute.

Krumhorn or Krummhorn. The double reed instrument, current in Middle Ages and Renaissance. Tube was curved at end, and reed was enclosed in capsule through which player directed breath without having direct contact with reed. Made in several sizes.

Kuchipudi. The Kuchipudi style of folk dramas which are typically Andhra are enacted in their crude form of drama style before the village elite, under the shade of trees or open air moon—lit sky, in the most thrilling and exquisite manner. The peculiarity in this is, that the men actors themselves take up the female role also and do it. They belong to a particular community and hail from a place called Kuchipude in Andhra.

Kullervo. Symphonic poem for soprano, baritone, male chorus and orchestra by Sibelius, op 7.

Kutchka (Russ.). Lit. 'Handful'—alternative name for the Five.

Kutchka. Handful—alternative name for the 'five'.

Kyrie. Short for 'Kyrie eleison' (Gr.). 'Lord, have mercy'. First part of Ordinaro of Mass. Only part of Mass in Greek.

L

L. The symbols in Tonic Sol-Fa notation for the sixth degree (submediant) of the scale, pronounced lah.

L.H. Abbreviation of left hand (e.g., in piano-playing).

La. The note A (in Latin countries, and formerly elsewhere); cp. Lah.

Lah. In Tonic Sol-Fa, the spoken name for the 6th degree (submediant) of the scale, written I. Cp. La.

Lakhshana Geetas. These are little songs first composed by Pt. V. N. Bhatkhande and later by Pt. S. N. Ratanjankar and several other modern composers. These songs give the picture of the raga in which it is composed. Even a stranger can at once form an idea and the formalities and conditions laid down for it to be observed from this description of the particular raga. It describes the lakshanas and hence it has come to be known as a "Lakshana Geet".

Lament. Refers to a piece of music which signifies grief especially at a death; and, specifically, a type of piece for bagpipes played at Scottish clan funerals.

'Lamentation' Symphony. The nickname for Haydn's symphony no. 26 in D minor, composed about 1767-1 (Hob. I : 26).

Lancers. A type of Quadrille which became popular in the second half of the 19th Century.

Landino. Alternative form of Landini's surname; Landino sixth, a type of cadence characteristically which is found in his music. In this the leading note falls to the submediant before rising from that note to the tonic; i.e., the 6th degree of the scale is inserted between the 7th and the 8th. Thus this term does not refer to 'a sixth' in the harmonic sense but to the melodic insertion of the 6th degree of the scale.

Landler (sing. or pl.). Type of dance in triple time originating in rural Austria and being a slow variant of the waltz.

Largamente (It.). Broadly—term usually denting a spacious and deliberate style rather than a clear indication of slow tempo. Cp. Largo, from which it is derived.

Large. The note of the largest time-value in the notation which grew up in the Middle Ages and gave rise to the present notation. It was divisible into either two or three 'longs'.

Largnetto. The direction indicating a speed not quite as slow as Largo.

Largo (It... broad). Slow; but cp. Largamente.

Lauda, Laude (It.). A song of praise; lauda spirituale or laude spirituale (pl., laudi spirituali), type of Italian religious song for several voices, having its own distinctive poetry and sung by a religious confraternity called the laudisti. This type of work is reckoned a forerunner of Oratorio.

Lay. The term is encountered for a purely instrumental work of that period, and in certain more general references (e.g., in Chaucer) it simply means 'a song'.

Leader. The directing member of an ensemble, e.g., a string quartet or a pop group.

Leading Seventh. Term which is in fact an abbreviation for 'chord of the minor seventh built on the leading note'—e.g., in C major, the chord B, D, F, A (reading upwards). It is characteristically produced by the harmonica, sucked.

Leading-motive. The English equivalent term for Ger. Leitmotiv (not-motif)—A theme used (particularly in Wanger's operas) recurrently to denote an object, an aspect of character, etc.

Leading-note. The seventh degree of the major scale, so called because it seems to lead upwards to the Tonic a semitone above it. In the minor scale this note is commonly used in ascending but not in descending.

Ledger Line. The short line written above or below the staff to accommodate notes outside the staff.

Legato (It., bound together). Smoothly, not Staccato—as a direction for performance.

Leger (Fr., light). The legerement; lightly; musique legere, light music.

Leggero, Leggeramente ((It.). Light, lightly.

Legno (It.). Wood; bacchetta di legno, (instruction to drummer to use) wooden-headed drum-stick; col legno, with the wood—instruction to string player to hit the string with the back of the bow instead of with the hair, producing a dry and rather grotesque sound.

Lesson. The term used in 17th—18th centuries for a short keyboard piece or a set of such pieces (i.e. a suite).

Libretto (It., booklet). The text of an opera—or sometimes of an oratorio or other non-stage work.

Licenza (It.). Licence, freedom, with some freedom(s) as to performance, or as to the construction of a work (when it does not follow 'strict' pattern).

Lieblich (Ger.). Lovely; lieblich Gedackt (organ stop), same as Gedackt.

Lied (Ger., pl. Lieder). Song; specifically, in the non-German-speaking world, the type of song with piano composed by, e.g. Schubert, Schumann, and Wolf. The term is dubiously applied also to songs not in German but of a similar king, e.g. by Grieg.

Liedertafel. Male-voice choir in German or German-descended communities, e.g. in U.S.A. and South Australia.

Ligature

(1) A slur-mark indicating a group of notes all sung to the same syllable (term sometimes also used in instrumental music when the Slur indicates that notes are to be phrased together);

(2) On the clarinet, saxophone, etc., the metal band which secures the reed to the mouthpiece.

Light. Term applied to music supposedly not requiring the listener's full concentration; light orchestra, orchestra providing this. So also light opera, imprecise non-technical term sometimes used by laymen in opposition to grand opera (also imprecise), and not clearly distinguishable from operetta.

'Linz' Symphony. The nickname for Mozart's symphony no. 36 in C, K. 425, composed in Linz and first performed there in 1783.

Lira (It.) :

(1) Lyre;

(2) The Vielle in its medieval sense (bowed-string instrument, not the hurdy-gurdy);

(3) Term used in various compound names, e.g. lira da braccio (.... for the arm), type of bowed-string instrument, with a less pronounced 'waist' than that of the violin.

Litany. An extended form of Christian prayer for pelp which is often set to music; and the term is sometimes used allusively in the titles of instrumental pieces.

Little Organ Book (Ger., Orgelbuchlein). A compilation by Bach of 46 chorale preludes for the organ, 1717.

Loco (It., place). Indication that music is to be performed at the pitch written, cancelling the instruction '8va sopra' (i.e. 'ottava...') or '8va bassa' indicating that music is to be played respectively an octave higher or an octave lower than written.

Locrian Mode. A mode that could be represented by the white keys of the piano beginning on B if it were not rejected as unusable in practice. (Unlike the other Modes, it would not include a note a perfect fifth upward from its 'final', B.)

'London' Symphony. The nickname for Haydn's last symphony, no. 104 in D (Hob. I: 104).

Long. The obsolete time—value of a note, in the system of notation which grew up in the Middle Ages and was superseded by the present one; a long could equal either a half or a third of a 'large' and was itself divisible into either two or three 'breves'.

Loud Pedal. The misleading name for the sustaining pedal.

Loure (Fr.). A type of rustic French bagpipe; and hence a French dance, usually in moderate 6/4 time. Hence also loure (derived from a technique of bagpipe—playing), a kind of bowing on the violin, etc., in which several notes are taken in one stroke of the bow but are slightly detached from one another.

Lur (Dan.). The prehistoric large bronze horn of which several specimens have been found, chiefly in Denmark.

Lute. The fretted stringed instrument plucked with the fingers (or, in the case of some earlier types, with a plectrum), much in the use for solos, song accompaniment, and ensembles.

Luth (Fr.). The lute; luthier, lute-maker—and hence, today, a maker of stringed instruments in general.

Lydian Mode. The mode represented by the white keys on the piano beginning on F.

Lyre

(1)The general name for a type of plucked stringed instrument in which the strings are fixed to a cross-bar between two arms;

(2)Ancient Greek instrument (Gk., lyra) of this type, rounded off at the foot (cp. Kithara).

Lyric. Relating to vocal performance with the lyre, i.e. sung; hence lyric drama, occasional synonym for opera (especially in French, as drama lyrique); hence also the lyric stage, i.e. the operatic stage; (2, of a poem) not epic, not dramatic, but fairly short and expressing the writer's own feelings.

M

M. In fonic Sol-fa = me, third note (or mediant) of major scale.

M. As abbrev. M. = medius, middle voice (in polyphonic music). M.M. = Maelzel's Metronome. M-S. = mezzo-soprano. M.d.= mano destra or main droite, right hand. mf = mezzo forte, moderately loud. mg = main gauche, left hand. mp = mezzo piano, moderately soft. m.s. = mano sinistra, left hand. m.v. = mezza voce, with moderate volume of tone.

M. Sop. Abbr. of Mezzo-soprano.

Machicotage (Fr.). The ornamentation of solo parts of plain song.

Machine Drums. The Timpani fitted with mechanism, such as foot-pedal, capable of making rapid and accurate changes of pitch.

Madrigal. Musical setting of poem in several parts.

Maestro (It, master). Title given in Italy to recognize conductors and composers.

Maestro al Cembalo (It.). Musician who directed performances of concertos etc. while seated at harpsichord.

Maggiore (It.). The major mode.

Maiden Quartets. Alternative name for Haydn's Russian Quartets.

Major, Minor. The terms contrasting with one another and having various musical applications:

(1) *Scales.* The major scale of C (i.e. treating the note C as its point of repose) has been as follows : (and the same notes descending).

The minor scale is divided for theoretical purposes into three types, of which the natural minor scale of C has been as follows . (and the same notes descending). The melodic minor scale of C differs in its ascending and descending forms :

The harmonic minor scale of C is (and the same notes descending). Similarly with scales beginning on the other notes; i.e. all major scales are internally alike, the distances (Intervals) between successive notes being the same, although the note of starting differs. All scales belonging to one of the three types of minor scale are, similarly, alike.

(2) *Keys.* The key of C major is that in which the notes of the scale of C major are treated as 'normal', other notes entering only for special purpose. The key of C minor bears a like relation to the scale of C minor : but, though there are three types of minor scale, there is only one type of minor key (the three types of scale corresponding to different aspects of it). The key-signature of a minor key is determined by the natural minor scale (above).

(3) *Chords.* A major or minor chord is one which, being built out of the major or minor scale, may serve to identify that scale. More particularly, the common chord of C major, or just chord of major, or C—major triad means to notes C, E, G—as contrasted with the common chord of C minor (chord of C minor triad), C, E*b*, G.

(4) *Intervals.* The Intervals second, third, sixth, and seventh are classified as either major or minor, the latter a semitone less than the former. Thus, measuring upwards from C, the major and minor intervals (in that order) are—second, C – D, C – D*b*; third, C—F, C—Fb; sixth, C – A, C. – A*b*; seventh, C – B, C – B*b*. Likewise, of course, measured upwards or downwards from any other note.

Malaguena (Sp.). The dance originating in Malaga, marked by singing; also instrumental piece of similar nature.

Malayalam Folk Songs. Malayalis also have any number of folk songs suited to dance and other avocations. Some of them are:

I. (1) Tiruvatirakkali (Dance songs).

(2) Kolkali.

(3) Cherumokkali.

(4) KaiKottikkali.

II. (1) Vanchipattu (During work).
(2) Vadakkanpattu.
(3) Kuravanpattu.
(4) Kummi Pattu.

III. (1) Tottam Ceremonies.
(2) Moplappattu.
(3) Oppana-pattu.
(4) Kalyanakkali.

IV. Festival and Devotional.
(1) Talattupattu.
(2) Keertanangal.
(3) Velanpattu.

These are just examples only. They have many other varieties.

Simple rural folk, scattered all over the land with contended and happy lives, spend their leisure singing these songs full of emotion. They describe the different stages of farming, watering the fields, collecting the corn, tilling the fields, etc. through their songs.

Their festive days like Pongal which of course is mainly a harvest festival some time in the month of January, and other festivals are enjoyed with seasonal mirth and gaiety.

Vandikkaran Pattu of the cow-boy, Talattu Pattu, and any number of devotional type of folk songs and the well-known Villu Pattu are of much interest.

Villu Pattu is a bow song. The pitcher, the bells, Udukku, Kattai, the whole orchestra, all tied in one on the bow-shaped bamboo-stick, playing while narrating themes of various kinds in a ballad form, is very interesting. Sometimes these are sung in a dialogue form with questions and answers.

Lavani is another popular variety in which extempore ability of the exposition is tested, like a debate in verse form. These are usually sung to the accompaniment of a large percussion instrument.

Malinocnia (It.). The melancholy.

Malkounsh (Rag). Rag Malkounsh is supposed to be an ancient melody. It must have originated, according to some authors, during the time of Malwa reign. Mal may have been derived from the name Malwa, and Kounsh must have come from Kaushik, i.e. Parwati's daughter.

This raga depicts—the unparalleled love and romance and portrays the intimate and close depth of love—in their warm feelings.

Malkounsh is a soft and delicate tune, which creates a pleasing and sweet feeling in the listener's minds. This is strictly speaking supposed to be a winter raga. But no one is strictly observing it in that way, and is now sung in any month of the year, well past midnight.

Mandola, Mandora. The obsolete lute-like stringed instrument, related to the Mandolin.

Mandolin (also spelt mandoline). The plucked stringed instrument of Italian organ, now usually of eight strings tuned in Paris (to the same four notes as a violin) and played with plectrum. Much used in informal music making and operatic simulations of this.

Manipuri. Manipuri is well-known for its graceful dances and music. There are sufficient traces of their traditional skilful craftsmanship which they have preserved to enable us to form an estimate as people with a national character and national art. Their typical costumes, hair styles and their very tender and soft movements reveal and speak to us about their ancient culture and the firmly rooted artistic activities.

But in their music we find a tinge of Western touch, which of course does not justify a nation's art. That shows that they were deeply interested in learning the arts of other countries. Therefore, their art formed sometimes a mixture of East and West, so as to transmute the borrowed gems into the already existing gold of her own to add to its charm and glow. Traditions of genuine rich folk culture is evident and is still in vogue in the interior parts. Manipuris resemble Burmese on one side with their Mongolian features and Bengalis too on the other to some extent.

Manual. A keyboard played with the hands—especially on the organ, as opposed to a pedal-keyboard; hence manualiter, bogus-Latin term for 'to be played on the manuals'.

Maraca. Latin American instrument, essential in rumba bands. Consists of gourd containing dried seeds and handle to shake it. Made in various sizes, and always in pairs.

Marcato (It.). Marked; marcato ki basso the basis to be played in a prominent manner.

March. A piece for marching, slow (usually 4/4) or quick (usually 2/4 or 6/8); transferred from military to other uses.

Marcia (It.). March; alla marcia in march-like style—term thus usually applied to 4/4, 2/4, or 6/8 rhythms.

Mariachi (Sp). Mexican folk group of varying size, but usually incl. 2 violins, guitar (jarana), harp (arpon), and large guitar (guitar ron). Word can also apply to solo folk singer.

Marimba. Latin American instrument, of African origin. It is similar to XYLO-phone in construction but with large resonators and usually made of metal. Pitched octave lower than xylo-phone, and more mellow in tone. Usual compass is 4 octaves starting from octave below middle C. There is also bass version.

Martele, Martellato (Fr., It.). Hammered, i.e. strongly accented— as applied e.g. to the piano and to a certain manner of bowing the violin and other strangled instruments.

Martellato. Term used in string-playing, indicating heavy, detached up-and-down strokes, played with point of bow, without taking bow from string. In piano-playing, indicates forceful, detached touth. Martele au talon indicates use of heel of bow.

Martenot. It is an Electronic instrument sounding only one note at a time, played with a keyboard. Brought out in 1928, it has achieved occasional usage as a solo and orchestral instrument – e.g. by Honegger in 'Joan of arc at the Stake'.

Masque, Mask or Maske. Elaborate court entertainment combining poetry and, dancing with vocal and instrumental music, and with scenery, machinery and costume.

Mass. In musical sense, setting of Ordinary, or invariable parts.

Mattinata (It.). The morning song.

Me. In Tonic sol – fa, the spoken name for the third degree (mediant) of the scale.

Meane or Mene. Term used for voice between treble and tenor (Lat., medius); also applied to middle part in 3-part keyboard music.

Measure. Also applied, more widely, to rhythm or time.

Mechanical Musical Instruments. The principle of revolving cylinder with protruding pins is applied to carilon and keyboard instruments. Addition of clockwork mechanism made it possible to apply to number of contrivances e.g. musical clocks, mechanical organs and orchestras, and musical boxes.

Mediant. The name for the third degree of the scale, e.g. E in C major—so called because it stands midway between the tonic (or keynote) and dominant, i.e. between the first and fifth degrees.

Medley. The mixture, miscellany, potpourri. Operatic medley is therefore, selection of excerpts performed non-stop. Term has long musical history, and was used in keyboard music.

Meera Bai. Meera, the ardent devotee of Lord Krishna, wife of Maha Rana Kumbha of Mewar, lived in the 15th century A. D.

She lived in the supreme divinity and talked to the eternal infinite Lord through her musical compositions.

Her life was a total dedication and surrender to Lord Krishna. She followed the path of noble devotion, holding the spiritual torch, immersed in the oil of music, high up, illuminating the whole universe with its bright rays of enchanting songs.

The story goes, that her husband the Rana and his sister troubled and tortured her for not behaving in the worldly way. They tried all the methods to make her agree to live in luxury and pomp befitting that of a queen. But their efforts were in vain.

Her resolve and firmness to lead a life of pure dedication, simplicity and her in calculable love for Lord Krishna, would not shake her.

At last, unable to bear the sufferings brought on her by her husband, she left for Mathura and Brindavan with a party of pilgrims (birthplace of Lord Krishna). She lived there in the temple, where she would sing and dance to the idol of Krishna.

When the husband heard about this he got furious and sent some poison in a cup to administered to her.

Lord Krishna who is always watchful and ready to save his bhaktas, at once turned the dreadful poison which the cup contained into sweet nectar (Amrit). Meera drank it smilingly most cheerfully dancing and singing with it 'Ghunguru Bandh Meera Nachi re-Nachi re', most melodiously.

The Rana, who was watching all this from a hiding place, was stunned to find that his wife did not die, in spite of the strong poison. He at once realised that it was her saviour Lord Krishna who protected and saved her. He came out of his hiding place and begged her forgiveness. The veil of ignorance had fallen from him and he became an entirely new man.

From that day onwards Meera's life was of pure song and devotional intoxication, unobstructed any more.

To her great joy and contentment the Rana, her husband, built many temples in his kingdom and helped the pilgrims by giving charities. What a transformation!

Ultimately, she revealed the eternal truth through her soulstirring devotional songs, composed by herself, and attained salvation.

Meera's inspiring songs move all young and old alike touching the core of the heart.

Some of her masterpieces are 'Mere to Giridhar Gopala', 'Chakara Rakhoji', 'Chalo mana Ganga' and so many similar songs.

There is no record to say how long she lived and till what age. It is presumed she did not live beyond fifty.

Meera attained her 'Niravana' union with Lord a few years after her reconciliation with the Rana.

Her glorious life is an example to the young girls.

Megha Malhar. Megha raga could be seen with precise associations. It is so intimately connected to the rains and clouds.

Literally 'Megha' means in Sanskrit 'Cloud'. Megha Malhar means Lord of clouds. This raga is supposed to produce rain when sung effectively.

The picture of this raga, as formed in the listeners' minds is supposed to be an image with four arms, blue complexion, denoting that of Lord Krishna Himself. Krishna seen dancing with a Gopika Radha, and, another Gopika Sakhi, standing with a drum accompaniment.

This being a raga of sultry summer day, makes the atmosphere slightly cool. Krishna has no flute in his hands. He dances pleasantly with the Gopika, having of background of trees, flowers, clouds and cows, etc.

There are many legends connected with this raga.

A girl is believed to have saved the crop, by her timely singing this Megha raga and bringing the rain in torrents.

Another story goes to say, how a maiden sang this very raga to save Sultan Akbar's burning palace, until rain poured forth and extinguished the fire, which was caused by singing Deepak raga. This raga portrays the majestic clouds and expresses the joyful feelings caused.

Mehrstimmigkeit (Ger.) Polyphony.

Mehta, Zubin (1936 -). Indian conductor. Has conducted Los Angeles Philharmonic Orchestra (1961-76), New York Philharmonic Orchestra from 1977; musical advisor to Israel Philharmonic Orchestra from 1968; and guest conductor of Vienna Philharmonic Orchestra.

Melisma (Gr., song; pl, melismata). Unit of melody sung to one syllable, esp. in plainsong. Also applied, more widely, no any florid vocal passage.

Mellophone. Type of brass instrument shaped similarly to an orchestral Horn and used as a kind of 'poor rotation' to it (e.g. occasionally in dance bands), being easier to play.

Melodie (Fr.).

(1) Melody;

(2) Song with paino accompaniment, French equivalent of German Lied.

Melodrama. The spoken words with musical accompaniment, either as complete work (also called monodrama or duodrama) or as part of opera, e.g. in Fidelio. Modern use of term, to denote violent or sensational play, is development of original meaning.

Melody. A succession of notes varying in pitch and having a recognizable musical shape. Thus the three 'dimensions' of music are often thought of as (1) melody, (2) rhythm, (3) harmony and counterpoint.

Membranophone. The term used in the scientific classification of instruments for those in which a stretched skin (or something similar) is set in vibration, by stick or otherwise – e.g. drums, etc.

Mensural Music. The medieval term for music with definite relative note-values, as distinct from plain-song (musica plana).

Mensural Notation. The system of notation formulated by Franco of Cologne in Ars cantus mensurabilis (c 1260) and used until gradual adoption of metrical rhythm with bar-lines during 17th century. In course of 15th century, black notes began to be written as white and red as black. In white notation, notes and corresponding rests were:

Their relations were governed by time-signature at beginning of part, and by signs of Proportions and use of black (imperfect, i.e. duple subdivision) notes instead of white (perfect, i.e. triple subdivision) in course of part. Relation of long to breve was called mode (or 'mood') and was normally imperfect; of breve to semibreve, time; of semibreve to mimim, proltion.

Menuetto. Term often written in scores by German-speaking composers under the impression that it is the Italian (correctly minuetto) for 'minuet'.

Mephisto Waltzes. The pieces by Liszt : no. 1 (well-known one) and no. 2 were written for orchestra and transcribed for piano and for piano duet; nos. 3 and 4 are for piano.

Messa (It.)

(1) A placing or putting.

(2) Mass (= Lat., Missa). So Messa dia Requiem, title used (e.g. by Verdi) for a musical setting of the Requiem.

Messa Di Voce (It., placing of the voice). The steady swelling and decreasing of vocal volume in one long-held note.

Messinginstrumente (Ger.). Brass instruments.

Mesto (It.). Sad.

Measure (Fr.).

(1) Bar;

(2) Time. Battre de measure, to beat time.

Metal Block. An instrument similar to wood block or small anvil; produces sound of indefinite pitch. Of recent origin.

Metallophone. The instrument of xylophone family, but made of bronze.

Metamorphosis. The term used to describe the way a composer may change a theme – altering tempo and rhythm, even notes, but preserving something essential and recognizable. This device has its obvious use in Illustrative Music, and is also used elsewhere.

Metre. Term used in prosody to cover the relationship between accented and unaccented beats, and sometimes similarly used in music – e.g. 3/8 and 6/8 being described as different kinds of metres. Usually the term Rhythm is so defined as to cover this relationship along with others; but some writers define rhythm and metre as mutually exclusive, metre concerned with the basic unvarying pulse (as above) and rhythm with the actual time-patterns of notes effected by the composer with reference to this basic pulse.

Metrical, of Metre. So (referring to the verse, not the music) metrical psalm, psalm translated and versified in a regular syllabic metre, and thus singable to an ordinary hymn-tune.

Metronome. A device which produces regular beats. Model in general use was patented by Maelzel in 1816 and adopted in following year by Beethoven to indicate tempo of his compositions e.g. ♩ = M. M. 60.

Indicates 60 crotchet beats per minute (M. M. is abbrev. of Maelzel Metronome).

Mezzo, Mezza (It.). Half, so mezza voice, at half voice, at half voice, i.e. with restricted tone; mezzo-forte (abbr. mf), midway between loud and soft; mezzo-soprano, type of female voice half-way between soprano and contralto range. The form mezzo-contralto is sometimes encountered, supposedly meaning a little lower than mezzo-soprano.

Mezzo (It.), half. Mezzo forte, moderately loud (abbrev. Mf). Mezzo piano, moderately soft (abbrev. Mp). Mezzo-soprano, voice between soprano and contralto in range. Mezza voice, with moderate volume of tone.

Mi. The note E (in Latin countries, and formerly elsewhere); cp. ME.

Microtone. An interval smaller than a semitone. (An alternative name is 'fractional tone'.) Quarter-tones have been systematically exploited by A. Haba and other Czechs, and have also had occasional use in more 'orthodox' contexts.

Microtones. Intervals which are fractions of semitone. Such intervals have always been part of theory and practice of tuning (Temperament), but only in modern times have they been introduced into compositions, e.g. by Haba and Ligeti.

Midday. The name given to one of a set of 3 symphonies by Haydn.

Middle C. The note C found at approximately the middle of the piano keyboard. It is commonly tuned to 261.6 Hz.

Middle Fiddle. Viola (term coined by Percy Grainger).

Mighty Five, The. An alternative English term for The Mighty Handful.

Mighty Handful ,The. English translation of Rus, moguchaya kuchka, term invented by Stasov, later applied to Balakirev, Borodin, Cai, Musorgsky, and Rimsky Korsakov. These five Russian composers took up a consciously 'nationalist' standpoint in music, drawing much on Russian history, literature, folk-music, and folk-lore generally. They are thus contrasted with composers thought to look more towards Western Europe, e.g. Tchaikovsky and Anton Rubinstein.

Militratrommel (Gr.). Side drum.

Military Symphony. Nickname for Haydn's symphony no. 100 in G having 'military band' effects from bass drum, cymbals, and triangle.

Mime. Acting without speech; a stage piece consisting of such (sometimes given with music).

Min. Abbr. for minor (scale, etc.).

Miniature Score. Score containing all voice and / or instrumental parts of a piece of music, but in smaller type and page-size than full score. Also known as pocket score or study score.

Minim. Time-value of 1/2 semibreve (whole-note).

Minimalism. Style of music arising in late 1960s characterized by constant reiteration of short rhythmic figures and phrases which are built up through minute variations into large structures.

Minipiano. Trade name for a type of small upright piano with a less extensive keyboard than normal.

Minnesinger. Type of minstrel flourishing in guilds in 12th and 13th century Germany. By social origin these singers were aristocratic; the Mastersingers who flourished afterwards were of the merchant class.

Minor. Term opposed to 'major' and applied to scales, keys, chords, and intervals.

Minore. (It). Minor mode.

Minstrel. General term applied in modern usage to a type of medieval musical performer, usually singing to his own accompaniment, and usually belonging to a guild or other recognized company; in medieval times such performers were classed more particularly.

Minuet, Minuetto (Eng., It.). The dance in triple time of French rustic origin, 'promoted' to court use and becoming widely fashionable in the 18th century. It is normally in AABA form, the 'B' being in contrast and called 'trio' because of the French custom (long since dropped) of writing it in only three parts.

Minuet. French dance, of popular origin, in 3/4 times at moderate pace. First introduced as stylized form by Lully c 1650, and appeared throughout baroque period. Became one of regular movements in classical sonata and symphony, always in ternary form (minuet-trio-minute).

Miracle, The, nickname of Haydn's symphony no. 96 in D (Hob- I: 96).

Mirliton (Fr.). The wind instrument consisting of pipe with one end closed by thin parchment or skin and hole in side into which performer sings. Produces tone similar to bleating of sheep. Now called 'kazoo', and regarded as toy.

Mirror Canon, Mirror Fugue. A canon fugue in which two or more parts appear on paper simultaneously both the right way up and upside down – i.e. as if a mirror lay between them, making one the reflection of the other.

Mirror Composition. Term applied to composition using either Retrograde Motion or contrary motion.

Missa (Lat.). Mass. So – missa brevis, either:

(1) A setting of the Mass in unusually concise musical form, or

(2) A setting of the Kyrie and Gloria only, in obsolete Lutheran usage; missa parodia (erroneous term).

Missa Solemnis (or solemnis) (Lat.), solemn Mass. Title is usually reserved for Mass of particularly exalted character, esp. Beethoven's in D (op 123).

Misura. A measure (in various senses); senza misura, not in strict time (e.g. of a passage in which bar-lines are omitted).

Misura (It.). Measure term which can be used in English sense of 'bar', but is more usually applied to regularity. Thus alla misura, in strict time; senza misura, not in strict time (i.e. bar-lines are usually omitted); misurato, measured.

Mixed Chorus, Mixed Voices, etc. A body comprising both male and female (adult) voices.

Mixed Voices. The Chorus comprising male and female voices.

Mixolydian Mode. The mode represented by the white notes on the piano from G to G.

Mixolydian Mode

(1) In ancient Greek music, equivalent of white notes on piano from B to B.

(2) From Middle Ages onwards applied to equivalent of white notes on piano from G to G. Sharpening of seventh note makes it identical with modern major scale.

Mixture. Type of organ-stop simultaneously sounding two or more of the higher tones (other then octaves) of the Harmonic Series A stop sounding two such tones is said to be a mixture of two ranks (and so forth); and the number of ranks is indicated in organ specifications by Roman figures. The mixture is used in conjunction with 'normal' stops to add richness to the tone.

Mock Trumpet. Early English name for chalumeau or early clarinet.

Mode. Refers to set of notes which form material of melodic idioms used in composition. Medieval (also called church or ecclesiastical) modes may be represented by scales of white notes on piano. They bear names derived from Greek musical system, though neither this concept of mode nor application of names corresponds to Greek theory:

I Dorian, compass D – D, final D, dominant A
II Hypodorian, compass A – A, final D, dominant F
III Phrygian, compass E – E, final E, dominant C
IV Hypophrygian, compass B – B, final E, dominant A
V Lydian, compass F – F, final F, dominant C
VI Hypolydian, compass C – C, final F, dominant A
VII Mixolydian, compass G – G, final G, dominant D

VIII Hypomixolydian, compass D – D, final G, dominant Cfx

Following modes were added in 16th century.

IX Aeolian, compass A – A, final A, dominant E

X Hypoaeolian, compass E—E, final A, dominant C

XI Ionian, compass C – C, final C dominant G

XII Hypoinian, compass G – G, final C, dominant E

Final of mode is note on which its melodies end; dominant is reciting note (tenor). Those modes prefixed 'Hypo-' are called plagal, the others are called authentic; distinction lies in range of melody.

It occurs frequently in plainsong melodies and secular songs of Middle Ages in form of F mode with flattened B. Intervals are thus identical with thode of Ionian mode. Practice of sharpening seventh in Mixolydian mode resulted in similar identity. Minor mode was conflation of Dorian and Aeolian modes, with seventh sharpened as required.

Moderato (It). At a moderate pace. It is also used after another tempo-direction, e.g. allegro moderato, implying 'a moderate allegro', i.e. that the word 'allegro' is not to be taken in an extreme sense.

Modinha. Type of Portuguese (and hence Brazilian) popular song mainly flourishing in the 18th and 19th centuries.

Modulate. To change from one key to another in the course of a composition – such a change being accomplished by 'continuous' musical means (i.e. not simply by starting afresh in another key) and having a definite validity in the structural organization of the music. Hence modulation.

Modulation. Bascially, change of key, process being achieved by logical harmonic progressions. At its simplest, establishment of new key is effected by perfect cadence in that key.

Modulation is often effected by passing through 'pivot' chord, i.e. chord with 2 or more notes belonging to both keys concerned, on way to dominant of new key, e.g. from C to E minor, pivot chord (A – E – A – C) is sub-mediant chord in C, and sub-dominant chord in E minor. Such pivot chords exists, and may be similarly used for modulation, between every major key and key of its supertonic minor, mediant minor, and sub-dominant, dominant, relative minor, and leading-note minor. e.g. between C and D minor, E minor, F, G, A minor, and B minor.

Chords of which root and fifth are common to 2 keys concerned are equally effective as pivot chords. Such chords exist between every 2 major keys, except those of which key-notes are tritone apart. Modulation which takes its departure from minor key may be effected along similar lines.

Modulation may also be effected by using as intermediate:

(1) chords which, since they divide octave into equal parts, are inherently capable of assuming as many key-contexts as they have notes (e.g. augmented triad and diminished seventh chord);

(2) Chromatic chords which have by historical usage established themselves within key (e.g. Neapolitan sixth and augmented sixth chords). In mediant chord of minor mode with sharpened fifth, which is augmented triad, any one of 3 notes may be used as dominant.

If modulation is repeated from new key as starting point, i.e. transposed into that key, result is modulating or 'real' sequence.

Such formulae as are given above may be basis of modulations which are momentary (sometimes called 'transitions') and are soon followed by return to original key, or are modulations or 'transitions') on way to further modulation, or are part of large total design. Technique and art of modulation is fundamental to artistic use of effects of tonality, to control of tonal design, and thus to art of composition.

Modulator. The diagram used for instructional purposes in tonic Sol-fa, for practice in sight-reading and modulation.

Monochord. Scientific instrument consisting of a single string with a movable bridge, used (since the time of Ancient Egypt) for showing how, by altering the ratios in which the string is vibrating, different notes may be produced. These are the notes of the Harmonic Series. A musical instrument based on this principle in the Trumpet Marine.

Modus Lascivus. The key of C major.

Monodrama.

1. Dramatic work involving only one character;
2. In particular, work for speaking voice with instrumental accompaniment.

Monody (from Gk. For 'single song'). The term used to describe the melody-and-continuo style of writing in contrast to the earlier polyphonic style when all parts were held as of equal importance (none simply as accompaniment). So also monodic.

Monophony. The music, which consists of melody only, without independent or supporting accompaniment.

Monotone. Refers to recitation of words on single note.

Monter (Fr.). To tune (instrument) up in pitch.

Montre (Fr.). Refers to one of name for 8ft open diapason stop on organ.

Mood. English term of 16th, 17th centuries. For note relationships (mode, time, prolation) of Mensural Notation.

Moog, Robert (b. 1934). The inventor of Synthesizer name after him.

Moog Synthesizer. Type of Synthesizer developed by Robert Moog in 1960s.

'Moonlight' Sonata. The name given (not by composer) to Beethoven's Sonata quasi una fantasia in C minor for piano, op 27, no 2(180).

Morbido. (It.). Soft, delicate, gentle; morbidezza, softness, delicacy, gentleness.

Morceau (Fr.). A piece (of bread, music, etc.)

Mordent. An obsolete musical ornament represented by sign over the note. This is the upper mordent. In the lower mordent the second note is the one below, not above, the principal note—in the above example it would be C. These two are sometimes called respectively inverted mordent and just mordent; and in German Mordent means only the second, the first being called Pralltriller.

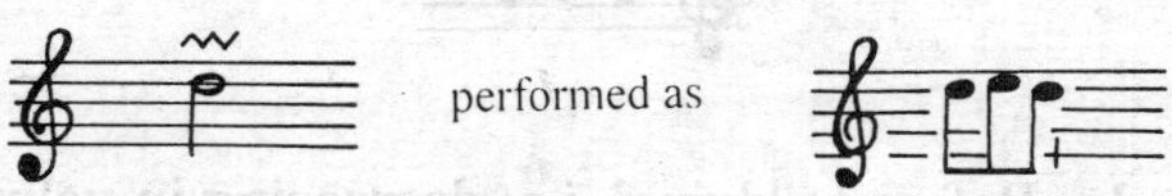

Mordent Lower. The ornament played by alternating written note rapidly once or twice with note below it. Speed number of alternations depends on length of written note, having regard to tempo in which it occurs. It is indicated thus:

And performed thus:

Mordent, Upper or Inverted. English term for ornament introduced c 1750 by CPE. Bach and called Schneller until c1800, and Pralltriller thereafter. Generally occurs on upper of 2 notes in descending second, and is indicated thus:

And played thus:

Morendo. Refers to 'dying', i.e. decreasing in volume (and poss. also speed) at the end of phrase or composition.

Moresca. the dance of 15th, 16th centuries., most often sword dance representing fight between Moors and Christians. Related to English morris dance.

Morning Heroes. Symphony by Bliss—work for orator, chorus, and orchestra, on texts by various authors, in memory of the composer's brother and others killed in the First World War.

Morris. Type of English fold-dance associated with Whitsuntide, the dancers wearing bells; traditionally accompanied by Pipe and Tabor.

Motet. Type of church choral composition, usually in Latin, to words not fixed in the liturgy—corresponding in the

Roman Catholic service to the Anthem (in English) in the Anglican service; type of work related to the preceding but not exactly conforming to it.

Motif. (Fr.) Term sometimes used in English for Leading-Motive and sometimes simply for 'theme', etc.; better avoided because of its ambiguities.

Motion. The term describing upward or downward movements of melodic lines.

Motiv, Motive (Ger., Eng.). A short recognizable melodic or rhythmic figure—term used especially to indicate the smallest possible sub-division in musical analysis, one Theme possibly having several motives.

Motto or Motto Theme. The recurring theme which is used to special dramatic purpose in course of composition. Sometimes theme will have pictorial or symbolic significance, sometimes it will be metamorphosed on each of its appearances, sometimes it will have effect of self-quotation.

"Mourning" Symphony. The nickname of Haydn's symphony no.44 in E minor, C 1772 (Hob. I:44). Haydn wanted its slow movement to be played at his own funeral service.

Mouth Music. Type of singing, wordless but articulated, used in Scottish Highlands to accompany dances.

Mouth Organ. Small wind instrument, also called harmonica. Blown from side, one of pair of metal reeds for each notes being operated by blowing, other by sucking. Chromatic notes are produced by slide.

Mouvement (Fr.).

1. Time, speed. Au mouvement, in time. Premier (or ler) mouvement, at original speed;
2. movement (of sonata, symphony etc.).

Movable Doh. Refers to description of systems of sign-reading, etc. in which doh represents of the keynote, ray the note above, etc., whatever the key. (Opposite to systems wherein, as in Continental Solfeggio, do is C, re is D, etc., whatever the key).

Movement. The primary self contained division of a large composition—usually each having a separate indication of speed, hence the name. A large composition without any such division is said to be 'in one movement'.

Movimento (It.). Motion (not 'movement' in the preceding sense); doppio movimento, at double the preceding speed.

Muffle. To cover the surface of a drum with a cloth, producing an effect analogous to that of a mute.

Muffle Drum. The drum with piece of cloth or similar material placed on vibrating surfaces. Resulting tone quality is somber. Often associated with funeral music.

Multimedia. The term applied to mixtures of musical, visual, poetic and other events.

Mundharmonica (Ger.). The mouth harmonica or mouth organ.

Musette (Fr.). Type of bagpipe popular among French aristocracy. Name also given to dance movements incorporating drone bassnotes suggestive of instrument, and to 8ft reed stop on organ.

Music.

1. 'An arrangement of, or the art of combining or putting together, sounds that please the ear'.
2. An English name for a band of musical performers.

Musica Da Camera (It.). The chamber music.

Musica Falsa, Musica Ficta. Faisa former term was used by theorists in early Middle Ages in discussing use of accidentals which lay outside Guidonian hexachord system. Later medieval theorists applied latter term to trans-positions of hexachord whereby (in addition to B flat), E flat, A flat and D flat became necessary. The term is also now used in referring to accidentals which, it is presumed, singers in 15th, early 16th centuries supplied to provide B flat in mode on F and leading notes for modes on D, G and A.

Musica Figurata (It.).

1. The polyphonic music that is not hormorhythmic, i.e. parts have rhythmic independence;
2. The plainsong with decorated melody, also called musica colorata.

Musical (noun, as abbr. for musical play), term of the type of light stage entertainment (largely American-influenced) which succeeded the older Musical Comedy in the mid-20th century.

Musical Box. Toy in which pins on a rotating cylinder 'pluck' the teeth of a comb which, being of different lengths, emit different notes; several sets of pins allow several tunes.

Musical Comedy. The type of English and American light entertainment, prominent in late 19th and early 20th centuries—related to Operatta, but often less unified musically and using more than one composer.

Musical Glasses. Glass Harmonica.

Musical Switch. The medley of well-known tunes one tune being 'switched' (after a few bars only) into the next—of no artistic value, its only distinction lying in ingenuity.

Musica Plana. The medieval term for Plainsong.

Musica Reservata (Lat.). Term used in latter part of 16th century, supposedly to indicate music suitable for connoisseurs and pirvate occasions, and more particularly music which gave vivid and faithful expression to spirit of words.

Musica Transalpina. The first printed collection of Italian (i.e. transalpine) madrigals with English words.

Musica Master, The. One-act comic opera satirizing the singing-master's profession.

Musica Ricia. In old music (up to 16th century) the practice of treating certain notes in performance as though they were marked with Flat or Sharp signs. This practice was necessary to avoid certain harmonic anomalies that would otherwise result in polyphonic writing, and was carried out by performers according to the recognized conventions of the period.

Musicology. The systematic study of musical composition and its history.

Music Theatre. The name for musical-dramatic works, produced (usually) more economically than operas, and employing smaller forces. Such pieces, are suitable for production in concert halls and theatres as well as opera houses, and their composers have not only discarded name 'opera' but also many of its conventions.

Musicology. The musical scholarship—20th century word useful in such contexts as 'to study musicology', implying an academic discipline different from that in 'to study music'. So also musicologist (usually implying someone whose activity is more learned' than that of a mere critic), musicological, etc.

Musikwissenschaft (Ger.). Musicology.

Musique (Fr.). Music.

Musique Concrete. Type of music in which sounds required by composer are recorded on tape and may then be manipulated, combined or distorted by him.

Musique De Chambre (Fr.). Chamber music.

Musique De Chambre (Fr.). Chamber music.

Musique Mesuree I'antique (Fr.). The music in which

rhythm was rigidly governed by metre of poetry which it set, practised by composers and poets of Academie de Poesie et de Musique.

Mustel Organ. The keyboard instrument of the American organ type invented by V. Mustel (1815-90).

Muta (It.). Imperative of mutare, to change. Direction to wind player to change instrument or crook, or to timpani player to change tuning. Mutano is used where more than one instrument is concerned.

Mutano (It. they change). Term used as the plural of Muta.

Mutation. Change from syllables of one Hexachord to those of another in Solmization, i.e. king of modulation.

Mutation Stop. The organ stop sounding not the note struck but one of its Harmonic Series other than the octave—e.g. a stop called 'twelfth' sounding the twelfth above.

Mute. Any device used to soften or alter normal tone colour of instrument. On bowed instruments it is small fork-shaped clamp that first onto bridge, thereby reducing vibrations; on brass instrument, it is often made of wood or metal and is pear-shaped though wide variety are available for trumpets and trombones, each producing distinctive tone colour. Drums, esp. timpani, were formerly muted by placing cloth over drum head.

N

Naccherone (It.). The large kettledrum.

Nach. In the manner of, after, towards. Thus 'nach E' would be instruction to player to tune instrument to E.

Nach (Ger.). To, after so, e.g., E nach G (instruction to kettledrummer) 'change the tuning of the drum from E to G'.

Nachschlag (Ger., after-stroke).

1. The two extra notes which conventionally close a Trill;
2. An extra note (printed in small type) coming after a main note and robbing that main note of some of its time-value.

Nachtanz (Ger.). After-dance i.e., a quick dance normally used to follow a slow one, e.g., a galliard following a pavan.

Nachtstuck. (Ger.), night piece. Title used by Schumann for set of 4 piano pieces, op 23.

Nad. The chief and most important property in music is Nad (or sound).

We now know that music forms from the sound. This is recognized throughout India.

Nad is of two kinds, one musical and the other unmusical. Any irregular sound caused by any sudden loud unpleasant noise is called an unmusical nad (sound). But if the motion of the nad (sound) is of a milder, soft, appealing and pleasing and pleasant nature, with regular rhythmic intervals and beats, it becomes a uniform musical sound which appeals to the ear.

Nail Fiddle, Nail Harmonica, Nail Violin. Alternatives names/for a freak 18th century instrument having nails of graduated sizes stroked with a violin-bow.

Naker. Early English name for small, high-pitched kettledrum of Arabic origin, introduced into Europe in 13th cent. Used in pairs. Tuning could not be altered.

National Anthem. Song or hymn chosen by country to represent it on official occasions, either at home or abroad.

Nationalism, Nationalist. Terms applied to music which (usually through elements derived from folk-music) suggests supposed national characteristics.

Notural. The note which is neither sharp nor flat.

Natural.

1. Not sharp or flat not having valves, keys or other mechanism, and so producing only the notes of the Harmonic Series as determined by the length of the tube.
2. Also a type of harmonics in spring-playing.

Naturale (It.). The direction that a voice or instrument which has been performing in an 'abnormal' way (e.g., falsetto, muted) should return to its 'natural' manner of performance.

Natural Horn, Natural Trumpet. Horn or trumpet not furnished with valves or other means of altering length of tubing in use. Except where hand stopping can be used, such instruments are limited to notes of harmonic series.

Neapolitan Sixth. The name given to 6/3 chord on fourth degree of scale with minor sixth and minor third, e.g., in key of A minor, D – F – C flat.

Neck. The part of stringed instrument that supports higher-board.

Nei (Rom.). The panpipes, pandean pipes or syrinx. Ancient instrument, commonly associated with Greece, though use today is confined almost entirely to Romania. Consists of number of pipes of whistle type made of wood or reeds, graduated in size, and bound together in row.

Neo. The prefix (from Gk. for 'new') which is used, in classifying musical styles, to indicate the re-adopting (real or supposed) of apparently out-moded characteristics, suitably modified for a new era. So, e.g., Neoclassical; neo-modal, referring to the 20th century revival of the old Modes; neo-Romantic, referring to the inclination of some composers to Romanticism even after the 20th-century reaction against it.

Neo-Bechstern Piano. The electronic piano invented by Vierling in Berlin 1928-33, and later further developed. Played, and strings struck, in normal way, but sound is modified electronically.

Neo-classicism. Term for 20th century musical movement which (especially in 1920s) revolted against lush, emotional, chromatic romanticism of late 19th, early 20th century music. Aspects of neo-classical music were emphasis on clarity of texture, lightness of orchestration, coolness of approach, and back-to 18th century. (esp. back-to-back) respect for counter point and close-knit musical forms.

Neo-modalism. Use by some 20th-cent. Composers of harmony based on old 'modes rather than on major and minor scales. Used productively by e.g. Vaughan Williams.

Neum (e). The generic name for each of the various signs in medieval musical notation (superseded by modern staff notation) showing the note(s) to which a syllable of vocal music was to be sung. As surviving in plainsong notation, the neums give precise indication of pitch.

Neo-romanticism. The term for reaction by some 20th-century, composers against wave of neo-classicism which sprang up during 1920s. Term, however is not very specific.

Neuma or Pneuma. The phrase of melody used by medieval theorists to illustrate characteristics and range of Mode.

Neume (from Gr. for sign). The individual sign in notation used for Eastern chant and Western plainsong.

Niente. Nothing, so a niente, to nothing—term used e.g., after the sign>, indicating that the sound is gradually to die away entirely.

Nightingale. The imitative toy instrument used in the Toy Symphony mistakenly ascribed to Haydn.

Nineteenth. A Mutation stop on the organ producing a note at the interval of a nineteenth (two octaves and a fifth) above the note touched.

Ninth. An interval of nine steps (counting the bottom and top notes), e.g., from C upwards for an octave and a whole-tone to D (major ninth) or for an octave and a semitone to Db (minor ninth).

Nocturne. Ninth-piece. Name introduced by John Field—from whom Chopin adopted it—for piano pieces with cantabile melody, often elaborately ornamented, over arpeggiated or chordal accompaniment.

Node. A stationary point on a vibrating string or air-column—the vibrations taking place in opposite direction on either side of it.

Noel (Fr.). Christmas Carol or song.

Noire. (Fr., black) = Quarter—note, Crotchet.

Nonet. A composition for 9 instruments or 9 voices; if the former, it will probably be in some regular several-movement form—cp. Quartet.

Non-Harmonic Note. Term used in the theory of harmony for a note that is not part of the chord with which it sounds, and therefore needs its own 'explanation'—e.g. it may be a Passing-Note of Appoggiatura.

Nota Cambiata. A device in counterpoint by which an 'extra' Non-Harmonic Note is used on an accented beat. The leap from B to an Accented D, both non-harmonic notes, is the essential feature; or it might have been from D to B.

(a) (b)

Notation. The writing down of music so as to indicate its pitch and rhythm.

Note.

1. Tone of definite pitch;
2. Symbol for tone, indicating pitch and duration;
3. Key of piano or other keyboard instrument.

Note Cluster. Term coined for dissonant group of notes, lying close together and usually played on piano.

Note De Passage. (Fr.). Passing Note.

Note-row. In Twelve-Note music, the order in which the composer chooses to arrange the twelve notes comprised within the octave, this order serving as the basis for the particular composition.

Note value. The length of time a particular note is to be played in relation to other notes.

Notturno (It.), night-piece:

1. Title given by 18th-century, composers to music for evening entertainment;
2. In 19th century, Italian equivalent of Nocturne.

Novachord. The patented Electrophonic instrument: it has a 6 – octave piano-like keyboard, manual controls varying the tone-quality, and pedals for sustaining notes and for volume control. Chords and not merely single notes can be played.

Novetette, Novellette (Eng. Ger.). Title for a short instrumental piece supposedly the equivalent of a romantic tale.

Number. A self-contained item in an opera, a musical, etc. (so called because each such piece is separately numbered 1, 2, etc. in the written score); hence humber-opera, an opera in which this separation into self-contained items is followed, as distinct from those operas where a whole act is written out without internal divisions and thus without possible pause.

Number Opera. The opera consisting of 'numbers', i.e. arias, duets, ensembles etc., separated by recitative or spoken dialogue.

Nut.

1. On a stringed instrument, the ridge over which the strings pass between the pegs and the finger-board; movable nut, contrivance placed on the finger-board, having the effect of shortening all strings equally and thus raising their pitch at choice, to facilitate playing in various keys;
2. On the bow of, e.g., a violin, the device at the heel by which the tension of the bow-strings can be regulated.

O

Obbligato. Term refers to part, usually instrumental, which cannot be dispensed with in performance, as distinct from part which is optional, or ad libitum.

Obertas or Oberek. Polish round dance in fast triple time.

Oberwerk. (Germ.) Swell organ.

Oblique Motion. Term describing two melodic lines or parts, one of which moves while other stays on same note.

Oboe. The woodwind instrument blown through a double reed and having a compass from the Bb below middle C upwards for more than two and a half octaves; standard in the orchestra, and used also in the military band, in chamber music, and as solo instrument. Oboe d'amore, similar instrument of slightly lower pitch and less pungent tone, written for e.g. by Bach and (exceptionally in modern times) by Ravel ('Bolero') and R. Strauss; oboe da caccia—literally 'hunting oboe', though it is not clear why—predecessor of the English Horn, the present 'contralto' to the oboe's soprano. The lowest members of the oboe family are two different instruments each with campass approximately an octave below the oboe—the (French) baritone oboe, blown through a side tube like the bassoon, and the (German) Heckelphone, sometimes called (e.g. in Delius's scores) bass oboe. The oboe's predecessor in the Shawm.

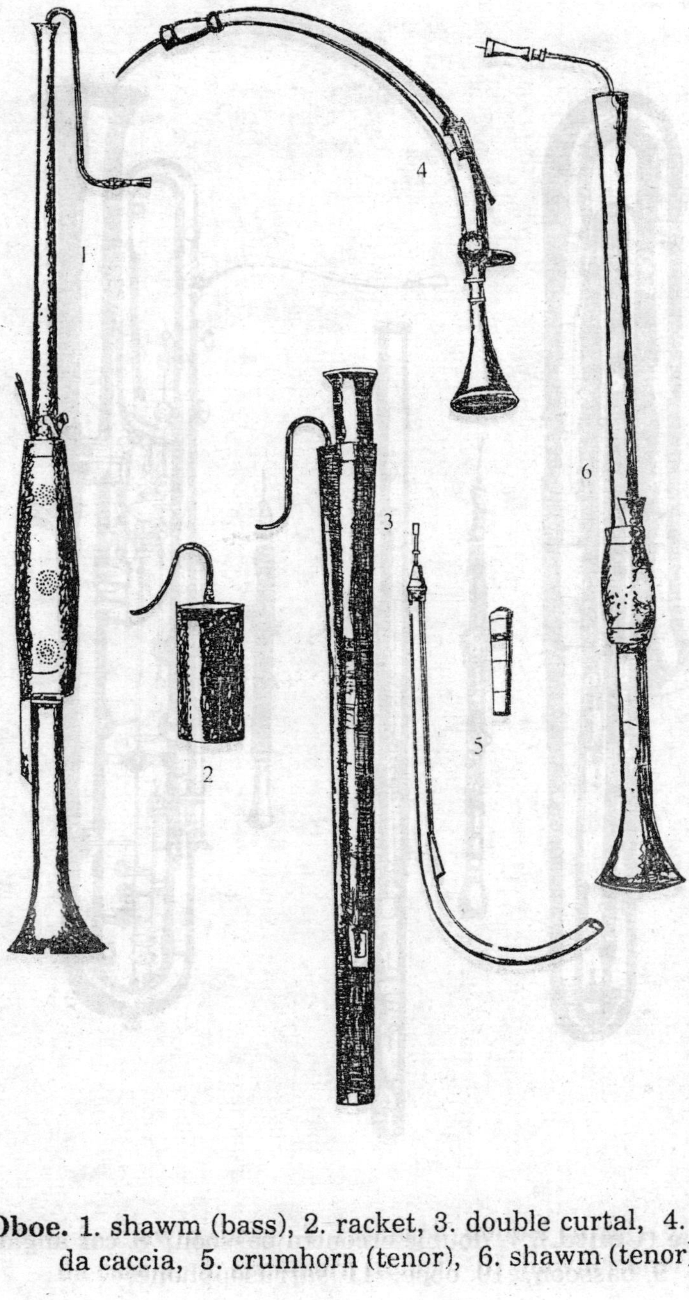

Oboe. 1. shawm (bass), 2. racket, 3. double curtal, 4. oboe da caccia, 5. crumhorn (tenor), 6. shawm (tenor)

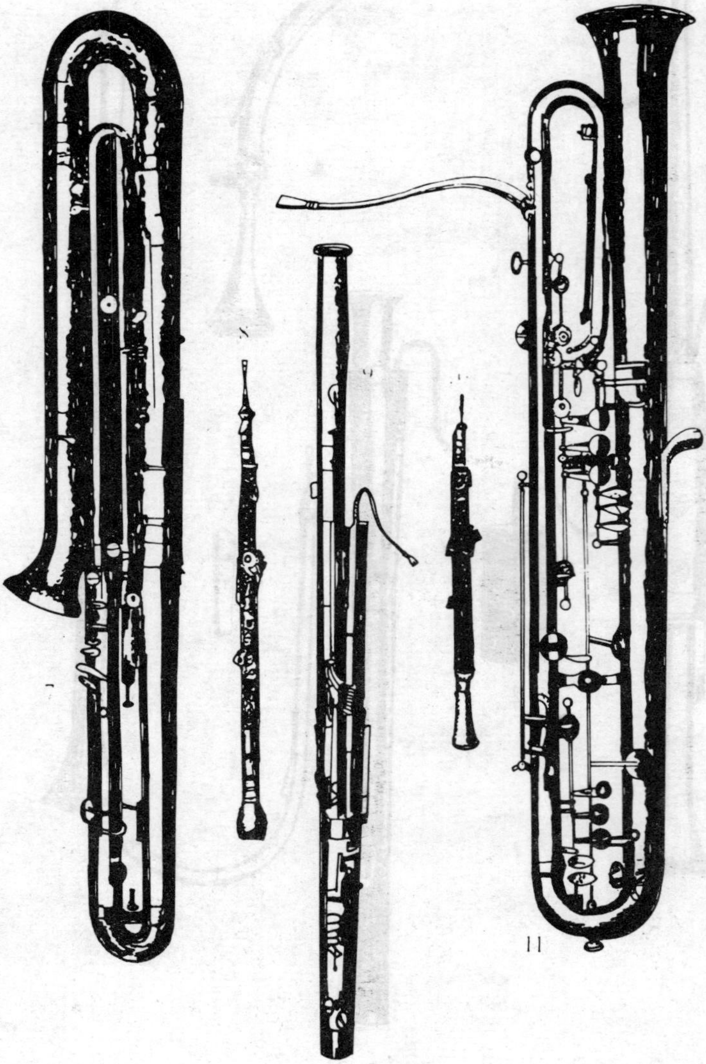

Oboe (Contd.). 7. double orcontra bassoon, 8. cor anglais, 9. bassoon, 10. oboe, 11. sarrusopphone.

Ocarina. Small pear-shaped wind instrument of recorder type and with similar tone quality. With its limited range it is hardly more than a toy.

Octave.

1. Interval between first and eighth notes of diatonic Scale. Notes which are octave apart are called by same letter name. Upper note is having exactly twice the frequency of vibrations of lower one and two notes have effect of mutual duplication and reinforcement. To play in octaves means that each note is doubled one or more octaves above or below;
2. 4ft diapason stop on organ, also called principal.

Octave Coupler. The mechanical device on organ which automatically doubles at octave above any note which is played. Sub-octave couples similarly double at octave below.

Octave Fiddle. The obsolete, small, 4-stringed instrument, tuned octave below violin.

Octet. The composition for 8 instruments or 8 voices; if the former, it will probably be in some regular several-movement from—cp. Quartet. Also a group of 8 performers.

Octobass. A huge bowed stringed instrument, larged and pitched lower than a double-bass, invented in 1849. It failed to win acceptance.

Octuor. Octet.

Ode.

1. Refers to the form of strophic poetry;
2. Also, refers to the vocal composition in honour of some person or occasion.

Offertoire. (Fr.)=Offertorium.

Offertorium, Offertory (Lat., Eng.). A plainsong or plyphonic setting of biblical works (in Latin) occurring after the Credo in the Mass of Roman Catholic Church while the Eucharist is being prepared and offered.

Oktave. (Ger.). Octave.

Oliphant. Small medieval horn made of elephant's tusk or of gold, a symbol of high dignity (e.g. that of knighthood).

Ondule. Effect, indicated by sign~used in violin playing in baroque period either on single note, or on several notes in Arpeggio, and produced by undulating motion of bow.

One-step. The US dance in quick 2/4 time, popular in early 20th century, but later ousted by slow foxtrot (or two-step).

Op. abbrev. of Lat. opus, 'work'. Term is traditionally used by composers to indicate numbering of their works in order of composition, e.g. op 95. If opus consists of more than one piece, it may be subdivided, e.g. op 59, no. 2.

Open. Not muted. In brass parts, indicates removal of mute, or discontinuation of hand-stopping (on horns).

Open, Fifth. Common chord without third is said to have open fifth.

Open, Form. The term used to describe certain composition (from the 1950s) in which the performer has the option of varying the sequence of component sections or may begin at any point and continue in circular fashion until reaching that point again.

Open Notes. On brass or wood wind instruments, notes produced without use of valves, keys etc., i.e. notes of Harmonic series.

When used of stringed instruments, term means notes not stopped by finger pressure (also called 'open strings'). Sign ° above note indicates that it is played on open string where poss, or as Harmonic.

Oper. (Ger.). Opera—also in the sense of 'opera company'.

Opera. The dramatic work in which whole, or greater part, of text is sung with instrumental accompaniment. Term is abbrev. of opera in music (musical work).

Opera-ballet. The stage work giving approximately equal importance to opera and ballet.

Opera-bouffe. (Fr.) The species of French comic opera.

Opera Bouffe. The type of light, often satirical opera or operetta, e.g. the operettas of Offenbach. Term taken from, but not historically quite the same as, Opera Buffa.

Opera Buffa. (It.). The comic opera.

Opera-comique. The 'comic opera', though applied in 19th century, to any opera with spoken dialogue.

Opera-oratorio. The term applied by Stravinsky to his 'Oedipus Rex', intended to be presented on the stage but in a static manner remote from ordinary theatrical practice.

Opera Semiseria (It.). The serious opera containing comic elements.

Opera Seria (It.). 'Serious' opera. Most prevalent operatic form of 17th, earlier 18th centuries, characterized by noble subjects, serious, elaborate arias, and general air of formality. Libretto was in Italian, and important roles were often given to castrato singers.

Opertta. The term used for an opera of a light type whether full-length or (like some of Offenbach's) in one act. The term is virtually synonymous with light opera'; and cp. Musical Comedy.

Ophicleide. The obsolete bass instrument made of metal and having keys; used in the orchestra (e.g. by Berlioz, Mendelssohn, early Verdi) as an improvement on the Serpent, but was itself superseded about 1850 by the tuba, on which instrument the parts intended for the ophicleide are now normally played.

Opus. the term used, with a number, for the enumeration of a composer's works supposedly in the order of their composition; if an 'opus' comprises more than one piece, then a subdivision may be used (e.g. 'opus 40, no. 2'). Occasionally the letters a and b are used to indicate different but equally valid versions of the same work.

Oratorio. The term used for setting of text on sacred or epic theme for chorus, soloists and orchestra, for performance in church or concert hall.

Orchester (Ger.). Orchestra.

Orchestra. A numerous mixed body of instrumentalists. The term theatre orchestra customarily indicates not an opera orchestra (which is ideally of 'symphonic' size) but a smaller orchestra used for musicals, etc., commonly including saxophones. A combination of wind instruments only, or any combination for dancing to, is commonly called not an orchestra but a band—the occasional 20th-century use of dance orchestra being pretentious. Although composers may vary both the kind and numbers of instruments used (variety being especially noticeable in the percussion section), the forces standardized by the requirements of 20th—century (and late 19th century) symphonic music are:

(a) Woodwind: 3 flutes, 1 doubling piccolo
3 oboes, 1 doubling English horn
3 clarinets, 1 doubling bass clarinet
3 bassoons, 1 doubling double-bassoon

(b) brass: 4 (sometimes 6) horns
3 trumpets
3 trombones (2 tenor, 1 bass)
1 tuba

(c) percussion: 3 kettledrums (1 player)
snare-drum, bass-drum, cymbals, gong, triangle, xylophone, vibraphone, etc.
(2 or more players)

(d)	unclassified:	2 harps 1 piano
(e)	strings:	first violins (about 14) second violins (about 14) violas (about 12) cellos (about 10) double-basses (about 8)

Orchestration. Art of writing for orchestra, concerned with tone colour, technical capacity, and effective range of instruments, with textures arising in combinations of instruments and with setting out of orchestral score.

Orchestrion. The mechanical instrument able to imitate sounds of various orchestral instruments.

Ordinary. The parts of Mass with invariable texts.

Orff-schulwerk. The collection of percussion instruments of simple construction designed by Carl Orff for educational purposes.

Organ

(1) The keyboard instrument in which wind is blown by a bellows through pipes to sound the notes; made in various sizes down to the medieval 'portative', i.e. portable, carried by the player.

(2) Term of each component tone-producing part of the instrument described about—e.g. the Great Organ, Pedal Organ, meaning the Great and Pedal keyboards plus the pipes controlled by them and the appropriate machinery.

(3) Term for an instrument controlled by keyboard, and imitative of the organ as described above, but pipeless—e.g. Reed-organ, Hammond Organ.

Organ Electronic. The instrument, of which Hammond organ and Compton Electrone are examples, with manuals and pedals in which tone is produced and amplified electronically.

Organetto (It.). The small medieval Portative Organ.

Organ Mass. The mass in which music of Ordinary is performed by singers and organ in alternating phrases. Singers sang plainsong and organist played polyphonic elaboration of it.

Organo Di Choro (It.). The choir organ.

Organology, (rare term for). The study of musical instruments in general (not just the organ).

Organo Pieno. The full organ.

Organ Point. Same as Pedal Point.

Organum. A medieval form of Part-writing based on a plainsong which was harmonized by the addition of one, two, or three (usually parallel) parts.

Orgatron. Electronic organ invented (1934) by Everett of Michigan.

Orgel Walze. Mechanical organ.

Orgue Expressif (Fr.). Harmonium.

Ornament. One or more notes considered as an embellishment of a melody, either:

(1) inserted by the performer (e.g. the opera-singer in Handel's time) from his knowledge of current conventions, without specific written instructions from the composer.

(2) Conveyed by a sign or abbreviation, or

(3) Written in full or ordinary notation, even when it could have been conveyed by a sign—as, e.g. the turn written out in full by Wagner and Bruckner.

Ossia (It.). Used to indicate alternative (usually simplified) to passage in composition.

Ostinato (It.). Refers to persistently repeated musical figure which may occur during section of composition or even throughout whole piece. Ostinato patterns very often occur in bass, so basso ostinato Ground Bass.

Ostinato. A persistently repeated musical figure or rhythm; so basso ostinato, a bass having this characteristic—i.e. a Ground Bass.

Otello. The form of name used by Italians for the character called Othello by Shakespeare.

Ottava (It.). Means octave. Abbrev. 8va. All' ottava or 8va, octave higher or lower (generally former); ottava alta or ottava sopra, octave higher; ottava, bassa or ottava sotto, octave lower; coll' ottava or con ottava, doubled at octave above or below. Indications are written above notes when they refer to higher octave, below when they refer to lower. Dotted line indicated how long indication is valid. When term 8va (or equivalents ceases to be valid, it is often contradicted by loco '[in the normal] place'.

Ottavino (It.). The modern Italian name for the small flute, elsewhere called Piccolo (itself signifying 'little' in Italian).

Ottoni (It.). Brass instruments.

Overblow. To blow a woodwind instrument harder, in such a way that its notes are 'stepped up' from those of its 'basic' pitch.

Overstrung. The method for positioning strings in pianos so that they are on 2 levels and cross each other diagonally. This allows strings of greater length to be used in small instruments than would otherwise be possible.

Overtone. The name for any notes of the Harmonic Series except the first ('fundamental').

Overture. The introductory music to opera, oratorio, ballet, play or other large-scale work. Concert Overture, however, is written as independent concert piece.

P

P. Abbr. For Pincherle (in numbering Vivaldi's works).

P. Abbr. of piano (It., soft); hence, as indications of increasing degrees of softness, pp, ppp, etc.—sometimes in even greater aggregations.

Padams. These are based on Sringara Rasa, of Bhakti of the highest order.

The kritis and the Keertanas followed the path of God to attain the good through sincere faith and devotion, praising the Lord. Whereas in the Padam you will find that it is all full of sentimental spiritualized love, the longing to be one in union with Him. Or some disappointment, they convey, on reaching Him sooner. For a layman, outwardly, only ordinary vulgar love of men is depicted in these songs called Padams. They cannot go deep to understand the real sense and the beauty it contains. It takes one, far beyond the realms of God with its inner philosophical meaning.

The inestimable devotion of the Nayaka Nayaki bhava, if understood in the proper way, is superb.

Nayaka is always understood as Bhagwan or the Guru, and the Nayaki as the devotee, begging Him for liberation.

Padams are just the replicas of Jaya Deva's Geeta Govindam of earlier times, both based on the highest theme of divine love.

They say that the composer of these Padams Kshetrajna, was the same Jaya Deva himself again reborn to give all these precious works. First as Jaya Deva in the past life, in Sanskrit language, and as Kshetrajna in Telugu language giving the same theme.

The feeling, the yearnings and the expressions of sorrow, of the pangs of separation from the Lord, are something which speak of the nobility and the true real love to God.

Kshetrajna has immortalized these padams with his unique way of presentation with bhava and bhakti.

He always gave his 'mudra' (signature) as Muvva Gopala, at the end of each padam. Padams which are all in Telugu language have also three divisions—Pallavi, anupallavi, charanam. Sometimes they contain three or four charanams too. These are sung with dignity and a flow of natural grandeur (respectable love) so as to bring the entire picture of the bhava or the sentiments if conveyed to the listeners' minds.

The union of superior love of individual soul with the godly universal soul is conceived in these compositions. It gives a lot of inspiration.

In the later years many other composers tried to imitate Kshetrajna, and composed some so-called padams. It is needless here to say they could not come anywhere near these great compositions.

The theme of the padams composed in later years by the other various musician-composers had been on different varieties of love. Some have expressed pure sringara of the mundane plane. Some have attempted on some humorous and other sorts of love songs, and some showed love of God.

Lately some Tamil musicians also have attempted successfully at composing some padams in Tamil language.

There are group padams also, just like group kritis.

Kshetrajna himself had left a set of five such group padams. He presented these Panch-Ratna-Padams to the Naik of Tanjore of those days, who was believed to be great lover of music.

Some noted Padam composers:		Mudra
1. Kshetrajna	...	Muvva Gopal
2. Saranga Pani	...	Venu Gopala (Primala Ranga, etc.)
3. Ghananam Seenayya Pedda Dasari	...	Maunam Ranga
4. Subbarama Iyer and one or two others.	...	Tamil

Pandiatonic (ism). The term coined (from Gk., pan, all) by the American musicologist Nicolas Slonimsky to indicate the pronounced use in chord-formation of all seven degrees of the Diatonic scale. Examples of such use are the Added Sixth in jazz and the chord C-E-G-B at the beginning of Deliu's on Hearing The First Cuckoo in Spring'.

Pandora (also bandora). The name given to many varieties of plucked instrument—especially a type of large, wire-strung Cittern used in the 16th-17th centuries as a continuo instrument.

Pan-Pipes. Refer to a series of simple short vertical pipes which are fixed side by side in order to give a scale when blown—an ancient, medieval, and 'folk'.

Pantomime. A play in dumb-show, a mime-play—either as a self-contained work.

Parameter. The vague term applied to such basic elements of a composition as loudness, duration, and timber—especially where such elements are subjected to a mathematical order, as in 'total serialism'.

Paris Symphonies. The term used for a set of 6 symphonies by Haydn (Hob. I: 82-7) composed in 1785-6, mainly for a series of concerts in Paris: no. 82 is nicknamed' 'The Bear', no. 83 'The Hen', no. 85 'The Queen'.

'Paris' Symphony. The nickname of Mozart's symphony no. 31 in D (K. 927), composed in Paris for performance there, 1778.

Parlando, Parlante. Either as a literal instrument (e.g. in opera), or as a direction in song indicating a near approach to a speaking tone.

Parody. The misleading term used by some musical authorities to denote a composer's straight forward imitation of adaptation of his own or someone else's work (without any implication of mockery).

Part.

(1) The music of a particular performer in an ensemble—the tenor part, the flute part, etc.; score and parts, expression contrasting the score (containing the music of all performers) with the music written separately for individual.

(2) An individual 'strand' of music, whether or not it is actually performed by one or more; a fugue in four parts or four-part fugue, etc.

Parte (It.). Part (1, 2); colla parte, with the (solo) part, i.e. the accompanying instrument(s) accommodating the soloist to allow some licence of tempo.

Partial. The name assigned to each of the notes of the Harmonic Series, the lowest or 'fundamental' being the first partial and the others (numbered upwards consecutively) upper partials.

Part-song. Any song written for several vocal parts, as distinct from a solo or unison song.

Part-writing. Refers to the laying-out of a composition so that each part progresses euphoniously.

Pas.

(1) step in dancing.

(2) Balled science of dramatic nature.

Pasodouble. The modern Spanish dance in quick 2/4 time.

Passacagia. An instrumental piece (originally a dance) in which a theme stretching over several bars is continually repeated, usually but not necessarily always in the bass.

Passage. Refers to a section of a musical composition with the implication of not having much structural importance.

Passing-note. In harmony, this terms refers to a note which forms a discord with the chord with which it is heard, but which is 'justified' because it is melodically placed between two notes which are not discordant.

Passion. The term used for a musical setting of the biblical story of the suffering (Lat, passio) and death of Jesus, properly to be sung in churches in the week before Easter.

Pasticcio. Refers to the operatic work with music drawn for the purpose from works by different composers.

Pastiche.

(1) Pasticcio;

(2) A piece which is composed deliberately in the style of another composer.

Pastoral.

(1) Term or nickname for music evoking (e.g. by instrumentation or verbal label) a rustic subject.

(2) Obsolete terms for a stage entertainment with a rustic setting.

Pastourelle. The term used for the light French song of pastoral character, cultivated especially in the 18th century.

Patter-song. The type of comic song (especially in opera) dependent for its effect on the rapid enunciation of syllables.

Pause. Its meanings is that the note or rest so marked must be held longer than normally, to an extent determined by the performer's discretion.

Pavillon. The 'bell' (extremity opposite to the mouthpiece) of a horn, trumpet, etc. So, as direction to brass-players, pavillons enl'air, with the bells held high up so as to increase the volume. But for pavillon chinois (i.e. Chinese), Jingling Jobnny.

Ped. Abbr. for pedal: (1, in piano music) instruction that the sustaining pedal is to be depressed until a point when its release is indicated; (2, in organ music) indication of music to be played on the pedal keyboard.

Pedal.

(1) (In harmory) A note sustained below (i.e. at the foot of) changing harmonies: this is called a pedal or pedal point or pedal bass;

(2) The lowest ('fundamental') note of the Harmonic Series, especially with reference to the playing of brass instrument;

(3) A foot-operated lever.

Pedal Board. A keyboard played with the feet—such as is normally found on the organ, rarely on harpsichord, clavichord and piano.

Pedal-piano. A piano which is fitted with a pedal keyboard in addition to its ordinary one.

Penillion (Welsh, pl.). A type of traditional Welsh singing, in which verses either given or improvised are sung in counterpoint to a well-known melody played on the harp.

Pentatonic. The term used for a scale comprising only five notes-particularly that represented by the five black keys of the piano (or other notes in the same position relative to each other).

Percussion. The collective name for instruments in which (usually) a resonating surface is struck by the player—in most cases directly by hand or stick, but sometimes through leverage as in the type of bass-drum used in dance-bands, operated by a pedal.

Perdendosi (It., losing itself; accent on second syllable). The direction for performance indicating 'softer and softer until dying away'.

Perfect. The term used for the intervals of a fourth, fifth, and eighth (octave) in their 'standard' dimension—e.g. C up to F, to G, and to C respectively. They become Diminished if lessended by a semitone and Augmented if enlarged by a semitone.

Pezzo (It., pl. -i). A piece, a play, a musical work, etc.

Philharmonic. A term used as title of various orchestras and other musical bodies.

Phrase. A small group of notes which are forming what is recognized as a unit of melody.

Phrygian Mode. The Mode which is represented by the white keys of the piano, beginning on E.

Piano (It.).

(1) Soft, abbr. P; so pianissimo or pp. very soft.

(2) Common English word for the keyboard instrument called in Italian pianoforte (literally soft-loud)—the shorter term being more convenient than the longer, and no worse English. The instrument may be distinguished e.g. from harpsichord and clavichord by having its strings struck with harmmers. It was invented shortly after 1700 and by 1800 had almost displaced the harpsichord. The modern piano is iron-framed and normally has 88 keys: it is either upright (i.e.

strings are vertical) or grand (i.e. they strings are horizontal). It has a 'sustaining pedal' (wrongly called 'loud pedal') operated by the right foot to prolong the sound by holding off the dampers; and a 'soft pedal (left foot) lessening the volume by causing fewer than the normal number of strings to be struck or by bringing the hammers nearer the strings before they start their movement.

Pianoforte. The Italian name for the instrument more commonly called piano in English.

Pibroch. Type of Scottish Highland bagpipe music, in a kind of elaborate variation-form.

Picardy Third. The major third used at the end of a piece otherwise in the minor key, converting the expected minor chord into a major one.

Piccola. The small flute pitched an octave above the standard flute. It is used in the orchestra and military band.

Pifferaro. The term used for a player on the Piffero.

Pipe. A hollow cylinder or cone in which air vibrates, e.g. in an organ or a blown wind-instrument; (term also used for) type of simple wind-instrument itself composed only of such a cylinder or cone without mechanism.

Piston. Valve (on brass instruments.)

Pitch. Refers to the property according to which notes appear to be 'high' or 'low' in relation to each other—a property scientifically determined by the frequency of vibrations of the sound-producing agent. So concert pitch is the standard of the pitch to which instruments are normally tuned for performance.

Pizzicato. Refers to the direction that notes on bowed string instrument are to be plucked, not bowed; abbr. Pizz.

Player-piano. The general name for a piano which is fitted with the type of mechanism usually known by such trade names as 'Pianola'. By this mechanism the keys are depressed not by the fingers but air pressure supplied by bellows and pedals, or electrically: the air pressure is applied through performations on an unwinding paper roll, such perforations being arranged so that a composition is played.

Plectrum. The term used for the small piece of wood, metal or other material which is used to pluck the strings of lute, mandolin, banjo, etc.

Pneuma. A type of florid passage sung to a single vowed in plain-song.

Pochette. The small-size violin (small enough to be kept in a long pocket) formerly used by dancing-master: same as Kit.

Poem, Poema, Poeme (Eng. It., Fr.). Term which was brought into music by Liszt in the expression Symphonic Poem and which has since been somewhat extended usually implies music based on a narrative.

Point. The end of the bow opposite to that held by the hand.

Pointing. In Anglican Chant, the allotting of syllables to the notes on which they are to be sung.

Polka. A dance in 2/4 time for couples.

Polo. Type of Spanish dance, with song.

Polonaise. A stately Polish dance in 3/4 time.

Polymodal(ity). Terms used by some commentators to allude to an effect which would be Polytonality except that the composer is using not the scales of modern keys but the scales of the old modes.

Polyphony. The term literally meaning (from Gk.) any simultaneous sounding of different notes—and correctly used e.g. in reference to instruments; polyphonic synthesizer.

Polyrhythm. The systematic exploitation of several rhythms performed simultaneously sometimes with the aid of mechanical devices.

Polytonality. Refers to the simultaneous use of more than one key. Where only two keys are involved the more precise term is 'bitonality'.

Ponticello (It.). The term for the bridge of a violin or other stringed instrument; sul ponticello (literally, 'on the bridge') instructions to play with the bow as close to the bridge as possible, for the production of a special kind of 'nasal' or 'metallic' tone-quality.

Poong. It is an instrument, a type of drum. This forms a part of all music and dance items of Manipuri. This gives beautiful rhythmic patterns. During 'Poong Chalam' concerts, these instruments are played by several persons in a group in rhythmical patterns.

Pop. Abbr. For 'popular'. In older usage it carries the straight-forward meaning of 'appealing to a wide audience'. However, it usually refers to a non-classical, commercially promoted type of music of US derivation, consisting almost entirely of songs, whether delivered by solo or group vocalists. Pop in this sense, particularly as purveyed by radio and gramophone records, has assumed the role of a popular alternative to the classical tradition of composition and performance. Hence pop groups (performers), pop festivals, etc.

Portamento (It.). The term used for the 'carrying' of sound—e.g., on a voice or a stringed instrument, the transition from one note to another higher or lower without any break in the sound.

Posaune. Trombone but also trumpet.

Positif (Fr.). Choir-Organ.

Position. The term used to specify how far along the finger-board the left hand should rest in order to play a given passage—first position being that nearest the pegs; second, etc., progressively further away.

Positive. Type of small organ, which was placed (i.e. positioned) on floor or table, in context with the portative, a portable organ.

Post-horn. The brass instrument of simple design—a long tube which is made without valves or keys, and so able to produce only the notes of one Harmonic Series. Built in various shapes.

Postlude. A final piece-opposite of Prelude, and an equally imprecise term, but much less commonly found.

Post-romantic (ism). Terms applied to musical styles seeming to continue on Romantic lines even after the original 'wave' of romanticism in music apparently reached its climax in Wagner.

Pot-pourri (Fr.). The term used in a musical sense for a medley of tunes having little formal cohesion between them.

Prelude. Properly a piece preceding something or forming the first number of a suite, of forming the orchestral introduction to an act of an opera; but the term is also used for a short self-contained piece.

Preparation. Refers to a device in harmony by which the impact of a discord is softened: the actual note which in a chord, causes that chord to be discordant, is sounded first in the preceding chord where it does not form a discordant element.

Prepare. To 'set' an instrument ready to produce a particular effect.

Prepared Piano. A piano in which the strings are 'doctored' with various objects so as to produce tone qualities other than normal, sometimes with the addition of unusual techniques of playing – e.g. reaching over the keyboard and plucking the strings by hand.

Prick-Song. An old English term for music that was 'pricked', i.e., written down, as distinct from traditional or improvised music.

Primo, Prima. First. So primo, the top part in piano duets; prima donna, the chief woman singer in the east of an opera, etc.

Principal.

(1) The first of an orchestra's players of a particular instrument (e.g. 'principal horn');

(2) A singer who takes main parts in an opera company—thus 'principal tenor' does not mean the chief tenor, but any tenor who has attained the standing of a 'principal'.

(3) An organ stop of the open Diapason type but sounding an octave higher.

Programmatic, Music, Programme Music. The music interpreting a story, picture, etc.

Progression. The motion from one note or chord to the next, in accordance with a musically logical plan.

Progressist. The term used for self-description of those French composers (e.g. Durey, Nigg) who after the Second World War wrote music deliberately of 'mass' appeal in accordance with Communist doctrine on 'progressive' art.

Progressive Tonality. The term used for the systematic plan of beginning a movement in one key and ending it in another.

Prompt (in operatic performance). To supply cues to a singer—not merely, as in a play, when the performer forgets, but often supplying verbal and musical cues in anticipation throughout a performance.

Psaltery. Ancient and medieval stringed instrument.

Pult. A passage is to be played only by the fist two players that of section.

Q

Q. As Abbrev.,=quintus, quinto or quinto pars.

Quadrille. French dance fashionable in early 19th century. Danced by 2 or 4 couples. Had 5 parts in 6/8 and 2/4 alternately. Operatic music was often arranged as quadrille.

Quadruple Stop. The chord of 4 notes played on bowed string instrument. Term applies even if some of notes are open strings.

Quadruplet. Refers to a group of four notes (or notes and rests) of equal time-value, written where a group of three, five, or some other number of notes is suggested by the time-signature.

Quail. Toy instrument that imitates sound of quail.

Quarter Tone. Half a semitone, which is smallest interval traditionally used in Western music. Notes are indicated by modified forms of usual signs for accidentals.

Quartet.

(1) A performing group of 4 instrumentalists or singers: where the instruments are unspecified a string quarter is assumed – 2 violins, viola, cello; a piano quartet consists of piano, violin, viola, cello.

(2) A piece for 4 performers; if instrumental, and actually entitled 'Quertet', it will probably have the character of a Sonata for 4 performers, in several movements.

Quarttagott. The large bassoon pitched fourth below normal instrument.

Quartposaune (Ger.). Trombone pitched fourth below tenor trombone in B flat, i.e. bass trombone in F.

Quaver. The note which is half length of cretochet, and eight of semi-breve (whole note).

Quest Opera. The opera in which principal character(s) undergoes various hardships, tests or difficult journeys before reaching his goal.

Quick step. March, in quick steps; also, modern ballroom dance notable for quick beat.

Qualisma. Neume used in notation of plain song. Usually came between 2 notes a third apart, and was prob. sung with trill or tremolo in same way as later Plica.

Quint. The organs stop sounding a note a fifth (Lat., Quintus) higher than the key depressed. It is with the aid of thus stop on the pedals that the effect of a 32-ft stop is produced even without 32-ft pipes.

Quintadena, Quintation. Types of organ stop which sound not only the note of the key depressed, but also the note a twelfth (i.e. an octave plus a fifth) higher.

Quintet.

(1) A performing group of 5 instrumentalists of singers, a string quintet adds an extra viola or cello to the standard string Quartet, and a piano quintet usually adds a piano to this standard string quartet.

(2) A piece for 5 performers; if instrumental, and actually entitled 'quintet', it will probably have the character of a Sonata for 5 performers in several movements.

Quinto (It.). Refers to specific kind or trumpet, prescribed by Monteverdi in Orfeo.

Quintposaune (Ger.). Tromabone pitched fifth below tenor trombone in a flat; i.e. bass trombone in E flat.

Quintruple Time. 5 beats, usually crotches, in bar, i.e. 5/4 time.

Quintuplet. A group of 5 notes (or notes and rests) of equal time value, written where a group of 3, 4, or some other number of notes is suggested by the time-signature.

Quodlibet. The piece containing several popular tunes put together in unusual and (usually) ingenious fashion.

R

R. Abbr. For right, as in r.h., right hand (in piano music, etc.).

R. Abbrev. of Respond.

R. Symbol in Tonic sol-fa for the second degree (supertonic) of the scale, pronounced ray.

Racket, Rackett or Ranket. A double reed woodwind instrument which consists of solid body pierced by number of parallel vertical channels, connected alternately at top and bottom so as to form continuous tube. Holes pierced in side made limited scale available.

Racket (t). A double-reed wind instrument of various sizes.

Raddoppiamento (It.). Means 'doubling', usually to indidcate doubling of bass at octave below.

Radio-synthetic Organ. Electronic organ in which electrical waves are converted to sound.

Raga. Basically, Indian scale, but term refers more widely to piece of music which has raga as its basis, and whose mood and atmosphere is determined by constant use of certain notes of raga. Each piece has its own fixed scale material, used without modulation throughout performance.

A raga can be sung for hours together if the artist is a high class singer or an instrument player. A raga is very pleasing to the ears and if sung with effort, creating proper atmosphere, it can make the listeners spell-bound. The words used, to sing a raga, are occasionally 'ta-na-ri-na' of 'akara', only.

A raga must have at least five notes in it. There are three jatis connecting to this which I shall explain here. The three main heads are –

(1) Sampurna jati (7) notes (full).

(2) Shadav jati (6) notes (one less).

(3) Oudav jati (5) notes (two less).

These three heads are again sub-divided into six kinds: -

(1) A raga containing all the seven notes of the scale in order is known as the 'Sampurna'.

(2) If it takes six notes only, it is called 'Shadav' variety.

(3) If it takes five swaras only, it is knows as 'Qudav' order.

When all these varieties are mixed up together the following varieties are formed—

(1) When swaras of both "Aroh" (ascent) and "Avaroh" (descent) take all the seven notes both ways, it is called a Sampurna-Sampurna jati.

(2) When a raga takes all the seven notes while ascending and leaves out any one note out of the seven, while descending, it is known as Sampurna-Shadav jati.

(3) When all the seven notes are in the ascending and two notes are dropped out while descending, it is known as a "Sampurna-Oudav jati".

(4) When a raga omits any one of the notes out of the seven, while ascending and uses all the seven notes while descending, it is called "Shadav-Sampurna".

(5) When a raga leaves out any one note both in the ascending and in the descending, then it is called "Shadav-Shadav jati".

(6) And if while ascending, there are six notes and in the descending there are only five notes then it is called "Shadav-Oudav jati".

(7) Oudav-Sampurna jati takes five notes while ascending and seven notes in the descending.

(8) When a raga takes five notes while ascending and uses six notes for descending, it is called Oudav-Shadav jati.

(9) For an Oudav—Oudav jati we must take only five notes, both while ascending as well as in descending.

We have already earlier that two notes of the same kind should not be used consecutively one after the other.

R G M D and N notes sometimes are sung as flat notes and sometimes as sharp notes.

But there are also some ragas which contain both Ma's both Ni's or both Ri's as the case may be. These are exceptions. Of course, great care must be taken while singing such ragas which have two notes of the same denomination. It is not an easy feat to sing these prohibited notes without spoiling the beauty of the ragas. Only persons with thorough knowledge of this art will be able to render it correctly. If all artists who do not posses sufficient knowledge of music also try to sing ragas like this, it will sound unmusical and unpleasant. Great care and caution is necessary.

A Diagram showing the Jatis of Ragas

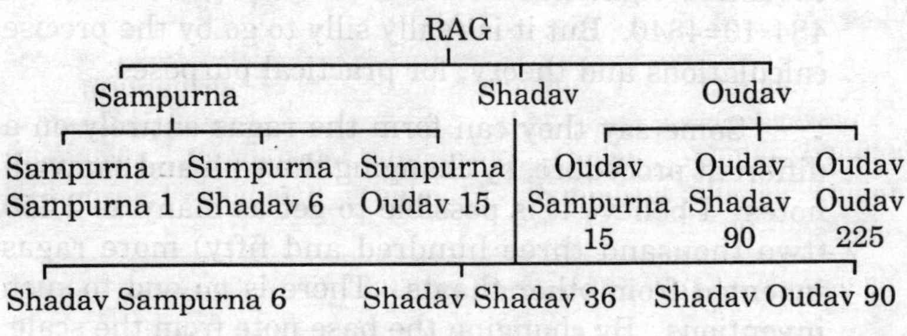

The above diagram shows the exact number of ragas which are easily produced from each jati.

(1) Sampurna-Sampurna is able to produce only one raga as indicated from the diagram.

(2) Six ragas are produced from Sampurna-Shadav jati.

(3) Fifteen ragas are produced from Sampurna-Oudav jati.

(4) Shadav-Sampurna jati produces six ragas.

(5) As many as thirty-six kinds of ragas are produced in the Shadav-Shadav variety 6×6=36.

(6) A large number of ragas derive out of Shadav—Oudav jati, which are ninety in number 6×15=90 as shown in the diagram.

(7) Oudav-Sampurna again gets only fifteen ragas.

(8) In the Oudav-Shadav jati another ninety ragas are formed.

(9) The largest number of ragas are formed in the Oudav-Oudav jati. 15×15=225. Two hundred and twenty-five ragas. Thus in this process we are able to produce 484 (four hundred and eighty four) ragas, that have sprung only from the Suddha notes,i.e. Bilawal thaat.

So, according to this theory, from the above-stated ten thaats of Hindustani system, we can get 4,840 (four thousand eight hundred and forty) ragas in all, i.e. 484×10=4840. But it is really silly to go by the precise calculations and theory, for practical purposes.

Some say they can form the ragas entirely on a different procedure, by changing the vadi and samvadi notes. I believe it is possible to get as many as 2,350 (two thousand three hundred and fifty) more ragas invented from other thaats. There is no end to such inventions. By changing the base note from the scale, we can get many new ragas. But I do not know how far these will be correct. For a theoretical purpose it may be interesting but if you have to observe everything in an orthodox way even in the practical purposes not much melody will be left.

RAGAS AND THE TIMINGS

The association of ragas with some particular seasons and timings had been a peculiar aspects of music. This is observed more in the North and is not so strictly followed in the South. In the Karnatak music they are not very particular now and they sing any raga at any time of the day or night.

But strangely enough for some reason or the other, the Karnataka raga Bhupalam, corresponding to the Hindustani vibhas, alone is always sung in the early hours of the morning even today in the South. All the songs composed specially for waking up of people at the time of sunrise, are set in this raga.

The musicians of the North in earlier days were more strict and orthodox about the fixed timings for Ragas than they are today.

According to our ancient Shastras also, each raga takes a particular form, with the change of time and season.

In addition to morning, afternoon, and evening and night ragas, there are Sandhi Prakash ragas also. These are sung only at the appointed hour and period, just before we enter morning (sunrise time) or into evening from the noon, (sunset time or dusk). There are midnight ragas and very early morning ragas too. But these rules are being relaxed now to a great extent.

The reason for this timing system of the raga to be retained so long in the North, was again due to the Persian influence they say.

It is believed that in Persia, Iraq and Iran this system of associating the ragas with particular timings of the day was prevalent. And naturally when they became our rulers, they were happy to find this system already in existence here.

Actually this system originated in India, and was somehow carried to those countries by trade through businessman on account of the two-way traffic. They liked the fixation of timings for the ragas and adapted it into their system and retained it.

Gradually the southern system which never had the influence of foreigners from those lands to the same extent, let it fade off.

There is a feeling that these ragas if sung specifically at the correct timings allotted to each, will have a special appeal on the listener's minds.

The following are a few ragas as examples: —

	Morning	*Noon*	*Evening*	*Night*
(1)	Bhairavi	Sarang varieties	Bhimplasi	Purya (later in the evening)
(2)	Bhirav	Desi	Purya Dhanashri	Khamaj Suddha-Kalyan
(3)	Hindol	Gunkali	Patdeep	Kamod
(4)	Jaunpuri		Pilu	Shankara
(5)	Todi		Multani	Behag
(6)	Bilawal			Bhageshri Molkouns Darbari

Some Sandhi Prakash Ragas are: —

Rag Lalit.........Early morning (before sunrise)

„ Ramkali „ „

Rag Shri.........Dusk time (sunset)

„ Marwar „ „

„ Purvi....... „ „

PORTRAYALS OR FORMS OF SOME OF THE RAGAS

It is queer to notice, how in our Indian music a picture of a particular raga formed in the mind's eye of the listener.

When a raga is being played on any instrument or sung vocally, a visual picture is formed according to the natural and the emotional sentiment and qualities of the music presented.

These musical pictures are portrayed in the most fascinating exquisite and expressive forms, symbolising the emotion thereby created and personifying each raga in its own splendour and glory.

It is the effect of the combination of notes which appear as the imaginary visual pictures and it is human reaction of either joy or sorrow of life being experienced.

Sometimes even a single note can express an emotional feeling. For instance, 'Sa', they say is a sound of joy. So is also 'pa'.

But Re, when produced by a cow, searching for, its calf, has a tinge of sadness in it. A peacock's 'Dha' at moments gives a feeling of trouble and creates an atmosphere of gloominess. A nightingale at spring time gives happy notes, feelings of joy and reunion.

Of course these visual pictures very according to one's own mood. It is not possible to give any literal translation of the raga in picture form accurately. Many ragas have changed their forms and the descriptions are not identical in every case. It is difficult to trace its origin now. However, these descriptions enable us to form the powerful associations of music with particular sentiments and moods and particular seasons of the year etc.

Indeed it is interesting to note how fundamental to Indian conception these ragas and raginis have acquired personalities of their own, can been from the few descriptions given below.

These descriptions as given here are by no means the accepted ones. Considerables difference of opinion on this subject has been raised among the scholars and art critics. Each one tries to present his own mental picture.

Raga "Ranjayati Ragh". It is so goes the Sanskrit saying, that means music which mainly consists of a raga (melody) must be pleasant, soothing, appealing and melodious to the listener. Otherwise, it is not music. If too much stress is given to the theory part of music with all mathematical calculations, the sweetness and charm goes.

"Yoyam dhwani Viseshastu Swara Varna Vibhushitah Ranjako jana Chittanam Saragaha Kashyate budhaihi".

A raga is a combination of swaras which has the pleasing effect on the listeners' minds. It is a melody consisting of Aroha and Avaroha, (ascent and descent, without which the raga cannot be formed. A thaat is the source of a raga:

(1) A raga must have at least five notes out of the seven notes in the scale.

(2) Two notes of swaras of the same nature, such as two Ri's or two Ni's or two G's must not come.

(3) Ma and Pa which are the Jeeva swaras cannot be omitted simultaneously. Either the Ma or the Pa, one of them must be there.

(4) A raga must have the ascending and the descending forms which are called the

combinations of 'Aroha' and 'Avaroha' Kramas. It must have "vadi and samvadi notes", which also must belong to the same thaat, to which the raga concerned is attached.

Nowadays, we find some musicians composing or inventing new ragas—missing both the Ma and Pa swaras. Of course that is not so far approved by the scholars.

So, we now know that a raga must derive from a parent scale and it must contain all the above-mentioned qualities to form into a raga.

Ragmala. There are 'ragamalas' consisting of a series of ragas all linked up into one composition. It is a string of melodies—meaning a garland of ragas. This sort of composition is more common in South India where these are commonly known as Ragamalikas.

Ragamalikas. Just like the ragamalika varnams mentioned earlier, these are ragamalika kritis, that is, a chain or a garland of ragas. These compositions contain different ragas in different sections. At the end of each raga swara singing also is done.

Even Slokas or poems can be sung in a ragamalika style, by changing the raga after every stanza. This is a common feature in the South Indian music.

These ragamalikas are lively and most enjoyable. In most of the ragamalikas the name of the raga, at the end of the charana, is sung. This gives the lakshana also in brief about the raga, and the listeners enjoy this immensely.

For instance, Nitya Kalyani a ragamalikas, a typical composition in eight different ragas, composed by one Sita Ramiah, is a very popular piece of a ragamalika.

There are many other ragamalika composition by several composers. Of all these, the noted Sata

Ragaratnamala of Thyagaraja himself, in hundred different ragas, is believed to be the most precious of all. The name of the raga and other lakshanas incorporated in this composition of Thyagaraja is an outstanding example.

It is of interest, to mention here, that there are ragamalikas combined with Tala Malikas too. Each section of song changes its metre. This is a unique example which explains the skill and the creative talents and the imagination of the composer. The names of the raga and tala also are incorporated in the sahitya.

Ragtime. The name given to an early type of jazz, particularly associated with piano-playing with characteristic syncopations.

Rank. A set of pipes belonging to one stop on organ. Word is most often used in connection with Mutation Stops; thus, mixture is referred to as 3-rank or 4-rank according to number of pipes which sound for each note.

Ranks. The 2 strings which are tuned to same note on instruments or like family.

Rant. Term applied to a wide range of 17th century English dances.

Ranz Des Vaches. Type of Swiss tune (name means 'cow-rank') sounded vocally or on an alphorn to call the cows; incorporated.

Rasa. Rasa is only what one experiences, i.e. Anubhuti. Just as a man is pleased with the taste of some delicious eat, we also get that emotional sentiment which comes according to the mental mood and experience then felt. These sentiments were of eight kinds.

Sringara, Hasya, Karuna, Roudra, Vira, Bhayanaka, Bibhatsa and Adbhuta. These are the same as already mentioned earlier. Later on, the ninth rasa also originated and formed a part of these rasas as Shanta rasa (peace).

Rataplan. Term for solos or ensembles in opera which have character of military march.

Rattle. The Ratched noise-making device which is occasionally used as an orchestral percussion instrument.

Ray. In Tonic sol-fa, the spoken name for the second degree (super-tonic) of the scale, written r. Dp. Re.

Real. Term used in opposition to tonal in special senses.

Realism. The stylistic term of at least two meanings:

(1) The use in opera of characterization and stories based on contemporary life as it is actually observed (not forgetting 'life in the raw').

(2) The philosophic attitude of mind considered 'correct' for composers under Soviet officialdom—showing optimism, sympathy with 'the people', to a desire to be comprehensible, an avoidance of such faults as 'Formalism', etc.;

Realize. To work out in full and artistically such music as was originally left by its composer in a sparsely-notated condition.

Rebec (k). The obsolete (medieval and later) bowed instrument with in 3 or 4 strings, a forerunner of the violin.

Recapitulation. A section of a composition which repeats themes which were originally presented in an earlier section but have interveningly undergone 'development'.

Recital. Refers for musical performance, usually by solosists or duettists, rarely by larger combinations.

Recitative. Refers to the type of speech-like singing which is written in ordinary notation but in which a certain freedom in rhythm (and sometimes also in pitch) is allowed in performance; used particularly in opera, oratorio etc. as preliminary to a (so 'recitative and air', etc.) and for dialogue.

Reciting Note. Refers to the note on which intermediate words of each verse of psalm are sung in plainsong. It is dominant of Mode in which psalm-tone is written.

Recorder. Type of woodwind instrument, without reed which was much used in 16th-18th centuries but ousted by the more powerfully toned 'ordinary' flute, which it resembles except for being blown at the end and held downwards instead of crosswise.

Recte Et Retro. The use of a theme performed normally, in counter point with that same theme performed backward.

Reduction. The arrangement (e.g. for piano) of piece of music that reduces or simplifies composer's original scoring.

Reed. A vibrating 'tongue' of thin cane or metal, used to set the air-column vibrating in certain types of mouth-blown wind instruments, certain organ pipes, etc.

Reed-organ. The name covering many instruments, both old and modern, which have no pipes and use free-beating reads (one for each note) to produce their notes.

Reed Stops. The organ stops controlling reed pipes.

Reel. The quick dance for two or more couples—found chiefly in Scotland, Ireland, Scandinavia, and N. America.

Reel. The dance which is practised in northern countries of Europe, in which dancers stand face to face and perform figures of eight. Music is usually in quick 4/4 time and in regular 4-bar phrases.

Refrain. The lines in song that recur at the end of each verse, usually set to same music.

Regal. Type of small portable keyboard instrument of Reed-organ type (15th-17th centuries); in church it was employed to regulate the singing.

Reggae. Type of West Indian popular music having 4 beats to the bar, upbeat being strongly ascented.

Register.

(1) A set of organ pipes which are controlled by one particular stop; so to register a piece for the organ is to select the stops appropriate to it;

(2) Part of an instrument's compass appearing to have a distinct tone-quality of its own, e.g., the Chalumeau register of the clarinet;

(3) A part of the compass of the voice giving its own distinctive sensation to the singer.

Registration. Art of choosing and combining stops in organ playing. Indications given by composer may incl. changes of manual, particular type of solo stop, or relative weight of sound.

Related. The term which is describing harmonic relationship between keys. Thus D major and A major are closely related, because latter is dominant of former and there is difference of only one sharp between key—signatures. On the other hand, relationships between B major and E flat major is more distinct, and thus modulation between them would be harder to achieve.

Relative. The term which is used to indicate the fact that a common key-signature is shared by one major and one minor key: e.g. E minor is termed the relative minor of G major and G major as the relative major of E minor, both having a key-signature of one sharp, and modulations between them being accordingly of a simple kind.

Reminiseence Motive. A recurring theme in an opera identified with a character or emotion, etc.

Renaissance. The term used by music historians to denote a period of style between 'medieval' and Baroque—from early 15th century (e.g. Dunstable, Dufay) to early 17th.

Renaissance Music. The term flexibly used to refer to music composed from about the middle of the 15th century, to the early of the 17th century. The word 'Renaissance' referred particularly to the revival of the ideas of antiquity, but in music this aspect did not become important until towards the end of the period, mainly because of the lack of examples of Greek music.

Repeat (noun). A section of a composition which is having a repetition of a pervious section. To save the space of writing out the passage again, such a repetition is indicated by pairs of dots (called repeat marks) and a double bar. On reaching these the performer repeats from the previous pair of dots or (if there is none) from the beginning.

Repetiteur. The coach, generally in opera house, who teaches singers their parts.

Repetition (Fr.). Rehearsal, Repetition general, dress rehearsal.

Reprise. Refers to a re-taking-up, particularly a return to the first section of a composition after an intervening and contrasting section, or (in an operetta or musical, etc.) the further occurrence of a song which has already been heard.

Resolution. The term used in harmony for process by which discord progresses to concord.

Resonance. The term used for the creation by vibrating body of vibration in another body. Occurs in form of:

(1) Sympathetic vibrations in such cases as tuning forks of same pitch;

(2) Sung note acting on free strings of piano;

(3) Stopped string on violin acting on open string of same pitch;

(4) Overtones of vibrating string on piano acting on corresponding higher strings when sustaining pedal is held down.

Respond, Responsory. The term used for the plainsong chant sung by chorus alternating with one or more solo verses.

Rest. The term used for the notation of an absence of sound in a performer's part for a length of time corresponding to a given number of beats or bars. So eighth-note (quaver) rest, two bars, rest, etc.

Resultant Tone. The name given to either of two acoustical phenomena:

(1) When two loud notes are sounded, another note may sometimes also be heard, lower in pitch, which corresponds to the difference in vibration between the original two and is called 'differential tone';

(2) Another note, higher than the original two, may also be heard. Corresponding to the sum of their vibrations ('summational tone').

Retardation. The term used for Suspension in which dissonant note is resolved upwards rather than downwards.

Retrograde. The term used of a theme when performed backwards a device prominently used e.g. in the Middle Ages, in Bach's 'The Art of Fugue', and in Twelve-note technique.

Retrograde Motion. The use of retrograde, i.e. backwards, motion has been applied in composition both to melodies (melody is played backwards), as contrapuntal device, and to entire textures, as formal device.

Returning Note. The cambiata in which movement is back to original note.

R.H. Right hand.

Rhapsody. The title given by 19th, 20th-century, composers to instrumental works of heroic, national, or rhetorical character.

Rhythm. Refers to that aspect of music concerned not with pitch but with the distribution notes in time and their accentuation.

Rhythmicon. The term used for the electrical instrument incorporating photo-electric cell invented by Leon Theremin and Henry Cowell. Although possessing keyboard it is concerned not with pitch but with producing cross-rhythms, esp. couplex ones. Has character, therefore, of percussion instrument.

Ricercar. The term used in general sense of essay or study as title of certain instrumental compositions. Many are in imitative polyphony. Ricercar is based on one or more themes of rather abstract character, is usually in 4/2 time, and is not clearly distinguishable in style from contrapuntal Fantasia.

Ricochet. The kind of bowing in which upper part of bow is thrown on strings, producing rapid series of bouncing notes on down bow.

Riddle Canon. The canon in which composer deliberately supplies only one part, leaving it to performer to decide where and at what pitch other parts enter.

Rigadoon, Rigaudon. The term use for the old French dance of a lively nature in 2/4 or 4/4 time.

Rinforzando (It., reinforcing)**.** Refers to the direction that volume is to suddenly increased on a particular note or chord or a small series of these.

Rinforzando. The sudden strong accent on note or chord. More or less the same as sforzando.

Ripieno. Term refers to full body of orchestra, as distinct from soloist or group of soloists (concertino).

Ripresa (It.)**.** 'Repeat':

(1) Dance movt. for lute in form of variation;

(2) In later music, any Repeat of recapitulation.

Rispetto. Italian improvised folk-poem with inter-rhyming lines, sung to popular tunes.

Risposta (It.).

(1) Answer in Fugue or Imitation;

(2) Comes in canon.

Risvegliato (It.). In an animated (or re-animated) manner.

Ritardando (It.). Becoming gradually slower—equivalent of rallentando.

Ritenuto (It.). Held back (as to tempo)—effectively the same as Ritardando.

Ritmo (It.). The rhythm; ritmo di tre battute, in a rhythm of three bars (i.e. three bars are treated as forming a rhythmical unit).

Ritornello. A recurring passage e.g. an instrumental passage always occurring between the verses of a song; so also a passage for full orchestra (without soloist) in a baroque or later concerto, thought of as 'coming round again' even though the material may not all be literally repeated. Hence ritornello form, as of a movement based on such recurrences (in various keys), e.g. the opening movement of the classical concerto.

Rock. Type of popular music (originating from 'rock'n' roll') which from US roots has spread over the Western world since about 1950—based on solo voice and guitars (mainly electric), and mainly diffused by gramophone recording. Rock'n' roll is now applied only to a sub-type, with particular rhythmic and other features. Fusions with other popular music are indicated by such terms as folk-rock and jazz-rock. The terms pop overlaps but is not quite synonymously used; to rock practitioners, 'pop' may denote a more commercialised more juvenile, and more easily assimilable product than 'rock'.

Rock Music. See rock.

Rock'n' Roll. See preceding.

Rohrflote. Organ stop of flute type; pipe is stopped at one end, but stopper is pierced by hole, in which metal tube or chimney is inserted.

Rohrwerk (Ger.). The reed stops on organ.

Roll. A very rapid succession of notes on a drum, approximating to a continuous sound. The technique varies between types of drum; on the side drum each hand gives a double stroke.

Romance. The title used occasionally—and somewhat vaguely – for lyrical piece of instrumental or vocal music.

Romanesca. The particular harmonic bass line used as basis for variations in same way as was Passamezzo bass, which differs from romanesca only in first note.

Romantic Music. The romantic era in music may be dated c 1820-c 1920. Broadly, change from classical age to romantic may be described as change of emphasis from universal to individual, from conservative to liberal, and from abstract to poetic.

Rondeau (Fr.). A musical (and/or poetic) form suggestive of a circle or of recurrence.

Rondo. The form of instrumental music with recurring section. May occur as single piece, or more often as last movement of sonata, symphony or concerto.

Root. The lowest note of a chord when that chord is in what is regarded as its 'basic' position—e.g. for the chord of C major (C, E, G) the root is C, which is regarded as the basic note of the chord.

Rosalia. The name sometimes given to a 'real Sequence'.

Rosin. Hard brittle resin, applied to bows of violin family to increase friction (and hence sonority) between hairs of bow and strings.

Rotary Valve. The special type of brass instrument valve.

Rote, Rotte, Rota or Rotta. The medieval instrument of

Lyre type, similar to Crwth.

Roulade. The ornamental vocal phrase, usually quite extended and traditionally (though not invariably) consisting of descending scale with intermediate notes rising by one degree.

Round. The type of short vocal 'perpetual Canon' in which the voices, entering in turn, all sing the melody at the same pitch (or at the octave).

Rovescio, Al. This may refer to either:

(1) A passage that can be performed backwards, or

(2) A type of Canon in which an upward interval in the original voice becomes a downwards interval (of the same distance) in the imitating voice, and vice versa.

Rubato. To be performed with a certain freedom as to time, for the purpose of giving the music suitable expression.

Ruggiero. Internationally known balled and dance tune of late 16th, early 17th centuries. Bass was used as pattern for variations and for new melodies in same way as were Passamezzo and Romanesca.

Rule of the Octave. The simple rule for harmonizing bass rising and descending stepwise through octave, used in teaching harmony in 18th century.

Rumba. Cuban dance in 8/8 time (3+3+2) which became established in ballroom dancing in USA and Europe about 1930. Occassional use in concert music – Jamaican Rumba.

Russian Bassoon. Brass instrument with cup mouthpiece, unrelated to bassoon, which paved way for and was then ousted by Ophicleida, Fingering was similar to that of Serpent.

Ruthe (Ger.). Refers to kind of birch occasionally used on bass drum, often while ordinary stick beats on other head.

S

S. Abbr. of Schmieder (in numbering Bach's works).

S. The symbol in Tonic Sol-Fa for the fifth degree (dominant) of the scale, pronounced soh.

Sackbut. An early English name for the trombone. (It is also used in older biblical translations for an instrument which cannot be identified with the trombone).

Salicional, Salicet, Salcional. Refers to soft 8ft metal organ-stop producing tone bearing some resemblance to that of string instruments.

Saltarello, Salterello. Type of Italian dance: in its most common meaning, a lively dance incorporating jumps, the music similar to Tarantella but not so smoothly flowing.

Samba. The term used for the dance of Brazilian origin, basically in 2/4 time but with syncopated rhythmic patterns. Traditional form of carnival music in Brazil, where it is danced by groups forming circle. In ballroom, danced by couples at more moderate tempo.

Sangeet. It is technical term generally used for vocal instrumental and dance music. It is impossible to separate them, although they are quite different in their characteristics from one another. Each has its own individual charm.

Now let us know them one by one:

Vocal music is what is sung by persons and which pleases the ears and refreshes the brain and carries the listener (if the music is good) to the realms of divinity and perfection.

Instrumental music also, if played well is pleasant to listen and can make the mind calm to remove all worries with its sweet melodious notes.

Dance. This third one is the one which attracts the eye first with rhythmic poses, combined with melodious background music and which makes the audience (spectators) thrilled and elevated.

Thus all these three arts jointly are known as Sangeet. This has been coming down from generation to generation and was very much appreciated and enjoyed by one and all throughout the universe alike.

Our ancient authors said in one of the old treatises about the appreciation of this art:

"Geyate Pariyate devah ssarwangah Parwati Pathihi Gopipatirannrtopi Vamasa dhwani vasamgatim Sama Geetirato Brahma, veena satya Saraswati Kimate Yaksha Gandharwa seva Danava Manava".

The combination of these beautiful notes or tunes have enchanting effect even on animal and reptiles like snakes, elephants, horses and cows, etc.

Sarabande (Fr.). The dance in slow 3/2 or 3/4 time, one of regular dances of Suite. Orig. seems to have been introduced from East to Spain.

Sardana (Sp.). The national dance of Catalonia, often in fast 6/8 time and performed in circle of pipe and drum accompaniment.

Sargams. These are only simple compositions set in tal, in simple swaras (notes) in each particular raga, like the alankaras, but in a simpler way, to enable the beginner to learn the fundamentals of a raga. This helps them to gain the correct "Swarajnana".

Sarngadeva (1169-1247). Sarnga Deva belonged to a Kashmiri Pundit family. He was a great scholar of Sanskrit and music and was the author of Sangeeta Ratnakara and Adhyatmika Viveka, etc.

His book Sangeeta Ratnakara consisted of seven chapters, each chapter dealing with different aspects of music elaborately.

We owe much of our knowledge to this eminent scholar's contribution as we often refer to his works even in the musical world of today.

Sarnga Deva lived some time during the period between 1169 and 1247 A.D. in the reign of Simhala Maharaja at Devagiri now known as Daulatabad.

Sarod. Indian stringed instrument, usually bowed but sometimes plucked; it usually has 4 strings but there may also be 8-12 sympathetic strings.

Sarrusophone. The family of double reed brass instruments with wide conical bore.

Satz. Term of several different musical applications in German, including:

(1) A musical setting; a composition;

(2) A movement;

(3) A theme or subject—so Hauptsatz, main theme; Nebensatz, subsidiary theme.

Saudades. Portuguese (plural) word of uncertain origin, but carrying the implication of wistful remembrance of things past.

Sausage Bassoon. An alternative and more informal name for the Racket(t).

Sautille. Type of bowing on the violin, etc., in which the bow springs rebound off the stirng.

Saw, Musical. Hand-saw held between knees and played with bow while left hand alters pitch by bending blade.

Saxhorn. The family of instrument spatented by Adolphe Sax in 1845. Invention resulted from application of valves instead of keys to Bugle family. Made in at least 7 sizes.

Saxophone. The name of a family of wind instruments having a reed resembling a clarinet's – and therefore classified among the Woodwind (not 'brass') despite a metal body. Invented by A. Sax about 1840. Made in various sizes, the lower-pitched ones in S-shapes or with additional curves (the alto exists in both S-shaped and straight forms).

Scale. A progression of single notes upwards or downwards in 'steps'. So scalic—e.g. 'a scalic figure', progressing upwards or downwards in steps.

Scat Singing. The jazz term for use of nonsense syllables and others wordless effects in course of vocal number.

Scena (It.). 'Scene':

(1) Stage (of theatre);

(2) Dramatic scene in opera, consisting of extended aria, usually of dramatic character;

(3) Concert piece for solo voice with accompaniment, similar in character to (2).

Schellen (Ger.). Jingles, sleigh-bells.

Scherzando (It.). Refers to playfully, in a light-hearted fashion.

Scherzando. Refers to direction that an impression light-heartedness is to be given. Cp. Scherzo.

Scherzo (It., joke). A type of lively movement which historically—chiefly through Haydn, and, especially, Beethoven—developed from the minuet as used in symphonies, string quartets, etc.

Schlaginstrumente (Ger.). The percussion instruments.

Schlagzither (Ger.). Type of Zither in which strings, instead of being plucked, are struck with hammers. In fact more like dulcimar than zither.

Schmetternd. Indication to horn players to use harsh, brassy tone.

Schnabelflote (Ger.). Obsolete name for Recorder.

Schottische. Type of ballroom dance similar to polka, popular in the 19th century. The origin of the name is unknown; the dance is not the same as the Ecossaise, despite the name.

Schrammel Quartet. Type of Austrian light-music combination of 2 violins, guitar, and accordion.

Scoop. The colloquial term for a fault in singing – to glide up to a note disagreeably from below instead of attacking it cleanly.

Scordatura. The tuning of stringed instrument to notes other than the normal, for special effect.

Scordatura (It.). Term used for tuning of stringed instrument to abnormal notes, for sake to effects.

Score. A Music-copy combining in ordered from all the different Parts allotted to various performers of a piece; so (e.g. in an orchestral library) score and parts, meaning both the combined music-copy (for the conductor) and the separate copies containing just the music for particular instruments.

Scotch Snap. The name for a rhythmic figure consisting of a short note on the beat followed by a longer one held until the next beat, e.g. Found in Scottish folk-music, but also elsewhere, e.g. in Hungarian folk-music, and in Purcell (as in the setting of English words like 'ruin'd').

Sec (Fr., dry). The direction that a note or chord is to be struck and released sharply.

Second. Refers to the Interval of semitone (minor second e.g. G-A flat), tone (major second *e.g.* G—A), or tone and a half (augmented second *e.g.* G-A sharp) when 2 notes concerned are having adjacent letter names.

Secondary Dominant. The 'dominant of the dominant', e.g. D in key of C (G being dominant).

Segue. The term used as a direction to the performer to proceed with the next section without a break.

Seguidilla. Type of quick Spanish dance in triple time, often accompanied by castanets.

Seikilos Song. The term used for one of few surviving examples of Greek music, inscribed on tomb of Seikilos (2nd or 1st century, BC) at Tralles in Asia Minor.

Semi-Chorus. A section of a choral body – not necessarily exactly half of the full chorus.

Semidemisemiquaver. An unusual equivalent of hemidemisemiquaver.

Semihemidemisemiquaver. The note with half time value of Hemidemisemiquaver, and 128th time value of semibreve.

Semi-opera. The modern term for certain 17th-and 18th-century English stage works (particularly Purcell's, e.g. 'King Arthur') in which music, although a principal element, is not so all-pervading as to justify the title of 'opera' as now understood.

Semiquaver. The note with half time value of quaver, and sixteenth time value of semibreve.

Semitone. Half a tone—smallest interval in regular use in western music. Can be regarded either as augmented unison (e.g. interval between G and G sharp) or as minor second (e.g. G and A flat) according to context. In Equal Temperament there are 12 equal semitones in octave.

Septet

(1) A performing group of 7 instrumentalists or singers;

(2) A composition for such: if instrumental, and actually entitled 'Septet', it will probably have the character of a Sonata for 7 performers, in several movements.

Septuplet. A group of 7 notes (or notes and rests) of equal time-value, written where a group of 3, 4, or some other number of notes is suggested by the time– signature, e.g. a 7-note group occupying a bar of 3/4 time.

Sequence. Refers to the repetition of a phrase at a higher or lower pitch then the original.

Serenade. Properly a piece of open-air evening music (cp. Aubade), e.g. lower's song outside his mistress's window, but now a term of the widest and vaguest significance.

Serenata. Title used in early 18th century for secular cantata or short opera written in homage to patron.

Serialism. The method of composition deriving from Schoenberg's Twelve – note System.

Series. Refers to the succession of notes presented in certain order, not necessarily to create melody, but to establish relationship between them.

Serpent. The obsolete wind instrument, bass of cornet family. Name was suggested by shape. Made of wood covered with leather.

Sesquialtera. A type of Mixture stop on the organ.

Seventh. Refers to Interval comprising first and last of any series of 7 notes in diatonic scale e.g. F – E. Major seventh is semitone less than octave e.g. C – B Minor seventh is tone less than octave e.g. C – B flat. Diminished seventh is 1½ tones less than octave e.g. C sharp – B flat. Since seventh is dissonance, chord containing seventh required resolution in traditional harmony. Most important chords containing sevenths are Dominant seventh and Diminished Seventh chords.

Sextet

(1) A performing group of 6 instrumentalists or singers:

(2) A piece for 6 performers; if instrumental, and actually entitled sextet, it will probably have the character of a Sonata for 6 performers, in several movements.

Sextolet, Sextuplet. The group of 6 notes to be performed on time of 4.

Sextúplet. A group of 6 notes (or notes and rests) of equal time- value, written where a group of 4, 5 or some other number of notes would be suggested by the time – signature, e.g. a group of 6 notes occupying a bar of 4/4.

Sfogato. Term used by Chopin and others to indicate any quality of playing.

Sforzando, Sforzato (It.). Giving strong accent on single note of chord.

Sfp. Abbr – signifying that a Sforzaddo is to be followed by a (sudden) softness of tone.

Sforzando, Sforzato. Refers to direction that a note or chord is to be played in a 'forced' manner, i.e. with special emphasis.

Shakuhachi. Type of Japanese end-blown bamboo flute.

Shankar, Ravi. Indian musician. One of greatest exponents of Sitar, has done much to arouse Western interest in India music.

Shanty. The word-song sung by sailors in days of sailing ships. Usually have decided rhythm and are in form of solo verses and chorus.

Sharp. The term indicating a raising in pitch – either:

(1) Indeterminately, as when a singer is said to sing sharp, by mistake; or

(2) Precisely by a semitone.

Sharp Mixture. The organ stops sounding high harmonics in addition to fundamental note, so giving bright tone ('sharp' refers to tone quality, not pitch).

Shawm. The obsolete double-reed woodwind instrument, forerunner of the oboe; made in several sizes, the larger (lower-pitched) ones being called Bombard or pommer.

Shepherd's Pipe. The primitive double reed wind instrument. Resembles bagpipe chanter.

Shift

(1) Change of position of left hand on stringed instrument;

(2) Change of position of slide of trombone.

Shofar, Shophar. Ancient Jewish wind instrument still used in synagogue. Make from ram's horn. Notes are produced in same way as on bugle.

Short Octave. The lowest notes on keyboard instruments in 16th, 17th centuries were often arranged so as to provide within compass of sixth (short octave) bass notes normally required, leaving out those which did not occur on account of restricted range of keys used.

Shoulder-viol. The viol midway in size between that of viola da braccio (arm viol) and viola da gamba (leg viol). It was played held in front of the body, and sometimes fastened to it. This made it suitable for playing while walking.

Shruti. It originates from the Sanskrit word shru to hear, meaning any sound that is capable of distinctly being heard by the ear.

From the time of our ancient scholars, it is quite clear that these were primarily selected for the purpose of fixing the scales. The names of twenty- two shrutis are mentioned in Bharata's Natyashastra, Sangeeta Ratnakara and Sangeeta Parijata, etc. almost in the same manner. But Bhavabhatta's Anupa Sangeeta Vilas gave a different set of names for these twenty-two (22) Shrutis.

The following tables will show us the different names of Shrutis, by its increasing order of pitch:

Chart Showing

Bharata and Sarngadeva's names of Shrutis

1.	2.	3.	4.	*Sapta Swaras*
Teevra.	Kumudavati.	Manda.	Chandovati.	Shadja.
	5.	6.	7.	
	Dayavati.	Ranjani.	Ratika.	Rishaba.
		8.	9.	
		Roudri.	Kordha.	Gandhara.
10.	11.	12.	13.	
Vajrika.	Prasarini.	Priti.	Marjani.	Madhyama.
14.	15.	16.	17.	
Kshiti.	Rakta.	Sandipini.	Alapini.	Panchama.
	18.	19.	20.	
	Madanti.	Rohini.	Ramya.	Dhaivata.
		21.	22.	
		Ugra.	Kshobhini.	Nishada.

Bhavabhatta's 22 Shrutis Chart showing names

1.	2.	3.	4.	
Nandana.	Nishkala.	Guda.	Sakala.	Shadja.
	5.	6.	7.	
	Madhura.	Lalita.	Kakshara.	Rishabha.
	8.	9.		
	Bhragajati.	Hraswagiti.		Gandhara.

10. Ranjika.	11. Chapara.	12. Purna.	13. Alankarani.	Madhyama.
14. Vainika.	15. Valitha.	16. Trishthana.	17. Suswara.	Panchama.
	18. Soumya.	19. Bhashangika.	20. Vartika.	Dhaivata.
		21. Vyapaka.	22. Subhaga.	Nishada

Siciliana (It.). Type of song or instrumental piece derived presumably from some Sicilian dance: much cultivated in the 18th century, it is in slow 6/8 (or sometimes 12/8) time usually in a minor key.

Side Drum. The cylindrically shaped drum, also called snare drum: smallest drum normally used in orchestra. Snares made of gut or metal are stretched across lower of 2 parchment heads, giving drum its characteristic rattling sound; snares can be thrown out of action instantly, giving totally different tone.

Sight. The system used for teaching choristers to descant, i.e. to extemporize simple part to go with plainsong melody. Singer imagined his notes to be on same staff as plainsong (tenor) but sang them at pitch suitable to compass of his voice. Thus, to treble descanter, who sang octave above his 'sight' pitch, third below plainsong in 'sight' actually sounded sixth above plainsong.

Sight Reading. The playing or singing piece of music at first sight.

Silver Band. The common name for brass band in days when instruments were silver plated.

Similar Motion. The movement of 2 or more parts or melodies in same direction, either up or down.

Simple Interval. An interval of an eighth (octave) or less; see Interval.

Simple Time. A scheme of time-division in which the beat -unit is divisible by 2-e.g. 4/4, in which the beat-time is the quarter note (crotchet) divided into 2 eighth-notes (quavers), Cp. Compound Time.

Sinfonia Concertante (It.). The orchestral work, normally in several movts., in which there are parts for solo instruments, generally 2 or more, usually, with less emphasis on display than in solo concerto.

Singakademie. The title used by certain choirs in German-speaking countries.

Sinfonietta. Short, small scale symphony. Sometimes also used as performing not a fall orchestra.

Sistrum. Ancient rattle-like percussion instrument with rings which jangled on a metal frame when the instrument was shaken.

Sitar. An Indian long-necked lute with movable frets, and originally with 3 strings, now with 4-7 and sometimes sympathetic strings also. It is played with a plectrum worn on the right forefinger.

Sitzprobe (Ger.). The term used in opera for a 'sitting rehearsal', i.e. one in which singers play their roles sitting down, with accompaniments played by orchestra.

Six-four Chora. The chord containing sixth and fourth from its bass note. It is second inversion of chord based on note which is fourth from its bass, e.g. 6/4 chord G - C-E is second inversion of C-E-G.

Sixth. The Interval comprising first and last of any 6 notes in diatonic scale e.g. F-D. Sixth may be minor e.g. F-D flat, major e.g. F-D, or augmented e.g. F-D sharp. Sixth, like third, of which it is Inversion, is imperfect consonance. Term 'sixth, chord' is sometimes used in referring to Six-three Chord.

Sixty-fourth-note. The note considered as a time-value. This term is standard N, American usage and, as mathematically corresponding to the element of time-signature represented by 6/4, should clearly be preferred to hemidemisemiquaver.

Six-three Chord. The chord containing sixth and third from its bass note. It is first inversion of chord based on note which is sixth from its bass, e.g. 6/3 chord E-G-C is first inversion of C-E-G.

Sketch

(1) A rough draft of a composition, or a musical jotting made by a composer as a 'germ' or reminder;

(2) A short piece usually interpreting pictorial or other extra-musical ideas.

Slatt. Type of composition (originally a march, but afterwards more broadly treated) played by Norwegian folk-musicians on the Hardanger fiddle.

Slapstick or whip. The percussion instrument consisting of 2 strips of hardboard hinged together but with spring that normally keeps them at an angle. Sound of strips striking each other resembles crack of whip.

Slatt. Type of Norwegian folk tune, often in march rhythm, played on fiddle.

Sleign-bells. The small metal bells containing steel ball. Normally fastened to leather strap, but for orchestral use they are fixed to steel frame connected to wooden handle, allowing for high degree of rhythmic precision when hand taps frame or vice versa.

Slide. A device on some brass instruments for altering the length of the tube (and thus the notes produced). The principal use today is on the Trombone.

Slughorn or Slughorne. Although mentioned by Browning and Chatterton, no such musical instrument has ever existed.

Slur.

(1) The curved line over or under group of notes indicating that they are to be played or sung

smoothly, or, on stringed instrument, in one bow. If slur is combined with staccato marks, indicates phrase should be performed semi-staccato;

(2) Purcell used term as equivalent of Slide.

Snare-drum. The smaller drum which is used in the orchestra, military band, dance band, etc. It has a skin at either end of a shallow cylinder, the upper skin being struck with a pair of wooden sticks and the lower one being in contact with gut strings or wires (called snares). These snares add a rattling effect to the tone; they can be disengaged at will.

Soap Opera. Not an opera but a radio or television serial story of a sentimental nature, designed to sell the sponsor's product, e.g. soap.

Soggetto. Subject of fugue or other contrapuntal piece which is short and of abstract of stock type, so distinguished from andamento and from attacco (Point of imitation).

Soh. In Tonic Sol-fa the spoken name for the fifth degree (dominant) of the scale, written s. Cp. Sol.

Sohal, Naresh (b. 1939). Indian composer, pupil in England of Goehr. Works with Indian or Sanskrit titles include 'Asht Prahar' (Sanskrit: 'asht' = 8, 'prahar' is a division of the day) for orchestra. Other works include harmonica concerto: Shades I (unaccompanied soprano saxophone) and II (unaccompanied flute); 'Hexahedron' for 6 players.

Solfege' Solfeggio. French and Italian terms for a method of ear- training and sight-reading by which the pupil names each note of a melody (do for C, sol for G, etc.) as he sings it.

Solmization. The designation of musical notes by a system of syllabic names – as applied to a nomenclature devised by Guido of Arezzo in the 11th century and now to a development of this. Such a development is represented by the current Italian do, re, mi, fa, sol, la, si (representing the notes from C up to B), parallelled in English Tonic Sol-fa by doh, ray, me, fah, soh, lah, te (though these are not fixed in pitch but relative, doh representing C in C major, D in D major, etc., the other notes ascending from it).

Solo (It, alone). A piece or passage performed by one performer – either alone or with others in a subordinate, accompanying role. So solo song normally denotes a song for one singer with piano accompaniment.

Solo Organ. The manual on Organ which incl. stops intended for solo, rather than combined, use. Found on organs of 4 or more manuals and is placed above swell. Its stops are enclosed in swell-box.

Solovox. The electronic instrument usually attached to piano, but with own keyboard. Imitates sounds of various instruments, but can only produce one note at a time.

Sonata. Originally any instrumental piece not in a prevailing forms (e.g. Canzona, Ricer car, or dance-form).

Sonata-form. Term used to describe a certain type of musical construction normally used in the first movement of a Sonata (above) and of a symphony (which is in effect a sonata for orchestra) and similar works.

Sonata-rondo Form. The combination of Sonata Form and Rondo Form.

Sonatina. The short sonata, usually elementary in its technical requirements.

Song. Any short vocal compositioe, accompanied or not – usually for one performer, but cp. Part-song.

A song is always supposed to consist of three or four divisions. They are Sthayi, Antra, Sanchari and Abhog.

Sthayi sequences (sangatis) in a song cannot go beyond the note Ma Then from Madhyama to top Sa the "Antra" sequences (sangatis) are taken.

Then, the mixture of all the notes from the (Mandhra) bottom, Madhyam (middle) and to the top (taara) notes are sung together, it is called a "Sanchari", and the last part "Abhog" utilizes from the middle to the top note. This fourth division is not so essential in composing a song. But the other three first divisions are very important in composing a song. All the composers have to observe this rule strictly.

Song Form. Basic form ABA, also used in many instrumental pieces, e.g. minuet and trio.

Sonore. The direction often used by composers to mean 'sonorously', apparently under the impression that it is an Italian word. It could be, however, either the French for 'sonorous' or (if written sonore) an abbreviation for the correct Italian sonoramente.

Sons Bouches. Stoped notes on Horn.

Sons Etouffes. Indication, most frequently found in harp music, meaning that vibrations should be damped by hand immediately after string(s) have been plucked, thereby producing dry sound.

Sopra. In piano music term used to indicate that one hand has to pass over the other.

Sopranino. Term used of instrument higher in range than soprano of certain families (e.g. flugelhorn, saxophone).

Soprano. The female voice or highest register with range extending approx, from middle C upwards for 2 octaves. Term is also applied to some instruments, e.g. soprano saxo phone. Boy trebles can achieve soprano range, as could castrati.

Sordino, Sordina. Abbrev. sord:

(1) Mute (of string or wind instrument). Can sordino, with mute. Senza sordino, without mute;

(2) Damper (in piano). Senza sordini indicates that dampers are to be raised, i.e. strings are to be left free to vibrate. This is done by using right-hand (sustaining) pedal-hence alternative indication Ped.

Sostenuto. The direction to sustain tone, usually equivalent to slowing tempo.

Sostenuto Pedal. Whereas sustaining pedal on piano removes all dampers from strings, sostenuto pedal (only fitted on more expensive instruments) enables player to pre-select specific notes he wishes to be sustained.

Sotto Voce (It., under the voice). The whispered, barely audible – term used of instrumental as well as vocal music.

Soubrette. Term used in opera to describe soprano who sings role of cunning servant girl.

Sound Board. The resonant wooden part of certain instruments, incl. piano, organ and dulcimer, over which strings are stretched. It vibrates sympathetically and so amplifies notes sounded.

Sound-hole. Hole which is cut out of the upper surface of stringed instruments to assist resonance – the violin and related instruments having two holes shaped like an f and called f- holes, the lute and some guitars having one hole cut in an ornamented manner somewhat like a flower and called 'rose'.

Soundpost. The piece of wood, usually pine, that connects 2 surfaces (belly and back) of stringed instruments. Purposes are to strengthen, and to distribute vibrations.

Sousaphone. The type of tuba made in a shape circling the player's body and ending in a big bell facing forward.

Speaker-key. Key on reed instrument, e.g. oboe or clarinet, which opens hole at such a point as to facilitate playing of notes which are sounded by over blowing at octave, twelfth or fifteenth.

Species. The name given to each of 5 types of academic 'strict counterpoint' progressively more complex (called first species, second species, etc.).

Speech-song. The type of vocal utterance midway between speech and song.

Spiccato (It.). Term used in string playing for light staccato played with middle of bow and loose wrist.

Spinet. (1). The wing-shaped keyboard instrument of harpsichord type, but smaller.

Spinto (It.). Pushed, urged on – especially in voice-classification lirico-spinto, a Lyric voice (tenor or soprano) which has been 'pushed' into more forceful singing.

Spiritual. The name given to a type of religious folk-song of the American Negro, usually of solo-and-refrain design.

Sprechgesang. Type of voice production midway between song and speech.

Springar (Norw). Norwegian folk-dance in 3/4 time, cultivated.

Springer. A musical ornament (used e.g. by Chopin) in which an extra note, notated in smaller type, robs the preceding note of part of its time-value.

Square Piano. Early form of piano, oblong in shape and strung horizontally.

Staatskapelle (Ger.). State orchestra.

Staatsoper (Ger.). State opera house and/or company.

Stabile (It.). Stable, firm; term used of an orchestra to denote 'permanent, regular, resident', etc.

Stabreim (Ger.). Alliteration; term for alliterative verse used by Wagner in his music dramas.

Staccato. A method of performance denoted by a dot over the note, and signifying that the note is to be made short – and thus detached from its successor – by being held for less than its full length; so the superlative staccatissimo.

Stadtpfeifer (Ger.). The performer on wind instrument employed by municipality.

Staff or Stave. The set of horizontal lines, each representing different pitch (as do spaces between them), on which music is written. 5 lines are now used for all music except plainsong, which uses 4. Leger lines are used for notes above and below staff, and Clef indicator pitch of one of lines and hence particular pitch-position of staff.

Stahlspiel (Ger.). The percussion instrument with steel bars and played with hammers.

Steg (Ger.). Bridge of stringed instrument.

Stimme (Ger.).

(1) Voice;

(2) Separate part, vocal or instrumental. Stimmbuch, part-book.

Stimmflote, Stimmhorn Stimmpfeite. The pitch pipe.

Stimmung

(1) Tuning;

(2) Atmosphere (in sense of 'prevailing mood').

Stochastic (from Gk.). Governed by the mathematical laws of probability – term applied by Xenakis to produces whereby, having determined a total massive sound, a composer makes a mathematical calculation (worked out by himself or by computer) to decide the distribution of its component sounds over many moments and/or performers.

Stock and Horn, Stock in Horn, or Stockhorn. The primitive Scottish instrument, fitted with single reed and played in same way as chanter of bagpipe. Made of either wood or bone and fitted to a cowhorn.

Stop (noun)

(1) Row of pipes on an organ, all put in or out of operation by one lever; or the lever itself;

(2) By analogy, the mechanism used in the harpsichord for similar purpose – e.g. 'sixteen-foot stop' for adding tone an octave lower, 'harp stop' for simulating harp tone.

Stop. On organ, handle or draw stop which controls admission of wind to particular register, or set of pipes. Term is also applied to register itself.

Stopped Pipe. On organ, pipe in which upper end is closed, so lowering pitch by octave.

Stopping. On stringed instruments, placing of fingers of left hand on strings, thereby shortening effective vibrating length and therefore raising pitch.

Stard. The colloquial name for an instrument made by the Stradivari family.

Strascinando. The dragging—direction referring not so much to tempo as to one note's 'dragging' the next behind it e.g. in singing Portamento.

Street Piano. The mechanical type of piano with barrel-and-pin action similar to that of musical box. Played in same way as barrel organ by turning handle and is thus sometimes called piano organ.

Stretta. The term used in some Italian operatic scores for the section towards the end of a long ensemble when a quicker tempo succeeds a slower one.

Stretto. Close, narrow, drawn together :

(1) Bringing in of overlapping entries of subject in figure 'closer', i.e. after shorter intervals of time than those at which they originally came.

(2) Quickening of tempo towards end of piece.

String (**s**). The lengths of wire or gut on which sounds are produced in many diverse instruments, incl. piano, harp, violin family, guitar, mandolin and lute; also used to mean stringed instruments, but in this case usually refers only to violin family and its predecessors.

Stringto. The direction to a performer to increase the 'tension' of the music – in effect, to increase speed, often as preparation for a new section of basically faster tempo than the old one.

Suring Orchestra. Band consisting of stringed instruments only, as distinct from wind or brass band.

String Quartet. The medium (and music for medium) of 2 violins, viola and cello. In effect it is Sonata in 3 or 4 movts.

Strophic. Term used of a song in which the same music is repeated exactly or almost exactly) for each successive stanza of a poem.

Study. An instrumental piece (usually solo) written to train or demonstrate the facility of the performer in certain specific points of technique.

Stump. Obsolete and now virtually non-existent type of Cittern.

Style. The tracing of the history of musical styles, and of the changes in social, technical and aesthetic ideas which accompany and interact with changes in musical style, is one of the chief objects of the study of musical history.

Subdominant. The fourth degree of diatonic scale, e.g. F in scale of C. Sub-dominant, dominant and tonic triads are 3 'primary, or principal triads in a key.

Subject. The theme (or group of notes) used as basis of musical form e.g. subject in fugue, and 1st and 2nd subjects (or group of subjects) in movt. in sonata form.

Submediant. The sixth degree of diatonic scale, e.g. A in scale of C major.

Suite. The most common name for an instrumental piece in several movements, usually (in older use) a sequence of dances.

Supertonic. The second degree of the scale, e.g. the note D in the key C (major or minor) – lying immediately above the Tonic (first degree).

Suspension. A device in harmony by which a note in a chord is kept sounding when that chord has been succeeded by another in which the prolonged note forms a discord. This discord is then normally resolved when the prolonged note falls to a note forming part of the new chord.

Swanee Whistle. The whistle with slide at opposite end to mouthpiece that can be pulled in and out by player, so varying length of tube and hence pitch of note.

Swell. A device for increasing and diminishing the volume of sound on an organ, or on certain 18th century harpsichords.

Swell Box. Box containing several organ pipes and fitted with Venetian Swell.

Swell Organ. The manual organ in which pipes are enclosed in Swell Box organs. In most moderns. Choir organ and Solo organ are similarly enclosed.

Swing

(1) Basic ingredient or jazz; quality differentiating good jazz performance from bad one;

(2) Specific era and style in jazz history.

Sympathetic. The term used in allusion to the capacity of strings and other bodies to vibrate (and thus give a note) when this note is sounded near them by some other agent.

Sympathetic Resonance or Sympathetic Vibrations. Refer to acoustical phenomenon that occurs when resonant body, e.g. piano string, glass or tuning fork, vibrates and sounds note without being touched when same note is played or sung nearby.

Symphonia. (Lat., from Gr. for simultaneous sound), (1) In ancient Greek theory (a) unison, (b) consonant interval.

Symphonic Poem. Term introduced by Liszt for an orchestral work which is approximately of the size and seriousness customarily associated with a symphony, but which is meant as an interpretation of something non-musical, e.g. a work of literature.

Symphony. Term literally meaning 'a sounding-together', formerly indicating:

(1) An overture, e.g. to an opera;

(2) The instrumental section introducing, or between the verses of, a vocal work.

Symphonic Study. The vague term used by Schumann for set of piano variations, and by Elgar for orchestral work Falstaff, and variously by other composers.

Syncopation. A displacement of accent on to a beat that is normally unaccented.

Synthesizer. The general word for an electronic apparatus by which any one of a number of musical sounds can be put together from its physical components (harmonic constituents, characteristics of attack and decay, etc.) at such a speed and with such convenience as to make possible the performance of a piece from a musical score; generally (e.g. Moog synthesizer) with a piano-like keyboard.

T

T. The symbol in Tonic Sol-Fa for the seventh degree (leading-note) of the scale, pronounced te. Cp Si.

Taan. Taans are the combination of swaras or notes in any particular raga. These notes are sung either in 'akara' or in the notation itself. These 'taans' in the end of the khyal as a finishing touch give dignity and grandeur to the song and at the same time reveal the talent and musical ability of the musicians. This requires a great deal of skill.

Tabla. The term used for the type of oriental drum beaten by hands. Indian and Arabic forms are most familiar. Indian version is single-headed, producing similar sound to tinpana; has clearly defined pitch and sets of up to 12, providing complete chromatic compass, have been used.

Table (Fr.).

(1) Belly, or upper part of sound box of string instrument;

(2) Sounding board of harp, rising diagonally from foot of vertical pillar to upper end of neck.

(3) Music for a banquet.

Tablature. A system of writing down music by symbols which represent not the pitch (as in ordinary modern notations) but the position of the performer's fingers.

Tabor. Small drum.

Tacet. Indication in part that performer does not play in particular movement or section.

Tafermusik. The music suited to convivial gatherings, e.g. for performance at or after dinner.

Tagore, Rabindranath (1861-1941). A Great Indian poet.

Taille (Fr.). Term used for:

(1) Tenor or middle part of composition;

(2) Tenor member of family of instruments.

Tala. It is another important aspect of Indian music. They say, rhythm originated from the primitive man, when he danced in ecstasy.

Rhythm gives beauty and colour and draws away the dullness, creating an atmosphere of briskness by its movements.

There are numerous works by various great authors on this subject, dealing with tala.

A tala is a time measure in Indian music. It is like the metre in Poverty.

There are innumerable varieties of talas in Indian music. Each song is set to a tala. Some songs in some talas and other songs in other talas. Each time measure has divisions of its own and has an individual character.

In India we call this rhythm and tempo, together as "Laya". According to Bharata of Natyashashtra, there are three Kalas in laya:

Dhrut (fast), Madhya (middle) and Vilambit (slow).

It is said that the Vedic period called this word 'Laya' as 'Vritti', to express rhythm and tempo. Laya is the unit of measurement, i.e. equal intervals of time measure.

Sarnga Deva says:

"Vishrantiyuktay Kale
Kriyaya manamishyate
Kriyantara Vishrantirlayak
Trividho Mataha

Thus, the rhythm is determined by the moving pauses. The oneness of the pause, is the meaning of the laya.

We count the matras (Akshra Kalas) in each section of the 'avarta' i.e. the whole line of a cycle, known as the full round of the tala, to come back to the same.

Sometimes, it is possible that different talas, may be having the same number of matras in it. But they are all different because they are patterned and designed separately.

Tala is described in the following way, in some granthas. "Tala is like the body of a man in which 'matras' (beats) are like the arteries, laya is like blood flowing in them. Strokes are like the various limbs".

There are any number of varieties of talas both in Karnatak as well as the Hindustani systems of music. The few important and more popular talas of both systems are given below:

Hindustani	*Karnatak*
1. Ektal.	1. Adi Tal.
2. Choutal.	2. Madhya Adi Tal.
3. Jhaptal.	3. Jampa Tal.
4. Deepchandi.	4. Triputa Tal.
5. Dadra.	5. Rupaka Tal.
6. Dhamar.	6. Matya Tal.
7. Trital.	7. Dhruva Tal.
8. Tilwada.	8. Ekatalam.

These are only a few as examples. In addition to these are any number of talas which are not so common.

A Mridangam, Ghatam or Kanjeera or any other purcussion instrument player, can exhibit his skill, with his varied creative ability, and his intellectual capacity, which by itself is a treat to the listeners.

India is the only country, so far which has found expression so systematically both in the tala system as well as the raga (melody) system.

The peculiarity of the Hindustani music is, as mentioned already, that it has its special important place in the tala, called (Sama), with the exception of just one or two talas, all other talas have 'Dhin' for the sama and the performer has to return to the 'sama', to catch the 'mukda', after an elaborate a alap and tan of his own creative ability.

Thus the tala system in India plays an important role in Indian music.

Talon (Fr.). Heel (of the bow of a stringed instrument), i.e. the end of the bow which is held by the player.

Tambourine. Type of small drum struck with the fingers and rattled with the hand; it has little jingles inserted into its wooden frame. It is of Arab origin but was known in Europe before 1300; brought into the modern orchestra by Weber, Berlioz, and later composers mainly to evoke revelry, gipsies, exotic scenes, etc.

Tambura (also tanbura, tanpura). A long-necked Indian lute having 4 wires strings and no frets; plucked with the fingers, it is used only to provide a drone.

Tamburo Piccolo (It.). Side drum.

Tampon (Fr.). 2-Headed drumstick held in middle and used with alternating motion of wrists to produce roll on bass drum.

Tamilnadu Folk Songs. A huge variety of Dravidian songs in the folk type is found in some places in Tamilnadu. There are the Tevarams, Tiruvaimozi, Tirupugash which are mysteries of sacred music. Some of these are now sung in the current system – with ragas with a little liberty to go a little outside the limitations of the raga to bring graces.

There Kavadi chindus and kummis have attained a degree of excellence and status among other compositions.

Of course the traditional characteristic inherent kinship to one another in the folk music is obvious and very close from region to region all over the land. But the four main races in the South of India, namely, the Telugus, the Tamils, the Canarese and the Malayalis bear the nearest relationship and resemblance in their music. All their songs are composed in very attractive tunes and have gained popularity.

Tam-tam. Variety of song.

Tangent. The metal 'tongue' which, on the clavichord, touches a string when a key is struck and so sounds that string. It remains in contact with the string for as long as the note sounds, unlike the hammers of the piano.

Tango. Argentinian dance which is supposed to have been imported by African slaves into the American continent; taken into general use in ballroom dancing about the time of the First World War.

Tansen. The most celebrated musician of the Hindustani Sangeet, and the most reputed musician gem that adorned Emperor Akbar's court, Miyan Tansen, needs no introduction to the lovers of music all over the world.

The greatness of Tansen and his fascinating stories are known even to a small child in the Hindustani realm of music world.

Tansen was born in a small village near Gwalior to a Brahmin couple, Pt. Makarand Pande and his devoted wife.

The story goes: "The couple did not have a child for a number of years and they prayed to a nearby renowned Fakir by name Muhammad Sufi Ghaus, who blessed them, and a male child was born". The little child was called 'Tanna, Ramtanu, and Trilochan, by different pet names.

When the child was slightly older, he was taken by the parents to the same Fakir Muhammad Ghaus to be blessed. The Muslim Fakir saint, while blessing the boy, put a little bit of the pan (betal) from his mouth, (he was chewing) into the boy's mouth and blessed him to be immortal.

From that day, he was converted into a Muslim, (on account of tasting the pan eaten by a Muslim Fakir) and had been given many Muslim names like 'Atah Ali Khan', etc. and was brought up as a Muslim child. However, this name Miyan Tansen was conferred on him by the emperor, at a later time.

As a little child even, he showed remarkable grasping power intelligence and talent. He could imitate all the sounds of the animals especially that of a lion. Playfully he used to scare away all those persons in his father's nearby fields by roaring like a lion.

Incidentally it is of interest to note here that Tansen's parents though of a high class Brahmin family changed their own religion and sect and became Muslims, for the sake of their beloved child.

At the same time, at Brindavan, the great Swami Haridas Baba was living and his great disciples happened to hear this small child's imitation of animal sounds and suggested to the boy's parents to send the child to the Swami for receiving musical training. An extraordinary ascetic-musician as he was, Haridas Swami whole-heartedly taught to every one that went to him in the quest of knowledge. He took pleasure in imparting this noble Vidya to all seekers of God.

Swami Haridas Baba of Brindavan was immensely pleased to receive the boy as his disciple.

He found incalculable talent in the boy and taught him all the science contained in music and in a very short time, made him outstanding.

Soon his fame spread far and wide and the Emperor Akbar sent for him. He was made one of the 'Nava Ratnas' (nine gems) in his Durbar.

It did not take long for Tansen to earn the affection of the emperor. He soon became the Emperor's favourite and was the recipient of many honours.

After joining Akbar's Durbar Tansen started composing songs in praise of the Nawab too, and somewhat paid less importance to the devotional compositions.

Once a small interesting episode happened just to remind him of God as an eye opener.

He was too engrossed and absorbed in praising a mere man (the Nawab) and forgot the Lord, during his numerous concerts held there. On one occasion, at the close of a splendid concert, a Maharajah (who was present) rewarded him with a large sum of money and a 'Kondi' (a cheap thing) on the top of the sum, saying, that the large amount of money was meant for Tansen, for his splendid performance and the small cheap "Kondi" was to be offered at the altar of the 'God'.

This opened Tansen's eyes and he at once began to compose beautiful songs in praise of all goods and goddesses (Hindu gods too) on his benefactor whose blessings brought him into the world, and on Swami Haridas Baba his most revered guru.

Here I may mention that Tansen, though a Muslim by conversion, remained loyal to the Hindu religion and served his guru Swami Haridas, like a worthy devotee.

Of course he continued his compositions in praise of his patrons, the Emperor, Rewa ruler and a few others too.

We find a number of his compositions in praises of Mahadev-Shankar, Krishna, Ganga, etc. in supreme devotion. He was permitted to enter the Hindu temples as a special privilege. Till day his devotional compositions are sung in some of the North Indian temples.

Tansen brought the Hindustani music to the celestial heights. He popularized and crystallized the Dhruvapads and earned a name in the Dhruvapad Gayaki.

His contemporaries were all the bright chosen gems of God, like Tulsi Das, Surdas, Baiju Bawra, Meerabai, Ramdass and others, and it is believed that Tansen paid occasional visits to some of them like Sur Das as they had mutual administration for each other.

Miyan Ki Todi, Miyan Ki Malhar, Miyan Ki Sarang, etc. were all his creations.

Tansens was not only a reputed musician and composer of delightful songs, he is said to have written two brilliant books: Sangeeta Sara, and Ragamala. He also knew the art of playing on plucked instruments like Veena (Vichitra Veena). His daughter Saraswati was a first class Veena Player and her husband was no other than the noted Misri Singh (a Veena player himself) who changed his name to Naubad Khan after his marriage with Tansen's daughter.

Tansen had four sons and only one out of them turned out to be a good musician acquiring some of his father's qualities. by name Bilas Khan a worthy son of a worthy father.

There is an interesting story as to how this Bilas Khan (the son) sang spontaneously a rag most pathetically with feeling and emotion near the corps of his father (when he left this world) in bitter grief, that the body, (corps) touched and moved by the excellence of the raga lifted its hand and blessed the singer, i.e.

the son. Since then this rag has come to be known as Bilaskhani Todi.

Tansen's other three sons did not attain any fame. The story of how the Emperor Akbar desired and went to listen to Tansen's guru, Hari Das Baba, and how Tansen deliberately did something to make Swami Haridas, sing before him and in what circumstances, is already narrated by me, with the life of Swami Haridas, which I need not repeat here.

Tansens's musical talents are well known to the musical world. He could bring rain in torrents, he could burn the lights and perform wonderful miracles through his enchanting music.

Tansen left his mortal coil to join the immortals when he was about fifty or sixty years of age. (The exact date is not known).

His entire family and the emperor Akbar himself were at his bed side at that time. Before he breathed his last, Tansen was believed to have expressed a desire that he should be buried at Gwalior. Accordingly his remains were brought to Gwalior for enternal rest, near the tomb of Pir Muhammad Ghaus and placed there.

There is a belief that the tamarind tree leaves near Tansen's tomb in Gwalior, if eaten, give melodious voice.

It was Pt. Bhatkhande the selfless servant of this noble art who took the trouble of going to Gwalior and with great effort got the deapidated tomb reconstructed and started the annual festivals there in Tansen's memory. All India Radio has taken up this burden of arranging the great musician's anniversaries at Gwalior every year.

Tanz (Ger.). Dance.

Tape. The term which in musical references stands for electronic-recording tape, particularly in reference to music which the composer has assembled from electronic components directly on to tape. The playback of this tape then constitutes the performance or is combined with 'live' elements: as in music 'for piano and tape', etc.

Tappas. These are typical Muhammadan songs, which mainly deal with love. These were first meant to be sung only by those separated from their lover, and were sung in a very rude and vulgar way. People coming from respectable families never sang these (in those days).

Nowadays these are sung in a more refined and polished way. These consist of two divisions only. These tappas, they say, were first introduced by a famous Muhammadan singer by name Shouri of Lucknow who lived about 1810 or so. A tappa when properly exhibited, can bring all the subtle graces which are expressed in the song. It is overloaded with melody when properly sung, with a marked rhythm.

Tarana. This is a peculiar piece of song. They say that when Amir Khusro first came to India as a stranger, he found it very difficult to pronounce all these high-flown Sanskrit words of ours, in the songs, and hence invented this style of his own, leaving all the words, and putting these meaningless words in those tunes like – "to, nam, Ri, tom nam, dri nam, ton, etc.", and called this as Tarana. This is how it has come into existence.

Tarantella. Very fast Italian dance in 6/8 time, usually with alternating major and minor sections. Long regarded as cure for bite of tarantula spider.

Tarbouka. North African drum used by Berlioz in Slave Dance in the Trojans.

Targato. Hungarian woodwind instrument with oriental origins. Orig. had double reed, now single. Resembles straight soprano saxophone in appearance and tone.

Tastatura. Keyboard.

Tastiera. The finger-board.

Tastiera Per Luce (It.). 'Keyboard for light', instrument invented by Rimington which projected colours. Had 12 notes 'tuned' to 'scale' of colours based on musical cycle of fifths.

Tasto

(1) Key of keyboard instrument. Tasto solo, in figured bass, play only bass notes without adding harmonies, above;

(2) Eret on lute, guitar, viol etc.;

(3) Fingerboard of stringed instrument. Sul tasto, Bowing.

Te. InTonic Sol. Fa, the spoken name for the seventh degree (leading-note) of the scale, written t. Cp. SI – the initial letter t was adopted in Tonic Sol-Fa because s would have brought confusion with soh (fifth degree).

Temperament. The system of tuning in which intervals are 'tempered' (i.e. slightly lessened or enlarged) away from 'natural' scale. Devised when gradual introduction of chromatic tones made inadequate systems based on physical laws, where intervals agree with those found by successive fractional division of string.

Temple Block. Type of hollowed-out wooden vessel, approximately in the shape of a human head; it is struck with a stick as a percussion instrument, particularly in modern dance bands.

Tempo.

(1) Time. Pace of composition as determined by speed of beat to which it is performed.

(2) Movement (of sonata, symphony etc.)

Tenor.

(1) The highest normal male voice.

(2) Name given, in 'families' of instruments, to that instrument considered to have a position parallel to that which the tenor voice has among voices – so tenor Saxophone, tenor Trombone, etc.;

Tenor Drum. The percussion instrument of similar type of snare- drum (and capable of similar rolls, etc.) but deeper in pitch, bigger, and without snares.

Tenor Horn, Tenorhorn. Name sometimes given to tenor Saxhorn and occasionally to corresponding member of Flugelhorn family.

Tenth. Interval of octave plus third. Treated as equivalent of third in theory of harmony and in figured bass.

Tenuto. Indication that single note or chord should be held for full value (or even longer) in context in which performer might be inclined to play it staccato. Abbrev. ten.

Ternary. In three sections; ternary form, classification used of a movement in three sections of which the third is a repetition (exact or near) of the first—i.e. a movement which may be represented as ABA or ABA.

Ternary Form. The form, represented by formula ABA, in which 1st section is restated, with or without modifications or embellishments, after middle section of different content.

Tertian Harmony. Harmonic system based on third or traid, i.e. standard western system of harmony.

Terzetto. Vocal trio. Also applied (rarely) to piece for 3 instruments.

Tessitura (It., texture). The compass of notes to which a particular singer's voice naturally inclines though exceptional notes may be produced outside it; similarly, the general compass (not counting exceptional notes) of a vocal part.

Tetrachord. An obsolete scale-pattern grouping 4 adjacent notes a whole-tone or semitone apart.

Thaat. A thaat or a Melakarta, is just one and the same. In South India the word Melakarta is more commonly used and in the North for the same thing we say a Thaat.

It is the current system, and was introduced first by Pt. Venkatamakhi originally for the (Karnatak) South Indian music and later to our Hindustani Paddhati. Since the basic principles of both the systems even now are common and as this was brought on an entirely mathematical calculation, it has been useful to both the systems equally well.

Pt. Venkatamakhi produced seventy-two (72) melakartas, and said "even gods cannot change these".

A Thaat is a combination of swaras by which a raga can be produced.

A Thaat must have all the seven notes in the scale and these must come in their proper order. Komal and Suddha notes may both be taken one after the other. It need not be pleasing to the ear like a raga.

Late Pt. Bhatkhande of recent times, who was an authority on Hindustani music, has selected only ten (10) thaats out of these seventy-two melakartas to make it simple for the Hindustani sangeet. Panditji said, these ten thaats are more than sufficient to produce the necessary ragas.

This is also one of the reasons for the two systems to be completely different from one another.

South India has retained the ancient system of seventy-two melarkartas in their original form as invented by Pt. Venkatamakhi. These have again been grouped under Chakras – about which I shall deal in detail in my chapter on 'South Indian System'.

Theme. Musical entity (consisting of group of notes, usually melodic) which is chief idea, or one of chief ideas, in a composition. Used esp. of idea is instrumental work which is used as basis for discussion, development or variation.

Theorbo. Type of archlute (bass lute) with long, off-the-fingerboard extra strings and an extra (S-shaped) neck.

Theory of Music. According to period when they were written, works on theory of music may deal with one or more of following aspects of the subject: acoustics, notation, melody, rhythm, harmony, counterpoint, composition, form, and musical aesthetics.

Theremin (or thereminovox). Type of Electronic instrument having an upright sensitive 'pole' which produces sound from the motion of the hand in space round it.

Third. Interval comprised by first and last notes of any. 3 notes in diatonic scale (i.e. 2 notes written on adjacent lines or spaces on staff), e.g. F – A. Major third has 2 whole tones (e.g. F sharp – A sharp), minor third has tone and semitone (e.g. sharp – A) and diminished third has whole tone (e.g. F sharp – A flat).

Third Sound. Tartini's name for the acoustical phenomenon he discovered, now known as a Resultant Tone.

Thirteenth. Interval of octave plus sixth. For 'chord of the thirteenth.'

Thump. Early Eng. word for pizzicato, esp. on lyra viol; also applied to piece so performed.

Thumri. The great Nawab of Oudh who was himself a musician, Nawab Wajid Ali Shah of Lucknow, is believed to have composed these songs, which are a mixture of khyals, and another type of songs known as 'tappas'. These are mostly based on love themes, and are supposed to be very romantic in their nature and style.

Lucknow and Varanasi (Banaras) are specially famous for 'thumris'. They generally mix up two or even three ragas sometimes, and make it lively and fascinating. They can keep the whole audience entraptured with their musical patterns mixed with a few gestures. Very high class music singers look down upon this romantic style of singing, as it is not so pure.

Thunder Horn. Early name for 'folded' as opposed to 'straight' trumpet.

Thunder Machine. Device consisting of hard balls inside large rotating drum, used to produce thunder effects.

Thunder Stick, Bull Roarer or **Whizzer.** Instrument consisting simply of flat piece of wood fastened to piece of string. When swung rapidly round head produces groaning or roaring sound varying in pitch was speed.

Thyagaraja. Thyagaraja, the glittering germ of the ocean of music, the immortal sage, poet, composer and musician of repute was born at Tiruvarur where the Telugu and Tamil cultures had both flourished, in the year 1759. (The date of birth of Thyagaraja is a matter of controversy). Some say it was 1767 and others think it was 1759; however, it is not a matter about which we have to strain our minds.

Thyagaraja was born in a Telugu Brahmin Vaikiki Murikinadu family of moderate means who belonged to the Telugu (Andhra) districts and who migrated later to the South to Tanjore district.

His father was Ramabrahman and mother Shantamma. Thyagaraja learnt his musical education from Shri Shonthi Venkata Ramaniah, or his way from and to the school.

He lost his father early in life and took to his father's profession of 'Uncha Vritti and led a pure simple life of dedication.

His wife Parwatamma also assisted him in every possible manner as an ideal wife.

It is believed, it was the cruelty of his elder brother that had partly led his mind towards God and Holy Scriptures. He passed through troublous times, which ultimately carried him to the heights of glory.

Being a born genius of music from the childhood, Thyagaraja became a 'Nadopasaka' of the highest order. He convinced the world through his songs (Kritis) that one can attain Mukti through music.

His compositions are of eternal value of rare musical excellence and brilliance, breathing the spirit of devotion of Lord Rama in each line.

Thyagaraja's compositions vary from the very simplest to the most complicated ones.

Thyagaraja poured out his soul's yearnings at the lotus feet of Sri Rama in the most exquisite ragas, full of bhakti and bhava. His celestial music had its recompense, for it is said that he had the fortune of having Sri Rama's Darshan' several times during his life.

The beauty of his Kriti compositions are, that they arouse a feeling of expectancy to know more about the descriptive nature of the meaning of the song as well as the crystallized sequences, Sangatis of varied modes with delight.

Of course, each language has its own beauty and musical appeal. But Thyagaraja had made this Telugu language pass and flow beyond its limits by his melodious thrilling songs.

Thyagaraja's songs are sung with immense delight, not only by the Telugu-knowing people but also by the Tamilians, Kannadas, and others in the South.

In fact it was our Tamilian brethren who were able to preserve this precious vidya and valued these songs of the great saint Thyagaraja as the best.

The Andhras are grateful to them for preserving this holy art of music, which but for them perhaps may have faded down and forgotten.

There are some very interesting incidents which happened during Thyagaraja's life.

It is believed that whenever Thyagaraja was in difficulties and doubts, a sanyasi invariably appeared to him and directed him to the right path.

Once Thyagaraja was invited to Srirangam, a holy place in South India, as the guest of a local Brahmin. One night a procession carrying a golden deity, seated on a chariot was approaching the house where he was staying. Thyagaraja looked at the procession and burst forth into a song, "Razu Vedale chutamu rare" meaning the Lord, like a king is coming in full glory, let us all go and see. It was a majestic scene, and Thyagaraja wanted to have a closer view of the deity. But the crowd made it impossible for him to move near the chariot. This greatly disappointed the musical sage and he was on the verge of tears.

The 'Ratha' (Deity on the chariot drawn by men) came to a standstill. It would not move, however much they tried to pull.

Then it occurred to the authorities and the priests, that some great devotee must be standing somewhere, and that they should find out and bring him to the deity. Everyone pointed to the corner where Thyagaraja stood in great grief. They at once knew it was he, and brought him to the chariot. Thyagaraja was visibly moved and sang the famous song "Vina rade na manavi" meaning will you not heed to my request? That request being, that the deity should now allow the chariot to move.

The movement he finished the song, the ratha began to move without any further effort.

At Tirupati. Another interesting episode was, when he visited Tirupati, where Lord Venkatesa resides, on the top of the Seven Hills.

Thyagaraja went there with a great desire to have the Lord's darshan. But when he entered the temple, after having bathed in the sacred tank, to his dismay, he found a curtain drawn in front of the image. Thygaraja took it to mean that the curtain between him and the Lord was his own pride. Then in deep humility he sang the Kriti "Tera teeyaga rada", which means Oh, Lord, will you not take away (remove) the screen and allow me to have your auspicious darshan?

At the conclusion of the song, the curtain fell as though by a miracle, and the Lord Venkatesa showed Himself in full splendour.

Thyagaraja was overjoyed beyond measure. Song after song poured forth from him in His praise.

The incident of robbers. Another celebrated story is the incident of the robbers.

On the return journey from Tirupati, after visiting Kovvur, Thyagaraja and his party commenced their journey. The chief of that place, out of admiration for this great composer saint, presented a bag containing one thousand gold sovereigns and placed it in Thyagaraja's palanquin without his knowledge. The disciples knew that this sum was given for being utilized for the holy celebration of Sri Rama Navami which Thyagaraja celebrated every year.

On the way, the party had to pass through a thick jungle. The place was noted for robbers. Thyagaraja's party was not spared, when the rubbers surrounded the group the disciples were in great fear.

When they sobbingly told Thyagaraja, he only said, "Why should we be afraid? What have we got?" The disciples revealed that the palanquin contained a bag of gold.

"Throw it away to the thieves", was his calm reply. When they told him it was meant for a good cause he said, "If it is God's money let Him come and take care of it."

He started singing the Kriti, "Mundu Venuka Iruprakhala todai", Come, come O Rama to our rescue from all sides to protect us.

Strangely enough, two young lads appeared and they showered arrows on the thieves. The robbers had to surrender themselves and ask for pardon.

The disciples ran and told Thyagaraja all that had happened, how two handsome lads had come and driven away the robbers.

Thyagaraja at once knew it was no other than Rama and Lakshmana, who had appeared to save them. He even praised the good fortune of the thieves and the disciples, for seeing the divine beings.

There are many more interesting incidents which have happened during his life.

Apart from the Kriti compositions which run into several hundreds including his valuable Pancharatna Kritis, Thyagaraja also wrote a few brilliant Telugu operas.

The operare "Nowka Charitram" "Prahalada Bhakti Vijayam, and "Sita Ram Vijayam".

(1) Nowka Charitram was his own imaginary account of a boat excursion done by Gopis in the company of Lord Krishna.

(2) Prahalada Bhakti Vijayam is the other opera he wrote after he had completed the whole of

Ramayana in the form of Kritis, and the opera of Sita Rama Vijayam relating to Uttara Ramayanam.

His Kritis were all on the Rama Avatara, of Lord Vishnu, "Prahalada Bhakti Vijayam" on Narasimhavatar, and the Nowka Charitram on Sri Krishna Avatara as the theme.

Thyagaraja lived up to his ripe old age. According to some scholars, Thyagaraja's age was 88 (eighty-eight). Some others estimated it to be 77 (seventy-seven) only. (1759- 1847).

It will take some generations again to find such a versatile genius with tremendous flood of musical ideas, all drenched in supreme devotion.

Tie. A line in musical notation joining two adjacent notes of the same pitch indicating that the sound of the first is to be prolonged continuously into the second, instead of the latter's being struck afresh.

Tierce De Picardie (Fr. Picardy third). Major third used in final chord of composition in minor mode, replacing expected minor third.

Timbre (Fr.). The quality of tone, also used in English as alternative to Tone Colour.

Tillanas. Just like taranas of the North India, we in the South India have these tillanas. These are songs with jatis. Some tillanas are songs in jatis, and some tillanas have first some sahitya (wordings) and then in the same notation the jati – like Tom-Nom-dadri, etc.

These also have the section – pallavi, anupallavi, charana, etc. Some tillanas omit the charana part completely. These have beautiful sangatis, and are meant to create an atmosphere of briskness to drive away the drowsiness if any, in the audience by suddenly taking up a tillana of a quick tempo.

These compositions are scholarly and are of smaller length.

H. H. Swati Tirunal, the Maharaja of Travancore, Pallavi Sesha Iyer and Patnam Subramanyam Iyer are some of the composers of tillanas with wordings also.

Time. Term used in music to classify basic rhythmical patterns: thus a movement is said to be in six-eight time (6/8 time), having 6 eighth-notes (quavers) to the bar. So also e.g. common time (4/4); waltz time (3/4, with a characteristic tilt); march time (usually 4/4 or 6/8); in free time, without any regular accent.

Time-signature. The sign at the beginning of a composition or movement (and thereafter only when a change has to be indicated) conveying by means of figures the kind of beats in the bar and (above it) the number of such beats. E.g. 3/2 indicates 3 half-notes (minims) to the bar; 3/8 indicates 3 eighth-notes (quavers).

Timpan. The string instrument used by Irish in early Middle Ages. Played with nails or plectrum.

Timpani (It., not tympani) = Kettledrums. (The singular timpano is not generally used in English, though it is standard Italian).

Tin-whistle. The rudimentary six-holed keyless wind-instrument of Recorder type but made of metal. Also called penny-whistle.

Tirade (Fr.), **Tirata** (It.). Baroque ornamental scale passage linking 2 notes of melody, or 2 chords.

Toccata (It.). An instrumental piece, usually for one performer and usually consisting of a single rapid movement exhibiting the player's touch.

Tom-tom. Snareless drum, usually with 2 heads but occasionally with only 1. Rarely found singly, sets of 7 being quite common.

Tom-tom. Type of high-pitched drum (imitation of African drum) used in Western dance-bands and in the orchestra—often in sets of 2 or more, either tuned to definite notes or otherwise. (Not the same as Tam-tam).

Ton (Fr.),

(1) Key, mode;

(2) Pitch;

(3) Equivalent of Tone;

(4) Demi-ton; semitone;

(5) Ton de rechange, crook (of brass instrument).

Ton (Ger.).

(1) Sound music;

(2) Note;

(3) Ganzton-Tone;

(4) Halbton, semitone;

(5) Equality of sound. Tonfarbe, tone colour;

(6) Kirchenton, church mode.

Tonada (Sp.). Tune set to poem or dance, usually with contrasts between slow and fast tempi.

Tonadilla (Sp.). Diminutive of Tonada. Term for type of scenic cantata, often with vocal, choral and instrumental movements, used in Spanish stage entertainment.

Tonality -key – especially in the effect made on the listener by the observance of a single key, as opposed (in the 20th century) to Polytonality (simultaneous use of several keys) or Atonality (absence of key).

Tone

(1) The quality of musical sound ('he plays with a pleasing tone');

(2) A musical sound consisting of a 'pure' note, as in acoustical analysis ('a note on the violin may be analyzed as containing several different tones');

(3) The interval consisting of 2 semitones, e.g. from C up to D;

(4) One of the plainsong melodies used for the singing of psalms in the Roman Catholic Church;

(5) A note (in such usages as 'a chord consisting of 4 tones'). It is because of this last use, derived from German and needlessly confusing, that there have arisen such American compounds as tone-row and twelve-tone (Eng., note-row, twelve-note).

Tone Colour (Fr., timbre; Ger., Klangfarbe). Refers to the characteristic quality of tone of instrument of voice. Effective combination of tone colour colours is chief art of Orchestration. Tone colour of note depends on number, selection and relative strengths of overtones of which it is composed these are different in different kinds of instruments.

Tongue. To articulate a note on a wind instrument with a certain use of the tongue.

Tonic. The first note of scale (e.g. C in case of C major and C minor) which is its key note and centre of its tonality, and key note of composition written in that tonality.

Tonic Sol-fa. English system of notation and sight-reading introduced in 1840s by J. S. Curwen (1816-80), though partly anticipated by others. According to this the notes of the major scale are named (ascending) doh, ray, me, fah, soh, lah, te – where doh is the keynote (tonic), and other notes being thus related to the keynote of the moment, not fixed in pitch as in ordinary (Staff) notation. Time values are indicated by barlines and dots, and there is other symbolization. The chief use of the written system has been in amateur choral music.

Tonus Peregrinus

(1) Medieval term what is now called the minor scale, not 'recognized' in the modal system then prevalent;

(2) The plainsong sung in the Roman Catholic Church to Psalm 114, being in the above scale.

Torch Song. The sentimental ditty of unrequited love, usually sung by a woman, and with jazz or pop associations. Idea is that singer is 'carrying a torch' for the loved one.

Touche (Fr.)

(1) Key of keyboard instrument;

(2) Fret on lute, viol, guitar etc.

(3) Finger-board on stringed instrument.

Tourte Bow. The normal type of bow used by string players, invented by Francois Tourte (1747 – 1835). Unlike earlier type, stick curves inwards towards hair instead of outwards.

Toye. Term occasionally used in English instrumental music of 16th, 17th centuries for piece of simple, playful character in dance rhythm.

Toy Symphony. A symphony of a simple kind in which toy instruments are employed. The best-known example is that which is usually ascribed to Joseph Haydn.

Tracker. The that strip of wood used as part of mechanism which connected key of organ with lid ('pallet') which admitted wind to pipe. Now replaced by some form of electric action.

Tract. The part of Proper of Mass, sung in penitential seasons in place of Alleulia. Tracts are among oldest part of plain song, and are all in 2nd or 8th mode. Words are from psalms.

Transcribe.

(1) To arrange a piece of music for a performing medium other than the original – or for the same medium but in a more elaborate style.

(2) To convert a piece from one system of notation to another, e.g. from medieval notation to the modern. So also transcription.

Transition.

(1) A passage serving mainly to join two passages more important than itself;

(2) A change of key, particularly one of a sudden kind, not going through the regularly ordered process called 'modulation'.

Transpose. To write down or perform music at a pitch other than the original.

Transposing Instrument. An instrument on which the player produces a sound at a fixed interval above or below the note written. The chief reason for this is the convenience of a player changing between different sizes of instrument.

Transposing Keyboards. The devices whereby keyboard Manuals could be moved in order to produce higher or lower keys. Player therefore had no need to transpose when music was required in key other than written one.

Transposition. The process of transferring music to a pitch other than the original.

Transverse Flute. The name for the ordinary flute, to distinguish it (as held cross-wise) from the recorder (of the same basic instrumental type but held downwards).

Traps

(1) Kit used by drummers in dance and jazz bands;

(2) In dance or theatre orchestras, devices used for special effects e.g. whistle, whip crack, cowbell etc.

Traner (Ger.). Mourning. So Trauermarsch, funeral march. So also Haydn's so-called Trauersymphonie (Mourning symphony); Mozart's Mauereische Trauermusik (Masonic Funeral Music); Hindemith's Trauermusik (mourning music), for viola and strings.

Trautonium. Trade name for a type of Electronic instrument invented in Germany in 1930; it produced only one note at a time. It could be fixed to a piano, one hand playing each instrument.

Traversa. The name occasionally found instead of Traverso.

Traverso. The name sometimes used in old scores as abbreviation of flauto traverse (It.)., i.e. the transverse flaute – to distinguish this instrument (the ordinary flute, held cross-wise) from the recorder, held downwards.

Treble

(1) Type of high voice – the term usually being kept today to children's voices, the adult female equivalent being 'soprano';

(2) The upper part of a composition, are the upper regions of pitch generally – especially in antithesis to Bass;

(3) Name given to high-pitched members of certain 'females' of instruments.

Treble Flute. Instrument approx, midway in pitch between ordinary flute and piccolo.

Tremolo. The rapid reiteration of single note or alternation of 2 or more.

Tremulant. The device used on organ to produce effect resembling Vibrato by alternately increasing and decreasing wind pressure.

Trepak. Lively Russian dance in 2/4 time.

Triad. A three-note chord consisting of a particular note plus its third and fifth – e.g. C – E – G, which is called the common chord' of C major, or no matter whether C remains the brass-note or is replaced by C minor.

Triangle. Three-cornered metal-framed percussion instrument, struck with a metal stick; its tinkling sound is without definite pitch.

Trill. A musical ornament also called shake, consisting of the rapid alternation of the written note and the note above.

Trillo (It.)

(1) Trill.

(2) An obsolete vocal ornament in which a single note was repeated, repetitions getting ever faster.

Trio

(1) Instrumental or vocal piece for 3 performers. Most frequent instrumental types are piano trio (piano, violin, cello) and string trio (violin, viola, cello).

(2) Middle section of minuet or scherzo after which 1st section is repeated Orig. written in 3 parts; title was retained after this custom was dropped.

Triple Stop. Any chord of 3 notes played on bowed string instrument, whether or not all 3 strings are stopped by fingers.

Triplet. A group of 3 notes (or notes and rests) of equal time-value, written where a group of 2, 4 or some other number of notes is suggested by the time-signature.

Triple Time. Time in which number of beats in bar is 3, e.g. 3/8¾, $^3/_2$.

Triple Tonguing. The method of tonguing on wind instruments in which consonants T-K-T are articulated.

Tritone. The interval of 3 whole-tones, e.g. from F up or down to B. This is a relatively awkward interval to sing, and its use in composition was formerly (in medieval and later practice) hedged round with various prohibitions.

Tromba. Trumpet.

Tromba Marina. The stringed instrument up to 2m (7 ft) long and consisting of single string mounted on thin and slightly tapered box. Player used how and had to stand; only notes he could produce were natural harmonics.

Trombone. Type of brass instrument, generally possessing a slide which serves to vary the effective length of the tube.

Trommel (Ger.). Arum; grosse Trommel, bass drum.

Tronco, Tronca (It.). Broken off short (of a note, especially in vocal music).

Trumpet. The metal wind-instrument, cylindrically bored, used for signalling, etc., from ancient times, and regularly appearing in the orchestra from the 17th century. The standard modern (form mid-19th century) has three valves.

Trumpet Marine. An obsolete bowed instrument (sometimes 6 ft long), one end of which rested on the floor. By the pressing of a finger at correct points on its single string, notes of the Harmonic Series could be obtained.

Trumpet Tune, Trumpet Voluntary. The pieces notes not composed for a trumpet, but imitating one – e.g. as solo for a trumpet-like stop on the organ.

Trope. Type of musical interpolation into traditional liturgical plainsong.

Troubadours (Fr., from Provencal, trobadors). The poet-musicians of early Middle Ages who lived in S France and wrote in langue d' or (Provencal).

Trumpet. The name applied to wide variety of instruments, some of which have little in common apart from being made of metal (usually brass) and having funnel-shaped mouthpiece.

Trumpet-cornet. The cross between trumpet and cornet, said by its exponents to combine tone of former with ease of playing of latter.

Tuba

(1) Type of bass brass valved instrument made in several sizes and shapes – when circular, called 'helicon', of which the Sousaphone is a variety. The standard orchestral tuba (or bass tuba) is in F, with compass from the F an octave below the bass clef, upwards for about three octaves, or in Eb, a tone lower.

Tuba Major, Tuba Mirabilis or simply tuba, 8 ft reed stop on organ. Although of great power, its range is considerably higher than orchestral tuba.

Tubaphone or **Tubophone.** The percussion instrument producing bell-like sounds when its metal tubes, laid out like piano keyboard are struck with hammers.

Tuning Fork. 2-pronged device for accurately giving pitch of single note. Sound given is practically pure note, without overtones.

Tune

(1) Melody, especially the upper part of a simple composition;

(2) Term (noun and verb) referring to correct intonation – so in tune, out of tune a piano, etc.

Turn. The musical ornament normally indicated by a special mark, as follows: played (and various similar indications).

Tutti (It.), 'all' (pl.). Term used, most often in concertors, to indicate entrance of full orchestra, as distinct from passages for soloist.

Tutti. It is an instrument called Tutti used by the folk people. A bag is made from the skin of a goat or a kid and this is blown by the mouth. The sweet and perfect Taara Shadja note coming from it is very fascinating. It serves to create a musical atmosphere at the very start. Until recently this was used in dance dramas, dance concerts and other puppet shows.

Tutto. All, so, in piano works, tutte le corde, all the strings, i.e. not with soft pedal.

Twelfth

(1) Interval of an octave plus a fifth;

(2) Organ stop of diapason quality and 2 ft pitch. Sounds produced are twelfth above notes played.

Twelve-note. Term used to describe a technique of composition in which all twelve notes within the octave (i.e. the seven white and five black notes of the piano) are treated as 'equal'—i.e. are subjected to an ordered relationship which (unlike that of the major-minor key system) establishes no 'hierarchy' of notes (but see below).

Twelve-note System. Method of composition, also known as dode- caphony, formulated by Schoenberg 1921 after period of experimentation in writing music without tonality and without using traditional ways of building chords. In it, basis of both melodies and chords of composition is arrangement of 12 notes of chromatic scale in particular order, called Note Row. This series is always used complete, but may be transposed to any of 11 other possible positions, inverted, reversed (Retrograde Motion), or reversed and inverted. It thus has 48 forms, and in addition any note of series may be used in any of its octaves.

Twelve-tone System. Twelve-note system.

Tzigane, Tsingane (It.). Term for Hungarian gypsies and their music.

U

Ubung (Ger.). Exercise'. Clavierubung, keyboard exercise.

Ukulete, Ukelete. A small easily-learnt 4-stringed guitar from Hawaii.

Unda Maris (Lat.). Organ stop of soft tone, tuned slightly flat, or which has 2 ranks slightly mistuned, so that beat results which has effect similar to vibrato. Also called vox celeste, vox coelestis or vox angelica.

Union Pipe. Form of Bagpipe which is popular in Ireland since early 18th century. Blown by bellows and has relatively quiet tone which makes it suitable for indoor use. Also called 'uillean pipe' (Gael. uillean = elbow).

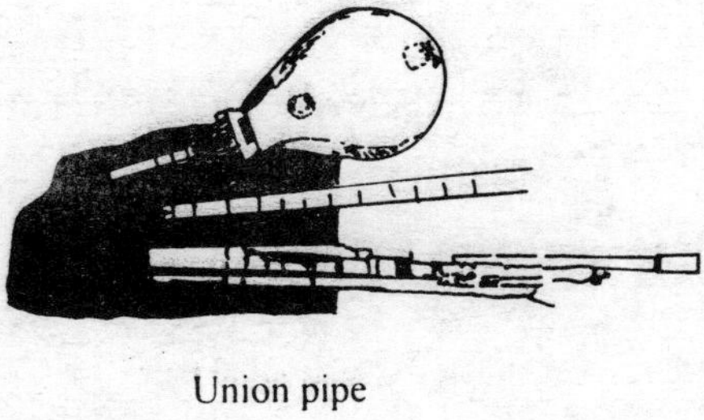

Union pipe

Unison. The combined sound of 2 or more notes of same pitch. Term 'singing in unison is used when song is performed by several voices, all at same pitch (or octave apart with male and female singers).

Unit Organ. Small organ constructed to save space and expense, with certain pipes shared by different stops.

Up-bow. Bow stroke on stringed instrument from point to heel.

Upright Piano. Ordinary domestic piano in which, to save space, strings are laid out vertically instead of horizontally as in grand piano.

Ut (Fr.). The note C. Also first note of Guidonian hexachord.

V

V. As abbrev., V. = violin,, voice. V. = verse (in Gergorian chant). Vc. = cello. Vla. = viola. Vln = violin. V.S. = volti subito.

Vadi.

(1) A vadi is a jeeva swara or the main important chief note, which is heard in the raga again and again.

(2) A samvadi is the next important swara of the raga and follows the king note that is vadi, like a Mantri or a Minister.

(3) There are also annuvadi and vivadi notes. Annuvadi is like a servant and the vivadi is considered as an enemy, because it produces discord.

The following sloka describes these four notes in this way:

"Svara Charturvidha seya Ragotpadana gocharaha

Vadi Samvadyanuvadi Vivadicha Chaturvidhaha

Vadi Swarstu Raja, syan Mantri Samvadi Samkshitaha

Swara Vivadi Vairy Syadanuvadicha Wintyavat'.

Hence these four above-mentioned notes which are meant to determine a raga are described in this way.

Value. The device enabling brass instruments to command complete chromatic compass. Used on horn, cornet, trumpet, flugelhorn, saxhorn, euphonium, tuba, and, less frequently, on trombone, where same result is normally achieved by slide. Valves either open length of extra tubing, so lowering pitch, or cut off length of tubing, so raising pitch: in this way different Harmonic Series can be used, so providing complete chromatic compass.

Vamp. To improvise an instrumental accompaniment or introduction e.g. to a song.

Varanams. These scholarly types of well-known compositions called varnams are next taught to the pupil. They are elaborate intricate melodies, the combination of which are specially built to suit this style. This is especially taught to help the rendering with perfect understanding, paucity of words in an artistic and stylish way. The high technique and a gradual development and the skill with which it has to be presented are some of its characteristics. The constant practice of these varnams gives considerable training and confidence and makes the singer a perfect skilful musician, with thorough swarainana.

There are two kinds of varnams: (1) Tana varnams, (2) Pada Varnams.

(1) A tana varnam furnishes very little of sahitya and is dominated by tana-jatis or phrases. These are taught to all pupils undergoing a study of music. These are sung at the commencement of concerts.

(2) A pada varnam is generally of a 'chouka', i.e. slow or a vilambit nature. The music is in a slower tempo, and is meant for dance concerts, with full of sahitya conveying the 'bhava' it contained thereby.

This type of varnam is very near to the 'padams' having similar 'similar sahityas' and theme. That is why they have come to be known as 'pada varnams'. These pada varnams are usually set in Rupaka tala of 6 matras. Whereas the tana varnams are found in various long measurement talas like Adi, Jhampa, Triputa and Ata etc. these tana varnams describe the feature and the nature of the raga also in a nutshell.

An instrumentalist can develop his finger-skill and capacity by practising varnams.

A varnam consists of a pallavi, anupallavi, the muktaiswara ettugada, and the charana swaras in it. The first part, i.e. the pallavi and anupallavi has the 'sahitya', the wordings which may relate to either 'bhakti' or 'stringara' or any other narration, is followed by muktaiswaras of a very high order. The second part starts with an 'ettugada' which usually has just one line of 'sahitya' (wording) and is followed by 'chitta swaras' of difficult passages progressively. At the conclusion of each swara sequence, the ettugada wordings are repeated after every 'avarta'. There are instances where the 'ettugada' swara passages are sung in a complicatedly arranged pattern in the order given by the composer, maintaining the formalities. This practice not only gives creative ability to the student but also improves his technique of execution. These varnams are usually sung at the commencement of a concert in an atmosphere of highly musical sentiments and an air of musical vibrations.

These are intended to be practised in three degrees speed (trikala) by the pupil.

There are also varnams which are composed in different ragas. These are known as Ragamalika Varnas. Different sections like the pallavi, anupallavi, muktaiswara charana, are all sung in different ragas. After each ettugada swara passage the charanam is repeated. Nritya (dance) with Abhinya (actions) is performed with this sort of a varna by the dancer. Veena Kuppier, Patchimriyam Adi Appiah, Shyama Sastri, Pallavi Gopala Iyer, Aswati Tirunal, Muthuswami Dixitar, Parameswara Bhagawatar, and Patnam Subrahmanya Iyer are some of the outstanding composers of tana varnams. Pallavi Sesha Iyer, Mysore Sada Siva Iyer and two or three others, have composed pada varnams.

Vaudeville. French theatrical term of varying meanings, among them that of a song with verses sung by different characters in turn, each verse followed by the same refrain as in the final number of Mozart's The Seraglio'.

Veloce (It.). Quickly normally a direction to give an impression of uninterrupted swiftness, rather than to increase actual speed.

Vent. (Fr.). Wind; instruments a vent, wind instruments.

Verbunkos. Hungarian military dance, once used to aid recruitment.

Form of slow introduction (lassu) followed by rapid section (friss) has been used as basis of various Hungarian rhapsodies (e.g. those of List and Bartok).

Verschiebung. Refers to the use of the soft pedal of the Diano.

Verse Anthem. Anthem in which important sections are assigned to one or more solo voices with independent accompaniment.

Verset (Fr.). A short organ piece, originally as an instrumental replacement for the verse of a psalm in Catholic Church usage.

Vial Viall. Alternative names for viol.

Vibhas. This raga illustrates the lovers who have fallen asleep at daybreak. They are disturbed and roused by the irritating cock. Hence dawn and cock are their enemies.

The picture shows the man attempting to shoot at the cock, which turns out into a floral arrow, which falls on the sleeping maiden kindling her love.

This is an early morning raga.

Vibraphone. The percussion instrument on which tuned metal bars (laid out on the pattern of a piano keyboard) are struck with small padded beaters held in both hands; beneath the bars are resonators which, constantly opened and closed electronically, impart a vibrating sound to the tone. Compass most commonly from F below middle C, upwards for three octaves. Used by modern composers occasionally in symphonic and operatic music and also in jazz, etc.

Vibration. The side-to-side motion of a string, a struck surface, or air column, by which musical sounds are produced.

Vibrato (It., vibrated). A rapid regular fluctuation in pitch-whether tasteful (e.g. as imparted by the oscillatory motion of a violinist's left hand) or exaggerated to a fault, as in a singer's wobble'.

Vielle Organisee. The 'organ' hurdy-gurdy incorporating set(s) of organ pipes.

Viertel (Ger., quarter) = Quarter-Note crotchet.

Vierhebigkert (Ger.). Term for musical phrases containing 4 bars or accents, or their multiples.

Vihuela. The old Spanish musical instrument, shaped like the guitar but strung like the lute; plucked either with the hand (vihuela da mano) or with plectrum.

Villanella, Villanene (It., Fr.). A countrified or rustic song (or an instrumental piece suggestive of such).

Viol. Type of bowed stringed instrument of various, sizes, current up to about 1700 and thereafter superseded by instruments of the Violin type; resuscitated in the 20th century, however for old music. The viols differ from the violin family in shape, in having frets, and in the kind of bow and style of bowing used. The three principal sizes (often encountered in ensemble) were the treble viol; tenor viol; and bass viol.

Viola. Bowed stringed instrument, a lower-pitched relative of the violin, invariably present in the orchestra and the string quartet (and used also as a solo instrument); its compass is from the C below middle C, upwards for more than three octaves.

Viola D'amore. Bowed stringed instrument related primarily not to the modern viola but to the Viol family but, unlike them having no frets, and played under the chin. It has (usually) 7 strings touched by the bow, and 7 'sympathetic' strings beneath them (hence the instrument's name) whose vibration is induced by the sounding of the upper set.

Viola Pomposa. (It.). Name apparently given to 3 different instruments that enjoyed brief existence:

(1) Small cello with additional top string.

(2) Viola with additional top string; predecessor of Viola Alta. Seems to be identical with violino pomposa.

(3) 4-stringed instrument irregularly tuned, lowest note being D below middle C.

Viol De Gamba. Organ stops imitating string tone.

Violetta Marina (It.). This rare and obsolete instrument was modified and presumably smaller version of Viola D'amore.

Violetta Piccola (It.). The name given by Praetorius as alternative for both violin and kind of small viol.

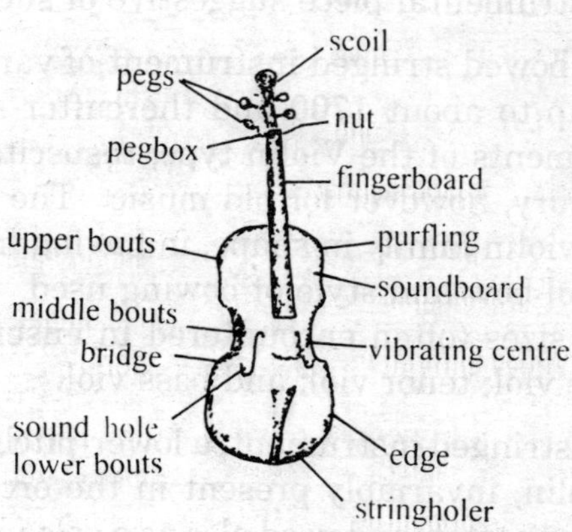

violin

Violin. (1) viola (2) viola d'amore (3) Hardanger fiddle (4) violin (5) cello (6) hurdy-gurdry (7) viola pomposa.

Violin. Bowed four-stringed instrument. The main types include the violin, the viola, cello, and double-bass, which has a superficial resemblance to the corresponding member (violone) of the viol family. The violin is prominently used in the orchestra (where the players normally divide into first and second violinists, a division usually corresponding to higher- and lower-pitched parts) and in solo and chamber music. Its compass is from the G below middle C, upwards for three and a half octaves and more.

Violin Diapason. The open diapason organ-stop imitating string tone.

Violino Grande (It.). Large violin, now virtually obsolete, with 5 strings, lowest tuned to C in bass clef, and other 4 as on normal violin.

Violino Piccolo (It., Ger., Kleine Discantgeige, Quartgeige). Small violin used tuned perfect fourth or minor third above normal violin.

Violoncello. (It., diminutive of violone; Fr., violoncelle; Ger, Violoncell, Violoncello). Bass of violin family. In non-Romance language normally abbrev. to 'celly'.

Violoncello Piccolo (It.). Small-sized cello for which Bach wrote obbligato parts in 9 cantatas.

Violon D'amour (Fr.). Obsolete instrument, used briefly in 18th century. Resulted from attempt to provide violin family with equivalent of viola d'amor, albeit at higher pitch. Had 5 playing string and 6 sympathetic ones.

Violone

1. Properly, double-bass Viol.
2. Also applied in 18th century, to double-bass violin, hence diminutive violoncello for bass violin.

Violotta. Modern but little used stringed instrument pitched between viola and cello. Tuned octave below violin.

Virginal (s). Term used for all types of keyboard instruments, including virginal proper.

Virtuoso. The performer of uncommon skill and technical mastery.

Vocalise. A wordless composition for solo voice, whether for training purposes or for concert performance.

Voces Musicales (Lat.). Notes of hexachord, sung to solmization syllables.

Voice

(1) The human (and animal) means of sound-production using the two vibrating agents called the vocal cords (not 'chords'); hence

(2) A separate 'strand' of music in harmony or counterpoint, whether intended to be sung or played.

Volti (It.). Turn over (page). Volti submito, turn quickly.

Voluntary. An organ piece of the kind used chiefly at the beginning and end of a church service.

Vox Humana (Lat.). The reed organ stops imitating human voice.

Vuoto, Vuota (It.). Empty – applied e.g. to a bar of music in which all performers' parts have a 'rest' (i.e. a 'General Pause'); corda vuota, open string.

W

Wagner Tuba. Type of instrument (more like a modified orchestral Horn than the usual tuba; Tuba), made in two sizes (tenor and bass), designed to Wagner's specification and used by him (two of each) in 'The Ring.'

Wait

(1) A salaried musician acting as town watchman, or as a member of a court band, etc.

(2) The old English name for Shawm, instrument much used by the medieval waits.

Wald Flute, Waldflote. The organ stop of flute-like tone.

Wald Horn. Hunting-horn, i.e. a 'natural' horn having no valves.

Waltz. Dance in triple time, slow or fast, with I beat in bar.

Washboard. Soundry utensil made of wood or metal, and played with drumstick or thimbles on fingers. Much used in early jazz bands.

'Wedgo' Fugue. The nickname for Bach's organ fugue in minor whose opening subject proceeds in gradually widening intervals.

Welte Photophone. The electronic instrument utilizing a photoelectric cell.

Whip. The percussion instrument imitative of the crack of a whip and consisting of two pieces of wood joined in V-shape; the player snaps the arms loudly together.

Whistle

(1) (verb) To produce a vocal sound through a small aperture in the lips, the pitch being governed by the shaping of the mouth as a resonating chamber.

(2) (noun) General name for various wind instruments, usually of primitive construction (and sometimes played with the nose) giving a sound similar to human wastling – a Western mouth-blown example being the Tin-Whistle.

Whithorn or May-horn. Very primitive type of oboe made from bark and wood of willow tree.

Whole-tone. The interval of 2 semitones, e.g. from C up to the adjacent D – divisible into the 2 semitones C – C≠ and C ≠–D. So whole-tone scale, a scale progressing entirely in whole-tones, instead of partly in whole-tones and partly in semitones like the major and minor scales and the old Modes. Only two such whole-tone scales are possible – one 'beginning' on C, one on C≠, though in fact each scale can equally well begin on any of its notes, since (owing to the equal intervals) there is no note which presents itself as a point of rest equivalent to a note.

Whole-tone Scale. The scale consisting of series of intervals of whole tone. May begin on any note. There is no tonic or any other implicit relationship between notes of series. 2 such scales are possible, notation of which may vary according to convenience: C – D – E – F sharp – G sharp – A sharp – A sharp – B sharp (or C); and D flat – F – C – A – B – C sharp (or D flat). Scale starting on D is obviously part of same series as one starting on C, and so on.

Wind Band. The ensemble consisting of mixed wind instruments i.e. both wood-wind and brass. Term is sometimes applied to Military Band.

Wind Instrument. The generic name for musical instruments in which the sound is produced through the vibrations of a column of air which is set in motion by the player's breath – such instruments being commonly divided into Wood Wind and Brass.

Wind Instruments. There are many kinds of wind instruments too, some made of bamboo, some made of horns and some of brass or any other metal.

This sort of instrument is held tightly by the teeth or the mouth, and is blown vigorously, giving the necessary sound. He plays with his fingers at the places provided there, while blowing from the top, to give different notes. Some tribal class call this the mouth music. There are big, small and all sorts and sizes of this instrument. It is said they believe in playing this instrument. It is said they believe in playing this instrument specially when the crop is ripe and it is weeding time.

It is supposed that when the crop hears this musical note, it grows quicker.

Wind-machine. Theatrical 'effects' machine simulating wind (usually by means of the rotation of a fabric-covered barrel) used in a few musical works.

Wire Brush. Type of drumstick with a head of several stiff wires, used to give a 'brushing' sound to a side-drum-an effect chiefly used in dance-bands.

Wolf

(1) A jarring sound sometimes occurring through unintentional vibrations on stringed instruments;

(2) An out-of-tune effect occurring in certain keys on old organs tuned in 'mean-tone temperament'—not in 'equal temperament' by which all keys are equally 'in tune'.

Wood Block [or Chinese Block]. A rectangular block of wood, hollowed out for resonance and used as a percussion instrument in certain 20th-century works. A related type is the Temple Block.

Wood Chimes. Also called bamboos or wood chimes. Consist of large number of different-sized hollow bamboo canes suspended together. Played either with hand or wooden stick (or some-times by wind) and give out dry sound that continues as long as canes remain in motion and so hit each other. Occasionally hard wood is used, giving more brittle sound.

Wood Drums. Although various kinds exist all over the world, they are rarely seen in concert halls. The 3 most important types are described. The log drum or wooden going is large, cylindrical in shape, hollowed out, and has slit running almost whole length of centre. The slit drum is similar but differently shaped, and can attain definite pitch. Wood plate drums are virtually tom-toms with single head made of wood; they are higher-pitched than other than 2 types.

Woodwind. The collective name for those types of wind instrument historically and generally made of wood—either blown directly (e.g. flute, recorder), or blown by means of a reed (e.g. clarinet, oboe), and in either case consisting basically of a tube with holes which, closed or opened by the player's fingers, shorten or lengthen the vibrating air-column and thus vary the pitch of the note emitted. The term wood wind is also used of instruments conforming to this made of metal (e.g. saxophones, and some models of flute and charinet).

Wurlitzer Organ. Type of Unit Organ at one time much used in cinemas.

X

Xylophone. A percussion instrument consisting of hardwood bars, laid out like keyboard and set in frame. Nowadays instrument is fitted with tuned metal resonators that help to enrich and sustain tone. They do so only to limited degree, in order not to counteract characteristic hard and bright sound. Tone produced depends on weight and hardness of mallets used by player. Range of instrument varies: large ones have compass of 4 octaves upwards from middle C, but many are limited to 3 octaves and fifth or 3 octaves and tone (lower range being curtailed).

Xylorimba. The percussion instrument (name combining xylophone and marimba), combining the compass of xylophone and marimba, about five octaves.

Y

Yodel (Ger., Jodel). Type of singing for men alternating between natural voice and falsetto, practised particularly in the Tyrol (in Austria). It is used for simple dance-like tunes.

Z

Zapateado (Sp.). Vigorous Spanish dance for a single performer, in which the heels tap out rhythmic patterns.

Zarzuela (Sp.). Type of traditional Spanish musical stage entertainment, with spoken dialogue, often satirical.

Ziehharmonika (Ger.). = Accordion.

Zilafone (It.). Xylophone.

Zimbel (Ger.). A medieval chime-bell.

Zither (1) Arab kanun, modern form of the Middle Eastern Zither from which the European psalteries developed (2) 19th century German concert Zither.

1

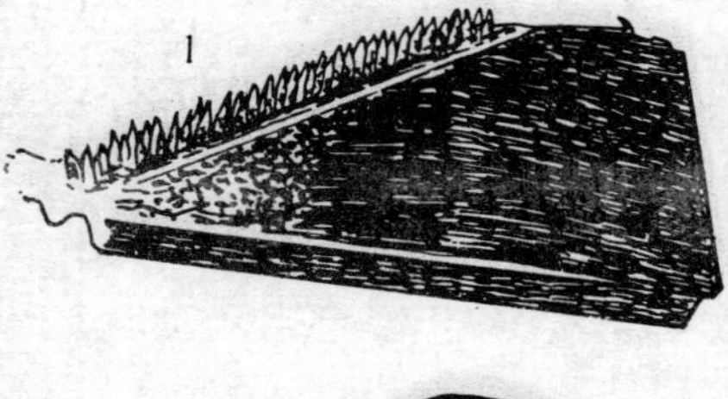

2

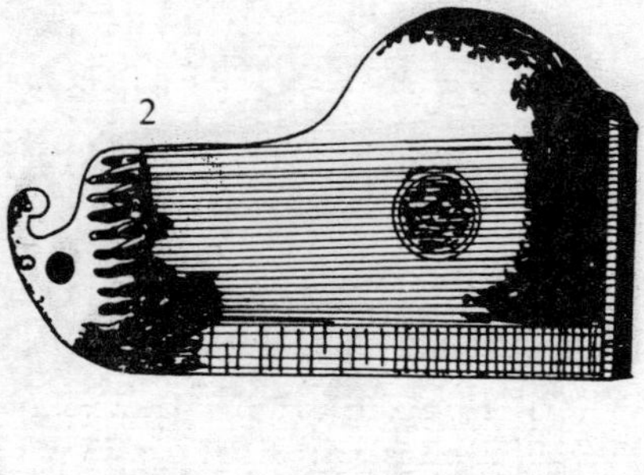

Zither. A stringed instrument laid on the knees or table; and plucked; usually, some strings can be 'stopped; (as on a violin), and others are fixed in pitch and used for accompaniment. It is a 'folk' instrument native to Central Europe but widely adopted elsewhere.

Zither Banjo. Small sized Banjo with wire strings.

Zoppa (It.). A limp; alla zoppa, term used of music have a prominent Scotch Snap or a pronounced regular syncopation.

Zugposaune (Ger.). A slide (as opposed to valve) Trombone.

Zukunftsmusic (Ger.). Music of the future.

Zunge (Ger.). Reed.

Zuruckhaltend (Ger.). Holding black, i.e. slowing down tempo.

Zymbelstern (Ger.). Percussion stop found in baroque organs.

Zwolf (Ger.). Twelve; Zwolftonmusik, Twelve-note music.